IRENE MONROE

Shaping New Vision
Gender and Values in American Culture

Studies in Religion, No. 5

Margaret R. Miles, Series Editor

Professor of Historical Theology
The Divinity School
Harvard University

Other Titles in This Series

Shaping New Vision
Gender and Values in American Culture

IRENE MONROE

Edited by
Clarissa W. Atkinson
Constance H. Buchanan
Margaret R. Miles

The Harvard Women's Studies in Religion Series

U·M·I Research Press

Ann Arbor / London

Produced and distributed by
UMI Research Press
an imprint of
University Microfilms, Inc.
Ann Arbor, Michigan 48106

Library of Congress Cataloging in Publication Data

Shaping new vision.

   (Studies in religion ; no. 5) (The Harvard women's
studies in religion series)
   Includes bibliographies and index.
   Contents: The power to heal / Karen McCarthy Brown —
Finding a self / Anne Carolyn Klein — A loving league
of sisters; class, race, gender, and religion in
Louisa May Alcott's *Work* / Amy Schrager Lang — [etc.]
   1. Women and religion—United States.   2. United
States—Civilization—20th century.   I. Atkinson,
Clarissa W.   II. Buchanan, Constance H.   III. Miles,
Margaret Ruth.   IV. Series: Studies in religion
(Ann Arbor, Mich.)   V. Series: Harvard women's studies
in religion series.
BL458.S495   1987   291'.088042   87-13854
ISBN 0-8357-1803-4 (alk. paper)

IRENE MONROE

Contents

Preface

Like the first volume, this second volume in the Harvard Women's Studies in Religion Series presents current research of a number of the scholars who in recent years have held appointments in the Women's Studies in Religion program at Harvard Divinity School. With the generous assistance of the Ford and Rockefeller Foundations, the program helps to support and guide development of the new field of scholarship on gender, values, and culture. The earlier volume focused on examination of the relationship between religious images of the female and women's social condition in various cultures and historical periods. This new volume presents research that illustrates the fruitfulness of gender analysis for unmasking and reassessing fundamental values that shape contemporary American life.

This volume and the series in general reflect the interdisciplinary discussion among outstanding scholars that it is the purpose of the Women's Studies in Religion program to cultivate. The involvement of Ford and Rockefeller has enriched immeasurably development of this discussion. Without the officers from these foundations who encouraged the Divinity School in its pursuit of the innovative aims of the Women's Studies program, this volume and the series itself would not have been possible.

The program's aims are embodied in the research of its visiting scholars. Those scholars who have contributed to this volume want to register, in addition to appreciation for the support they received, warm expressions of gratitude to their colleagues in the program—many of whom contributed to the first volume or will contribute to future volumes. It was in the lively community of visitors, students, and faculty at the Divinity School in recent years that the research presented in the following pages took shape.

Clarissa W. Atkinson
Constance H. Buchanan
Margaret R. Miles

Cambridge, Massachusetts
January 1987

Introduction

Clarissa W. Atkinson

As participants in the global women's movement of the last two decades, feminist scholars have sought to understand, to analyze, and to
critique the revolutionary reconstruction of gender roles and relationships. Their work includes the shaping of a new social vision for the
future and the construction of a more adequate account of human experience in the past and the present. With increasing complexity, feminist
scholars are demonstrating that in research as in society, questions of
gender are inextricable from questions of value. The analysis of gender
uncovers and allows the reassessment of basic patterns of human value
and meaning. By making possible the examination of women's lives,
such analysis contributes new resources for the evaluation and reinterpretation of fundamental social and cultural systems. This process of
evaluation and reinterpretation requires careful attention to the values
implicit and explicit in the method of study as well as in its object.

The essays in this volume advance the discussion of central issues in
women's studies and simultaneously identify the lingering patriarchal
assumptions that inhibit the development of new feminist insight. In
some instances, traditional patterns of thought and unexamined
assumptions have persisted in feminist formulations—for example, the
set of assumptions buried in the notion of "women's experience." That
concept, central to much feminist theory, can mask or deny essential
differences among women, especially differences of race and class. The
construction of women as One may be as oppressive and stultifying as
the traditional construction of men as One (and women as the Other).
Several of these essays confront essential questions about experience
and diversity. The authors have selected topics vital not only to the field
of women's studies, but also to the development of contemporary
understandings of human beings and the world.

The essayists examine issues of concern in the United States in the 1980s. Some of them deal with contemporary social problems, including aging and violence, and some with scholarly formulations such as the uses of "women's experience" in feminist theology. In one way or another, all these essays involve a reappraisal—a new look at assumptions about sex and gender, and at developments within the field of women's studies. Sharply aware of the radical alterations of vision that have marked their own lives and work, feminist scholars tend to be particularly conscious of perspective, and of the shaping of scholarship by social location. While they work toward new formulations, these authors keep watching for the submerged presence of inconsistent and outmoded ways of thinking and of posing questions.

The contemporary revolution in sex and gender relations and ideologies, which is at its heart a revolution in values, has had dramatic consequences in many areas of American life, from national politics through large and small communities to individual consciousness. No area is untouched, but because this movement *is* primarily a revolution in values, its implications are especially serious and far-reaching in the area of religion—in religious activity, and (within scholarship) in religious studies. Religious institutions and ideologies are major arenas of conflict; religion supplies many of the resources for the struggle, and for the analysis of the struggle in terms of language and symbol, private morality and public policy. Most important, perhaps, religion has been primary in the shaping of gender assumptions and sex roles as well as a major arena of women's activities. Scholars in many fields are now aware that in order to make sense of the revolution in gender construction, they must look carefully at religious structures, beliefs, and behavior. Historians are coming to appreciate the centrality of religion in the lives of women in the past; social scientists concerned with gender relations must focus on values. In the study of literature, scholars engaged in the battle over the "canon" (of texts accepted as central to scholarship) are increasingly fascinated by once-despised pious works that shed light on women's writings and female consciousness. Amy Lang provides an example of this in her reconstruction of a woman's utopian vision in nineteenth-century New England, focussing on Louisa May Alcott's novel, *Work*—little known even to readers of *Little Women*, but marvelously illuminative of nineteenth-century American religion and society.

The new wave of feminist scholars of the 1970s discovered the impossibility of defining or confining their work within traditional academic disciplines. They could not ask, much less answer, their own questions without resources and approaches drawn from many fields, and new methodologies were developed to deal with new issues.

Within religious studies, scholars for whom gender was a crucial category of analysis had to work with theology *and* history, psychology *and* ethics, and with more than one religious tradition. The authors in this volume do not limit their questions to those that can be answered with materials drawn from one discipline. Margaret Miles asks about the origins and persistence of violence against women in Jewish and Christian history and in modern culture. She examines the patristic texts that occupy traditional historical theology, but as these texts—being part of the problem—cannot adequately address the question, Miles expands her sources to include visual images whose use demands the tools and training of the art historian as well as those of the theologian. Through the use of visual images, Miles demonstrates that pornography is not unique in American culture in its "eroticization of violence," and that "the most pervasive foundations of violence against women are so ordinary, so unexceptional, and therefore so unnoticed that they are seldom challenged." Using new materials, and combining her materials in new ways, Miles perceives that the endemic violence of our society has deep roots in our religious traditions.

Feminist historians, critics of the status quo, soon encountered the limitations of traditional sources and methodologies and began to discover new archives and approaches. Aligning themselves with social historians in the tradition of the French *Annales* school, American feminists focussed on sources that included women and on the places where women were: on material culture, on *"mentalités,"* on the family, and on religion. The historical fields, thus expanded, continue to provide rich ground for feminist scholarship in religion. Biblical and historical scholars uncover achievement as well as oppression; they are empowered by the discovery of female creativity in its myriad forms throughout many historical eras and areas.

Much of the significant feminist scholarship in the United States is historical in intent and method, perhaps in part because women are determined that their history will not again be obliterated from memory. In the early 1960s, the record of past women's movements—even the heroic struggle for women's rights in nineteenth century America—had been forgotten. The accomplishments of earlier feminists were ignored or trivialized; an entire movement was consigned to a joke, or to a footnote in the textbooks. This is not likely to happen again, for contemporary scholars have attended carefully to women's history. Although her central interests are in philosophy and ethics, the feminist theologian Mary Daly wrote her first book about the history of the Christian churches in relation to women.[1] For Daly as for many others, the first question was, "How did this happen?" They turned eagerly to examine the Jewish and Christian traditions, pointing to blatant and subtle forms of sexism in the religious heritage of the West. It was essential to reappropriate the past—to remember and reflect upon the achievements of women in earlier times—and to look at patriarchal traditions from the new vantage point of feminist consciousness. Margaret Miles does what earlier students of the Hebrew and Christian traditions could not or would not do: she draws essential connections between the rape and murder of the nameless concubine of Judges 19 and the rape and murder of countless women in modern American society.

Students of historical Judaism and Christianity identified some of the sources of women's oppression in the teachings and institutions of those traditions. The realization that certain texts and teachings are careless or hostile toward women and other less privileged people forced them to ask basic questions about authority. If the scripture, the church, or the synagogue was oppressive, where might a liberating religious truth be found? What sources of authority would admit the experience of persons who were ignored in traditional teachings? It is not surprising that feminist theologians turned to experience, and specifically to women's experience, as a theological starting point and authoritative principle.

Much innovative scholarly work has been accomplished in the few short years since the beginning of this wave of feminism. In history, in theology, and in many other fields, the identification and revalorization of "women's experience" have served to expand and enrich the discourse of religious studies. However, "women's experience" is not a solution to every question; the concept is problematic, and oppressive in its turn, if it assumes an unwarranted collectivity and commonality. In our search for ties that bind women together, and in our eagerness to appreciate the distinctive elements of women's history, we have sometimes overlooked crucial differences of race and class, age and sexual preference—differences constitutive of "experience" itself. In 1979, the poet Audre Lorde said:

> It is a particular academic arrogance to assume any discussion of feminist theory without examining our many differences . . . The failure of academic women to recognize difference as a crucial strength is a failure to reach beyond the first patriarchal lesson.[2]

Lorde's comments, which were published in an article aptly entitled "The Master's Tools Will Never Dismantle the Master's House," warn of the danger of falling into the patriarchal habit of collapsing many into One by overlooking difference.

Several of the essays in this volume deal directly with the vital correction of feminist theory in the direction of diversity. Writing on "The Limits of the Appeal to Women's Experience," Sheila Davaney examines the writings of Mary Daly, Rosemary Ruether, and Elizabeth Schüssler-Fiorenza. Davaney insists that because *all* experience is historically and socially conditioned, feminists must not claim a privileged ontological status for women: to assert such a privileged status for any group is to fall into an ancient error. Until we deal with the issues of race and class that divide us, we may not claim a common experience even of patriarchal religion, nor place all women within one historical struggle, assuming that they share even a common history – much less a common nature or consciousness. Emily Culpepper, whose essay focuses on "Contemporary Goddess Thealogy," approaches this point from a different perspective. She argues that feminists who collapse all sacred female being into a "Great Goddess" or "Mother Goddess" participate in the ancient male construction of the "Eternal Feminine." Furthermore, they risk the loss of the affirmation of difference, and the inspiration of variety, that ought to distinguish their cause from patriarchal monotheism. Culpepper's sympathetic critique of contemporary feminist spirituality warns against the oppressive return of the One – the One that is always predicated upon an excluded and rejected Other.

The accent on diversity, which warns against any easy reference to "women's experience," is made in another way by Cheryl Townsend Gilkes. Gilkes's portrait of women within the Afro-Christian tradition reminds us that women have *not* been invisible in Black American churches, but consistently and powerfully present in prayer and music and testimony – even, to some extent, in preaching, the most exclusively male component of Black church life. Patriarchal church history recounted the history of Christianity without attending to race, and feminists risk a similar failure when they generalize without looking carefully at Black as well as white churches. A critique of "Christianity" as a whole on behalf of "women" as a whole does not take into account the experience of women in the Afro-American religious traditions.

Writing on " 'A Loving League of Sisters,' " Amy Lang examines certain intersections of race, class, gender, and Christianity in the imaginative construction of a female author in the nineteenth century. Lang believes that to replace *theology* with *thealogy* is to leave intact the root, *Logos* – the single Word of Western monotheism. It is not the gender of the divine, but its singularity, that is problematic for Lang, who claims that Western feminists tend to reconstruct the One as rapidly as they deconstruct patriarchal traditions. The problem of monotheism is precisely the problem of difference that besets feminist theory. In the novel *Work*, Alcott posits gender as a common ground unifying women of different age and race and class. But to banish these distinctions, or to submerge them in a gendered Christian utopia, is in fact to proclaim the triumph of white, middle class values. "In the broadest sense, then," Lang argues, "*Work* describes the inevitable return of pluralism to monotheism, the retreat from *logoi* to *logos*. And in this same sense, it stands as a peculiarly instructive tale for modern feminists." The novel demonstrates that as an ultimate or transcendent reality, gender overlooks the essential diversity of women and thus allows race and class oppression to thrive.

For feminist theory, the life and work of an individual woman may be as illuminating as "women's experience." Karen McCarthy Brown does not risk over-generalizing in her essay on "The Power to Heal" in Haitian Vodou. Considerations of race, class, and gender are crucial to Brown's analysis of the Vodou priestess Mama Lola, but they do not replace the individual at the center of the discussion. However, Brown's essay is not about diversity, but about power and authority and healing. The "root metaphor" of the First World—property—extends to healing; doctors possess a "power to heal" that inheres in their control of drugs, medicines, and machinery. Western professionals "own" the special knowledge required to heal the patient, who is essentially a passive participant in the system. In her case study of Vodou healing in contemporary Brooklyn, Brown analyzes the dynamics among a priestess, her client, and the spirits. A client's difficulties with a job, with chronic stomach pains, with a parent or child—symptoms we might divide into "social," "physical," and "emotional"—are viewed as continuous, and all are understood as disruptions in relationship. Mama Lola and her client are both figures within a constellation of relationships (with the dead and the spirits as well as the living); within that network, power does not belong to one party to be used on or for another. Ultimately, the Vodou system is effective in part because it does not deny the realities of desperate social conditions, of human infirmity, or of death itself. Mortality, poverty, and weakness are aspects of life—as are laughter, growth, sexuality, and power.

The attitudes of middle-class North Americans toward infirmity and death are very unlike those of Mama Lola and her clients, and the vast difference is nowhere so obvious as in attitudes and practices concerning aging and the elderly. In "The Fall of Icarus," Constance H. Buchanan examines the complex relationships of aging, gender, and religion. It is expected that one out of five Americans will be sixty-five or older by the year 2030. Women live longer than men—generally seven or eight years longer—so that issues of gender are inseparable from issues of age. Even against evidence to the contrary, Americans tend to assess older people as victims of severe and particular disabilities. Religious thinkers apparently believe that old age is "characterized chiefly by universal and inevitable decline—by dependence." Karen Brown spoke of a root-metaphor or property in relation to healing; we might speak also of a root-metaphor of acquisition and loss in relation to the American notion of the life cycle. The image of growth to a peak in mid-life followed by increasing debility is reinforced by theological discussion and the practices of religious institutions.

If the metaphor for age is loss, Buchanan asks, what is it that is lost? In the religious culture of middle-class Judaism and Christianity, as in the secular culture, what is lost is the "self"—or personhood, based primarily on independence, but also on potency, on meaningful activity, and on the status derived from such activity. The model, clearly, is drawn from the experience of privileged males—the persons in our society who have power, whose work is valued as meaningful, and who stand to lose a (socially-constructed) "self" in old age. Our culture identifies aging and old age with the loss-experience of middle-class men. Buchanan points out the inadequacy of this model of the self, arguing that it is not appropriate outside the narrow circle of the privileged "selves" who traditionally have constructed our social and theological models.

The notion of the self has been and remains a major point of discussion in feminist theory. The ancient ideal and assumption of women's "selflessness" was traditionally based either on belief in an essential female nature with fixed characteristics, or on the expectation of fixed patterns of feminine socialization. In her essay, "Finding a Self: Buddhist and Feminist Perspectives," Anne Klein points out that although feminists have sought identities free from rigid role-expectations, they have not necessarily wished simply to follow the lead of privileged men. Individuation has particular historical meanings in the modern West, where the self has been maintained through strict differentiation and exclusion of the Other. The Western "I," requiring the existence (and inferiority) of a despised and rejected Other, depends on an individuation characterized at least potentially as racist, misogynist, and chauvinistic. At the very beginning of modern feminism, Simone de Beauvoir described some of the outlines of this historical and philosophical quandary of *The Second Sex*—the gender construction of women by men.

Klein believes that we may be assisted in our exploration of the possibilities of self and selflessness by increased appreciation of aspects of the traditions of Indo-Tibetan Buddhism, which offer an extended awareness of possible subjective states. We may learn creative approaches to the traditional western split between knowledge and experience, shedding light from a new direction on the problems of "women's experience." In Buddhist meditative practice, one begins with an "awareness of one's own experience," and the desired goal of "empti-ness" requires affirmation of the self—the "contingent, dependent, interconnected, and non-autonomous self" of Buddhist discourse. To appreciate the Buddhist sense of self, and the meaning of emptiness, is to acquire new options for the construction of a self, to be assisted philosophically and psychologically out of certain dilemmas of western feminism.

Women who participate in new ways of seeing and action, or share in shaping new vision, have worked toward social, political, economic, and religious change in the direction of greater equality for women and for other persons with limited access to power and participation. Femi-nist discourse has been predicated on the necessity for change, and on the expectation that women will participate as leaders of change. In the presidential election of 1984, for the first time in American history, a woman was a candidate for national office on a major party ticket.

Geraldine Ferraro, the Democratic candidate for Vice President in 1984, is a Roman Catholic as well as a woman. In her essay on "Ferraro, the Bishops, and the 1984 Election," Mary Segers reminds us that it was widely believed in 1984 that Catholicism had not been a problem for American political candidates since the election of John F. Kennedy in 1960. However, during the 1984 campaign, an influential group of Roman Catholic bishops departed from precedent by making Ferraro the target of vituperative attacks from the pulpit and in the press. They publicly denounced her stand on abortion, which (with the help of the bishops) became a major issue in the campaign. They reacted much more strongly to Ferraro's pro-choice position than to similar stands taken by male Catholic politicians, perhaps because, as Ferraro herself said, "Mario Cuomo could talk about abortion. I could actually have one."[3] For the hierarchy, Ferraro came to represent danger and discord, not only in the national political arena but in the Roman Catholic Church. The discord was not limited to the matter of abortion; it included the role of women in the church and the world. Segers fears that American Catholic leaders have not in fact accepted women's equal-ity as a goal, and that their attempt to turn back the tide of social change may have far-reaching implications for their church and for American politics. It is clear in any case that prejudice against women who step out of traditional roles, inherited in part from historical Christianity, plays a significant part in American politics and in the present-day experience of American women.

The feminist theory developed in the last twenty years, focussed on complex and difficult issues of value and meaning, has formulated ground-breaking questions within a field of discourse mined with traditional patriarchal assumptions. In order to recognize and appreciate diversity, to make useful claims about power, or to establish a "self" that does not posit a rejected other, we must avoid old ways of thinking and of posing questions shaped by the experience of privileged males. The authors of essays in this volume, inspired by earlier feminist work but aware of certain vital shortcomings, turned for assistance to many kinds of historical and contemporary resources, new materials and new approaches. Some of the essays focus on the theoretical phase of the struggle; others on the more practical or active role of feminism in the world—in relation to aging, or violence, or national policy and politics. All of them represent attempts to break through the intellectual and social dilemmas of twentieth-century American feminism, to establish the new visions on which our new lives depend.

Notes

1. Mary Daly, *The Church and the Second Sex*, rev. ed. (New York: Harper & Row, 1975).

2. Audre Lorde, *Sister Outsider* (New York: Crossing Press, 1984), pp. 110, 112.

3. Geraldine A. Ferraro with Linda Bird Francke, *Ferraro: My Story* (New York: Bantam Books, 1985), p. 222.

Violence against Women in the Historical Christian West and in North American Secular Culture: The Visual and Textual Evidence

Margaret R. Miles

Let's start with a story, an old, old story, not really one woman's story, but a story repeated in some or all of its details numberless times in the lives of countless women. The story from the Hebrew Bible book of Judges relates the story of a nameless woman who was betrayed, raped, tortured, murdered, and dismembered. The concubine of a powerful ruling-class man, this nameless woman was offered by her master, as the text calls him, to some men who threatened violence against *him* as they travelled through a foreign territory.

> So the man seized his concubine and put her out to them; and they raped and abused her all night until the morning. And as the dawn began to break, they let her go. As the morning appeared, the woman came and fell down at the door of the man's house where her master was, till it was light.
>
> And her master rose up in the morning, and when he had opened the doors of the house and went out to go on his way, behold, there was his concubine, lying at the door of the house with her hands on the threshold. He said to her, "Get up, let us be going." But there was no answer. Then he put her upon the ass; and the man rose up and went away to his home. And when he entered his house he took a knife, and laying hold of his concubine he divided her, limb by limb into twelve pieces and sent her throughout all the territory of Israel.[1]

He did this, according to the text, to protest this cavalier treatment of his property. Commenting on the story in her book, *Texts of Terror*, Hebrew Bible scholar Phyllis Trible writes: "Of all the characters in scripture, she is the least. Appearing at the beginning and close of a story that rapes her, she is alone in a world of men. Neither the other characters nor the narrator recognizes her humanity. She is property, object, tool, and literary device. Without name, speech, or power, she has no friends to aid her in life or mourn her in death."[2]

This is an old story, but is it not also a current story? Parts of it sound strangely contemporary for a story about two thousand years old. In the United States today, a woman is raped once every six minutes; one in ten women will be a rape victim sometime in her life; 20–30 percent of girls now twelve years of age will suffer violent sexual assault in their lifetimes. In the first three years of the 1980s, there were approximately three-quarters of a million attempted or completed rapes, according to FBI statistics.[3] In addition, a woman is beaten every eighteen minutes in the United States; each year three to six million women are beaten by their sexual partner or ex-partner. In one state alone—Massachusetts—a woman is murdered by her husband or partner every twenty-two days.[4]

Sexual violence against women is also a racist crime: black women are nearly six times as likely to be rape victims as white women.[5] And it is a class crime: the incidence of violence against women is significantly higher in poor families, in racial minority families, and in urban families.[6] Violence, far from being a thing of the past in our enlightened age, is on the increase, and women are its primary victims. But violence against elderly people, children, and vulnerable men is also growing in American culture. Rape is only one form—though a particularly heinous one—of the pervasive violence that is a major threat to Americans, draining human resources and requiring massive strategies for containment and the rehabilitation of its victims and perpetrators. Analysis of the ideological rationalization of and support for violence toward those most affected—women—will help us to begin to unravel the complex cultural strands that keep violence at record highs in American culture.

Women who are fortunate enough never to have been sexually molested often do not realize how much we adjust our lifestyle to avoid victimization. These "precautions" constitute an implicit recognition of the danger; the threat of assault and rape is enough to make us rearrange our lives, reflecting our constant state of terror. Yet our precautions are often futile efforts to lessen the possibility of attack. A high percentage of rapes take place in somebody's home, many of these by assailants known to the victim. There is no possibile way for any woman to be thoroughly enough protected that we can feel safe; there is no "safe" way to dress, no "safe" way to behave that will guarantee that we will never be victims of a sexual assault.

Is rape a universal crime, simply a biological fact of life? Because of its distance from us in time and space, the story with which we began seems to imply that rape has been prevalent in every society in every time. If rape is universal, surely there is nothing we can do about it except hope that some *other* woman will be in the wrong place at the wrong time and become a victim. Rape is not, however, a universal crime. The misconception that rape is universal is one of the factors that keeps women feeling passive and helpless in the face of the statistics. Peggy Reeves Sanday's cross-cultural studies of rape revealed that in 40 percent of the societies she studied rape was absent or rare. Rape is not universal but is, Sanday writes, "a learned response which comes from the way societies are organized."[7]

Similarly, Beryl Lieff Benderly, in her article "Rape Free or Rape Prone," writes:

> Certain behavioral patterns and attitudes are common to rape-prone societies. These societies tolerate violence and encourage men and boys to be tough, aggressive, and competitive. Men in such cultures generally have special, politically important gathering spots off-limits to women . . . . Women take little or no part in public decision making or religious rituals: men mock or scorn women's work and remain aloof from childbearing and rearing. These groups usually trace their beginnings to a male supreme being.[8]

North American Christian and post-Christian culture is certainly not unique in its record of violence against women; it is, however, the serious common moral duty of women and men in all rape-prone societies to identify the ideas and images, the attitudes and practices that support, promote, and rationalize violence. If rape is not universal—something we must resign ourselves to and learn to live with—then we must be prepared to detect the images and ideas in American culture that formulate and support the misogyny that results in violence against women.

The second misconception that keeps us feeling helpless in the face of the startling figures on violence against women in our own culture is that rape has a biological cause in the powerful sexual urges of males, that it is, in some sense, "natural." This idea is without basis in fact, according to Sanday's cross-cultural studies which identified societies in which rape occurs rarely or not at all. Nevertheless it is pervasive enough in western culture to come from places as various as the Marquis de Sade—and my mother. Men can't "help themselves," my mother told me when I was a teenager, and thus it was "up to me" to see to it that I didn't arouse them. The Marquis de Sade wrote:

> It appears beyond contradiction that Nature has given us the right to carry out our wishes upon all women indifferently; it appears equally that we have the right to force her to submit to our wishes . . . . It is beyond question that we have the right to establish laws which will force women to yield to the ardors of him who desires her;

violence itself being one of the results of this right, we can legally employ it. Has not Nature proved to us that we have this right, by allotting us the strength necessary to force them to our desires?[9]

Sexual violence against women is not universal and it is not hormonal, whether the biological basis is construed as an irresistibly powerful sexual urge or as superior physical strength. Moreover, sexual violence is not sexual. Marie Marshall Fortune, in her book *Sexual Violence: The Unmentionable Sin*, calls rape a "pseudosexual act motivated by aggression and hostility."[10] Clinician Nicholas Groth in his study of rapists quotes what he describes a typical description of a rape by the offender:

I was enraged when I started out. I lost control and struck out with violence. After the assault I felt relieved. I felt I had gotten even. There was no sexual satisfaction; in fact, I felt a little disgusted. I felt relieved of the tension and anger for awhile, but then it would start to build up again. The crime just frustrated me more. I wasn't sexually aroused. I had to force myself.[11]

Marie Marshall Fortune writes: "The belief that male sexual aggression is natural, biologically driven behavior and is 'so overwhelming that the male is the one to be acted upon by it' is a myth that we can no longer afford to perpetuate." Implicit in this myth of male helplessness in the face of a massive biological drive is a pessimistic view of men. Ironically, it is feminists who question this helplessness hypothesis most strongly. Believing that rape is neither inevitable nor natural to males, feminists insist that men "take responsibility for their sexual and aggressive behavior."[12] If particular social practices—such as male gender conditioning that trains boys to be tough, aggressive, and competitive—are connected to the rape-prone societies studied by Benderly, it is clear that these practices must be identified and changed if misogyny is to be healed. But the dominant ideas, values, and visual images of the American public must also be scrutinized by feminists since these inform social practices.

Patriarchal Order: Eve as Derivative

What are the ideas and images of historical Western Christianity and contemporary secular culture that constitute the particular conceptual foundation of violence in American culture? My analysis will not exhaust the subject but will aim, rather, at stimulating further work to identify, protest, and change the concepts, images, and conditions that promote violence against women in our society. Moreover, instead of exploring some of the dramatic cultural support for violence against women—such as pornography—I will focus on ideas and images that support violence simultaneously in more readily accessible and more foundational ways. The most pervasive foundations of violence against women are so ordinary, so unexceptional, and therefore so unnoticed that they are seldom challenged. Pornography, an industry larger than the record and film industries *put together*, may be enormously important as the major eroticization of violence of our culture,[13] but there are other rationalizations of and support for violence against women. These are more superficial in that they lie more on the surface of American culture; at the same time they are more foundational in that they are built into the assumptions and institutional structures of American culture in the family and child rearing, in educational institutions, and in churches, synagogues, and government.

It is important also to recognize that misogynist ideas and images are not the only messages given in Judaism and Christianity to and about women; there are other ideas and images that were often used by women for their empowerment, as validations of their activity, and as warrants for a degree of independence. Historical Christianity, on which I will focus in discussing medieval and Renaissance visual images, is a frustrating mixture. If it were unambiguously misogynist, feminists could feel free to reject it; if it presented a comprehensive affirmation of women, feminists could find in it tools for present empowerment. Since Christianity carries both possibilities simultaneously, it is necessary to do a painstaking job of identifying the misogynist *and* the useful and usable strands, the history of oppression *and* of women's creative use of ideas and images that gave them credibility and leverage in relation to their societies. It is well to keep in mind that a kind of anachronistic violence against historical women can be done by historians who assume that they tolerated and masochistically enjoyed a religion and culture that oppressed and persecuted them. A respectful attitude toward the struggles of historical women requires that we remain open to seeing the possibility that they were often able to create for themselves lives of amazing beauty and richness by the creative use of their religious and cultural resources.[14]

It is not, however, the project of this chapter to explore the resourceful selective interpretations by which women constructed their self-images and ideas of relationship, world, and God with the help of Christian ideas and images. Our project is the identification of the most common biblical concepts contributing to misogyny and the continued use of these concepts in the present. It is astonishing to detect the continuity of rationales for the subordination of women across what we usually take to be the gulf between the historic religious cultures of the

West and contemporary American culture. Although patriarchal religious ideas and visual images are still strong in their religious setting in large sectors of the American public, their translation in the secular media has insured both their continuing influence and their constant availability to Americans. Secularization has not apparently rejected, but rather taken over many ancient religious judgments about the role and value of women. We will shortly take a closer look at this continuity.

First, let us consider three pervasive and powerful ideas of Jewish and Christian cultures that continue to contribute heavily to the misogyny in American culture that scapegoats women. The first of these ideas is that patriarchal order is the right ordering of society, reflecting cosmic order. Patriarchal hierarchy has been amazingly constant from the Ten Commandments of the Hebrew Bible which list a man's wife along with his cattle and house as one of his possessions, to the laws of modern American culture, which in most states, despite efforts to change them, still stipulate that rape within marriage is impossible since a husband always has the right of sexual access to his wife. Tertullian, an influential North African Christian author of the third century, explained the Genesis account of the creation of men and women like this: "This second human being was made by God for man's assistance, and that female was forthwith named woman."[15] In the texts of historic Christianity, the creation of Eve after Adam is repeatedly cited as "proof" of women's inherent need to be controlled by men. As several contemporary authors are showing, other interpretations of the creation myth are certainly possible; the consistent interpretation of Eve as a "second human being" created to help man, is puzzling unless we find political reasons why it was thus interpreted through centuries of patriarchal order in the Christian West. For example, John Boswell, the Yale historian, has argued that the creation myth of Genesis 1 clearly states an ascending progression of creation: first inanimate matter, then animals, then intelligent being—man, and, as the apex and crown of creation, intelligent and life-bearing woman. What seemed to Boswell as an "obvious" reading is one that is seldom found in the history of interpretation of Genesis.[16]

Most people in historic Western communities did not, however, write or read scriptural or theological texts. And, although they heard expressions of ideas of patriarchal order in sermons, in religious drama, in public readings of devotional texts, in hymns, scripture, and liturgy, the written and spoken word was perhaps not the most powerful communication of misogynist attitudes to illiterate people. Visual images, seen by everyone in the community every day on the walls of their local church, were a constant and fundamental source of instruction and conditioning for whole communities. Historical people did not have television, newspapers, magazines, or billboards. Thus the images they saw daily were few and usually remained the same throughout their lives. It is perhaps impossible for us to reconstruct from our own experience of a glut of media images the powerful influence of medieval "media," that is, religious paintings and sculpture. We cannot do more here than to suggest some characteristic visual themes and pictorial treatments that, seen repeatedly in the central community gathering-place, the church, contributed to and validated violence against women.

The texts written and ready by a small minority of culturally and educationally privileged people in historic communities might have been less influential had the idea of Eve's creation as a "second human being" not been visually reinforced and extended in many paintings and sculptures which show Eve emerging bodily from a gaping hole in the side of the sleeping Adam. Repeated depiction of this scene on the facades of cathedrals and in paintings in local parish churches enabled people not only to hear or read, but also to *picture* the secondary creation of the first and prototypical woman.

The establishment of patriarchal order in early Christianity, the exclusion of women from leadership roles in the church, and the theological rationalization of patriarchal order in family and society has been described by several feminist historians.[17] The preoccupation of church leaders with the danger of insubordination led them to urge the gender-specific "virtues" of docility, submissiveness, and obedience for women. Tyrannical domination, the complementary male role, was apparently less to be feared than female insubordination. In the early fifth century, Augustine, discussing the question of why the patriarchs of the Hebrew bible were permitted to have more than one wife, wrote:

> It was permitted for one husband to have several wives, [but] it was not permitted for one woman to have several husbands . . . For, by a hidden law of nature *things that rule love singularity*; things that are ruled, indeed are subjected not only each one to an individual master, but also . . . many of them are not unfittingly subjected to one master . . . just as many souls are properly subjected to the one God.[18]

"Things that rule love singularity" is followed by the justification and rationale, "just as many souls are properly subjected to the one God." The twin assumptions of male supremacy—through self-identification with God—and women as male property constitute patriarchal order. Rationalized as loving protection of the ruled, the bottom line of patriarchal order is the use of violence toward and even murder of the ruled for their protection. Augustine's epic *City of God* provides the explicit connection between rule and protection that allowed patriarchal rulers in families and states to justify their rule to those subjected as "for your own good."[19]

A contemporary example of the murder of a woman for her protection shows the continuity of patriarchal assumptions. James Michener's 1983 novel, *Poland*—thirty-eight weeks on the *New York Times'* best seller list—provides a contemporary example of the continuity of male justification of violence against women as clearly and vividly as if it were contemporaneous with the book of Genesis or with Augustine. After a battle, the protagonist finds in the luxurious headquarters of the defeated enemy the partially decapitated body of a beautiful young slave woman. Reflecting on this grisly scene, he muses that "the man who bought her had obviously loved her deeply, for he had killed her—rather than have her fall into the hands of others."[20] The author apparently expects readers of this novel to assume, along with him, that murderous violence is the ultimate proof of deep love. The short steps from patriarchal order, to ownership, to violence are all in place.

Woman, Body, Nature, and Sin

The second influential idea we need to examine is the identification, in Western Christian cultures, of woman with body and nature, and body with sin. From Eve, the instigator of sin, cause of the fall of the human race, to the actual women whose beauty tempted celibate males, women have been reduced in male eyes to body, visibility, and temptation. Just as images of women as sinful functioned as cultural sanctions for male domination, male supremacy ratified the domination, denudation, and use of nature.

Again, historical sculpture and paintings, the media of Western Christianity, encouraged medieval and Renaissance viewers to picture the sinful woman as naked and old, with swollen belly and pendulous breasts. Excessive female flesh was a consistent visual signal of "fleshliness"—a literalistic interpretation of St. Paul's use of "the flesh" as a theological term to designate the predilection to sin of the whole person, especially the soul. A facade bas-relief on the Modena cathedral, Notre Dame du Part, shows Eve, with swollen belly and exaggerated breasts, standing by Adam. His foot is placed on top of hers, a pictorial device for signifying superiority. Female nudity was symbolic of woman's "natural" proclivity to lust. If, in addition, the female body suggested pregnancy, it represented the biological result of male lust.

Since woman was seen as body, biology, and nature, she represented for men everything in themselves that they must discipline and reject if they are to achieve their potential to be pure intellect, mind, and spirit. Tertullian described male lust as the responsibility of women:

> *You* are the Devil's gateway. *You* are the unsealer of that forbidden tree. *You* are the first deserter of the divine law. *You* are she who persuaded him whom the Devil was not valiant enough to attack. *You* destroyed so easily God's image, man. On account of *your* deserved punishment, that is, death, even the Son of God had to die.[21]

These quotations from the Church fathers are not significant because they originated the ideas they express, but because they are tediously characteristic of the male ecclesiastical leadership whose perspective they represent. If these were novel ideas of Tertullian or Augustine, they would probably not have been influential, since in their own time theological texts were read only by a few culturally and educationally privileged males. They are important precisely because they were *not* novel but were, instead, extraordinarily clear statements of consensus male opinions.

Tertullian says, further, that he can be confident that he recognizes a woman's desire to attract him by the way *he* is affected by the woman's appearance. If a man is aroused by a particular woman, that woman means to arouse him: "Seeing and being seen belong to the selfsame lust."[22]

One result of the identification of woman with body, nature, and sin, is the exaggerated esteem of female virginity that Andrea Dworkin, in her book, *Woman Hating*, calls "a real sexual perversion."[23] If woman is body, sex, and sin, rejection of her "nature" as body/sex/sin is inordinately valued. Thus, although men rape and impregnate women, the woman they value is the untouched, untouchable woman. The virgin/mother of Christ is the prototype. The popular fourteenth-century devotional text, Jacobus de Voragine's *The Golden Legend*, follows the opinions of more esoteric theologians like Augustine and Thomas Aquinas that although the virgin was consummately beautiful, yet there was something about her that absolutely prevented any man from looking at her with desire.[24]

Paintings and sculptures of the Virgin strongly reinforce textual insistence on her obedience, submissiveness, and innocence. Her head is frequently shown with a side cant, a posture of humble acquiescence, as in Botticelli's Madonna of the Magnificat. An exaggeratedly high brow, large eyes, and a small mouth are iconographical features repeatedly employed by painters to represent her spirituality and lack of sensuality. Even in paintings of the nursing Virgin, like Rogier van der

Weyden's St. Luke Painting The Virgin, the potential sensuality of an exposed breast is controlled by her non-sensual facial features.[25]

Female Suffering as Salvific

The final rationalization of misogyny and violence against women that we will discuss is the idea that suffering is the path to transcendence and salvation. This notion has a complicated historical development that, to be fully understood, would require an equally complex examination of the concrete historical situations in which it came to be a prominent Christian idea. The glorification of suffering in Western Christianity has suggested that if suffering is potentially beneficial, even salvific, to impose physical suffering on another human being, far from being reprehensible, may sometimes even be helpful to the victim. From the fifth century B.C.E. forward, the spoken or unspoken law of Western societies has been that the strong take what they will and the weak suffer what they must. The Greeks, who articulated this description of aggression, did not attempt to sweeten it with the rationalization that it was good for the weak to suffer. No heavenly reward that would eventually compensate the sufferer was posited. The Greeks simply acknowledged a brutal law of the jungle.

In Christianity, however, imitation of and participation in the suffering of Christ, although variously interpreted, was seen as normative for Christians. Even the most tyrannical oppressor could claim enough suffering to warrant support for the principle that suffering is good for the soul. Suffering in life was seen especially in the medieval period as a way to preclude suffering after death. Present suffering ensured future bliss. Some notorious oppressors took this maxim quite literally. In fifteenth-century England, John, Lord of Arundel, before going off to war, paid a call on the local convent, carrying off sixty nuns to entertain his soldiers on the long sea voyage. Midway through the voyage, however, storms arose which necessitated lightening the ship's load. The nuns were thrown overboard and perished, to a woman. When John of Arundel died, his will left instructions for posthumous penance for this and other deeds of his adventuresome life. His body, the will stipulated, was to be beaten, wrapped in chains, and buried naked in the earth. The advantage of posthumous penance is obvious,[26] but even in its own cultural setting the notion that such undemanding "suffering" could atone for responsibility for the suffering of the raped and drowned women trivializes the real suffering of the murdered women.

Medieval religious painting, publicly accessible on the walls and altars of churches, repeatedly depicts the suffering of women as salvific—and not only for their own souls; it is their suffering that quali-fies them to be effective intercessors for others. The martyrdom of women saints was a favorite theme, a theme which often borders on pornographic eroticization of violence. Paintings of the martyrdom of St. Barbara by Master Franke (The St. Barbara Altarpiece, first half of the fifteenth century) and of St. Agatha by Sebastiono del Piombo (first half of the sixteenth century) show these saints having their naked breasts pulled off by giant pincers of sliced off by one burly executioner, while being whipped by another. Martyrdoms of the legendary St. Catherine of Alexandria, like the painting of this subject on the wall of the St. Catherine Chapel in San Clemente, Rome, show St. Catherine being beheaded. From these depictions of violent suffering to depictions of the fainting but dignified Virgin at the foot of the cross, the physical and spiritual suffering of women is shown as one of the primary ways for women to follow Christ. Excluded from emulating other roles of the human Christ, such as teaching or preaching, women often gained social and spiritual power by exaggerated and self-imposed suffering.

Male saints and scriptural figures—especially Christ—are, of course, also shown in texts and images as suffering, but their roles are not focused on salvific suffering. A much broader repertoire of activities is assigned to men than to women in religious images, while the primary religious participation and power of men was priesthood, religious images suggested to women that various forms of suffering were the surest route to participation in religious power. The reward for suffering was also a constant theme of religious paintings and sculpture. In this life, the reward was ecstatic mystical union, such as that shown in the later Bernini sculpture of St. Teresa in the Cornaro Chapel of Santa Maria della Vittoria in Rome. In the next life, present suffering was rewarded more dramatically; bodily assumptions of the Virgin and Mary Magdalen, as well as Coronation of the Virgin scenes, depicted the fulfillment of patient suffering in this life.

Women as Subordinate, Evil, and Suffering

The most dramatic historical example of the confluence of the three ideas and images we have explored occurred in the fifteenth through the seventeenth centuries in an oppression and persecution of women unparalleled in the history of Christianity. The phenomenon of witch-hunting in the late fifteenth through the early seventeenth centuries is too diverse and complex on the one hand, and too local, petty, and sordid on the other hand to be illuminated by any single explanatory thesis. It is, however, a striking example of the co-operation of misogynist texts and images to produce massive violence against women. Figures for victims of witch persecutions can only be guesswork due to partial and lost records; the most conservative estimate is that of the 100,000 to 200,000 victims approximately 80 percent were women. Henri Bouget, writing in 1590, said that "Switzerland has been compelled to wipe out many of her villages on [the witches'] account," and that Germany was "almost entirely occupied with building fires for them."[27] The human suffering involved cannot be adequately suggested by statistics.

Manuals on witchcraft and its detection and prosecution, like Kramer and Sprenger's *Malleus Maleficarum*, codified and expanded older beliefs about women's moral weakness, gullibility, and wantonness, and concluded that the persecution and execution of witches was God-ordained and God-pleasing. Quoting patristic authors, the *Malleus* says that the root problem of witches and the reason they are mostly women is that such a woman "will not be governed, but will follow her own impulse."[28] Secondly, "All witchcraft comes from carnal lust, which is in women insatiable." The *Malleus Maleficarum* is a catalog of male projection: "The word "woman" is used to mean the lust of the flesh." Yet, oddly enough, although women cause men to sin through inciting them to lust, one of the chief accusations brought against witches was that they cause impotence. The witches' arrest, judicial torture, and execution by burning was prescribed as the only way to relieve the innocent who suffered from their powers. In fact, it was apparently genuinely believed that the only possible way to impress on a witch the evil of her ways and the urge to true repentance was the extreme suffering of burning; *in extremis*, it was believed, the witch might repent and thus, in spite of all, attain salvation. Therefore, the greatest possible favor one could do for a witch—as for any heretic—was to burn her.

The Inquisitor's witchcraft handbooks, horrifying in their logical impeccability and cool self-righteousness, however, were texts written in Latin and inaccessible to everyone but the educated. The *Malleus* was published in 1484, but it was not until the sixteenth and seventeenth centuries that the witch persecutions reached their most intense level. The manuals did not inspire the popular frenzy against presumed witches of the sixteenth and seventeenth centuries. Rather, the witch persecutions were a media phenomenon. They could not have happened before the invention of the printing press at the end of the fifteenth century. The first widely circulated printed "newspapers" were not pamphlets containing Protestant reformation theology but broadsheets distributing accounts of the trials, tortures, and executions of presumed witches. The dissemination of this "information" to towns and villages prompted the popular mania for identifying and persecuting witches.[29] When people were told that hailstorms, miscarriages, crop failures, accident, and disease were caused by witches, *and* when they were shown what witches looked like, they learned to look for the cause of their high and constant levels of misery in women familiar to them. As in paintings and sculptures of Eve with an abundance of flesh, printed drawings of witches on sixteenth-century broadsheets, etchings and engravings featured corpulent women epitomizing the lust that motivated witchcraft. Hans Baldung Grien and Albrecht Dürer are the most famous of the artists who obsessively pictured witches and their alleged activities. Not until ideas and images were brought together did witch-hunting become mass hysteria and popular sport.

Contemporary Women and Patriarchal Order

We have seen that the first newspapers were illustrated tirades against women; let us turn now to our present situation, to media images of our own time, and ask if traditional misogynist ideas and images are not still selling newspapers. Since media images of our own time are not usually religious images, the continuity of ancient biblical misogyny is masked in North American media. But is it not still there?

How do advertising images function to inform members of the present society of their relative value and position in the society? Verbal captions of advertisements proclaim, by seeming to address everyone, a rhetoric of social equality. Images, however, consistently present young, wealthy, slim, sexually attractive Anglo-Saxon women and men as the satisfied users of their products. The verbal text contradicts the powerful subliminal message of the image, which promotes sexism, racism, and ageism. By the endless repetition of visual cliches, it creates marginal people, both women and men, who can never realistically aspire to youth, wealth, the right skin color or sexual preference in order to qualify for the satisfaction promised by the image.

In advertising images, the valued and valuable members of the society are clearly identified; consistent and cumulative messages are given by which we measure ourselves and formulate self-images based on the degree to which we match the images. Both men and women appear in our daily newspapers, but, as one student recently discovered when she analyzed an issue of the Sunday *New York Times*, about 90 percent of the pictures of men appeared in news stories, while about 90 percent of the images of women appeared in advertising. On October 27, 1983—the day Grenada was invaded—the front and back pages of the first section of the *New York Times* illustrated vividly the complementarity of gender images. The front page shows photographs of men, brows furrowed, conferring with one another, and photographs of military men landing in Grenada, greeted with gratitude and enthusiasm. The back page shows a full-page sized "Cosmo girl," partially but inadequately draped, in a seductive pose. Our conditioned expectations that men think and act, while women fulfill themselves and gain whatever power they may have by being beautiful objects, are consistently nourished by media gender imagery.

The three ancient ideas about women examined above are alive and well in today's media. Male supremacy is daily reinforced in implicit if not explicit norms of patriarchal order; identification of women with body and temptation is a staple of media images, and the notion that suffering is salvific is also to be found in press photographs of suffering women and in advertising images: "Life looks better when you do," urges an advertisement for cosmetic surgery. The secularization of these messages makes them seem contemporary, but, as the French proverb has it, "the more things change, the more they remain the same." We have seen that it is precisely these traditional ideas, now artfully clothed in fashionable modern dress, that provide cultural support for misogyny and ultimately for violence against women.

In *The Body and Society*, Bryan Turner has argued that changes in the character of the family unit, industrialization, women's participation in the marketplace, and laws which have to a great extent dismantled the exclusionary practices that established and maintained patriarchy, have given rise to a contemporary American culture that cannot be realistically characterized as patriarchal. If patriarchy is defined as institutional and political subordination of women, we do not presently live in such a society. Yet institutional changes have not created an inclusive society; women still experience sexism, misogyny, and violence in everyday life. In fact, Turner argues, the demise of patriarchy has created the condition of "patrism," or ideological patriarchy. Although "patrism" is unsupported by laws and institutions, it is still a powerful force, a reaction by men who "find their traditional sources of power increasingly open to doubt ":

> The collapse of patriarchy has left behind it widespread patrism which is a culture of discriminatory, prejudicial, and paternalistic beliefs about the inferiority of women . . . . Patrism is expanding precisely because of the institutional shrinkage of patriarchy, which has left men in a contracting power position . . . . Institutionalized patriarchy has crumbled along with the traditional family unit and the patristic attitude of men towards women becomes more prejudicial and defensive precisely because women are now often equipped with a powerful ideological critique of traditional patriarchy.[30]

If Turner is correct in identifying a trend in the direction of increasingly inclusive laws and institutions in American culture, then it is important to extend feminist analysis beyond the structures of society to the more subtle oppression of women by patrism — male reaction to the loss of patriarchal laws and institutions. Traditional ideas and images, often in contemporary dress but essentially unaltered and undiminished in virulence, continue to be reiterated, reinforced, and extended in the public practices of everyday life as well as in the media. The ideas and visual images discussed above inform and rationalize numerous everyday occurrences that are too taken-for-granted to be easily changed — jokes, street taunts, sexist language, dress, and sexually-differentiated labor. Social change must still proceed, no doubt, by continuing to insist on laws that protect and institutions that include women. But public life is not the only arena in which change is necessary. Personal attitudes and behavior are also political activities. In making some suggestions about how a public ideology of misogyny can be addressed, then, let us speak personally.

What can we do about it? It is, of course, worse than useless to stand around deploring the communication media of modern society, perhaps the most common and constant carrier of misogyny in North America. The media are here to stay. Yet it is important to raise questions about the values implicit in the daily media dosage of a whole society. Until we are conscious of these implicit values, we are helpless victims. Until we are conscious of the messages we receive daily, we can neither choose those we find life-enhancing nor reject and protest those that promote injustice and violence.

There are two possible kinds of response to misogyny and violence against women. One response is that of providing help for victims of violence. As a result of the present women's movement, Mary Pellauer writes, "intellectual and institutional resources have been generated at an incredible speed. There are now more than 500 battered women's shelters and 1500 rape crisis centers around the country."[31] The difference between the passive voyeurism of the viewer of media violence and active engagement to eliminate violence and to heal its victims is crucial. Most shelters are staffed by volunteers, women who find the opportunity of "doing something about it" personally healing. We can address the moral deadening caused by seeing daily doses of misogynist and/or violent media images about which we can do nothing by offering our presence and help to women who are the victims of violence.

The second response aims at prevention, at the massive social transformation that will be necessary to change our situation as women.

Identifying the underlying and constant ideas and images that make violence against women possible and even, in the eyes of some, legitimate, enables us to speak against these ideas wherever we find them — in the home, in institutions, in the media, in churches, and in synagogues.

If our speech is to be effective, however, we must overcome the individualism that enables many of us to think that violence against women is not *our* problem. "I've never been raped, never been discriminated against, never been hurt," we hear. The crucial step for the creation of the solidarity necessary to protest and change the conditions in which we live as women is to stop thinking only in terms of "my own experience" and to self-identify with women as a "caste," in Mary Daly's term, with women who are always subordinated in patriarchal cultures and in cultures characterized by patrism. Once one has achieved identification with women as a caste, all one needs to do is to read the newspapers in order to feel as one's own the dramatic abuse of women, especially women of color, poor women, and third world women. Once one has made this self-identification, it will no longer do to blame the victim, to think, however unconsciously, that victims of so-called sexual violence have been assaulted because they dressed provocatively, because they "invited" it by going out alone at night, or even by living alone. Blaming the victim functions to keep women feeling safe, feeling that we will not become victims; it keeps us isolated.

How do we claim as our own the experience of another human being? How do we feel experiences we have not had? Feminist author Emily Culpepper once responded to these questions with a simple but profound reply: "We tell each other our stories," she said. In the commitment to listening with empathy and speaking with honesty, the experience of another woman can become one's own experience. The ability to feel the pain of others can then become an ethical resource, empowering women to overcome isolation, individualism, and fear. The first step toward protesting the misogyny and violence of present society and beginning to create a society in which we can love and play and work without fear, is to begin to think communally, collectively.

The second step has already been named. Women must replace paralyzed passivity with activity. The two steps are intimately connected. Women can act effectively only to the extent that we act collectively. Probably every woman has had the experience of speaking about an issue of personal importance in a public gathering. A great effort was required to do so, and after saying her piece she felt guiltily that she had been daring, subverted the discussion, and made an impact. Then the next person spoke, not in response or even rebuttal to her comment, but on an entirely new topic. The discussion went on as if the woman had never spoken. Perhaps a few minutes later someone else mentioned her comment, reinforced it by noting it, or restated it. Then and only then she feels and *is* heard. A single woman's voice in patriarchal and patristic cultures is inaudible, no matter how strong and loud it may be. But once two or several women have acknowledged or restated the comment, it begins to be heard. Only our collective voices are heard.

Finally, in a culture characterized by patrism, it is not usually by dramatic public statements against women that violence against women is justified and perpetuated, but by the small increments of sexism occurring constantly on a daily intimate level. Even the apparently humorous misogyny of everyday life desensitizes both women and men to misogyny. If misogyny is pervasive, however, it is also accessible; it can be named as it appears, and if it is constantly named and rejected by women it can be changed.

Only by exploration of the deep roots of misogyny in Western scriptures and religious images can the rationalizations for violence against women be recognized in their contemporary forms. For an historian trained to expect that ideas appearing to remain the same across time and space in fact do not act similarly in different cultural settings, it is startling to see the continuity of misogynist ideas and images and the similarity with which they operate to subordinate women in diverse cultures. The next surprise is that, in spite of the pervasiveness and rootedness of misogyny, the subordination of women, and violence against women in Western societies, women have still been able to change the institutionalized, legalized oppression of women in American culture still prevalent a few decades ago. Those real gains, however, cannot be consolidated and advanced unless feminists continue to unmask the patriarchal God as He appears in American culture. Where should women place our attention—on the progress, the fragile beginning of the creation of an inclusive society, or on the mighty forces within and outside individuals that persist in misogyny? We need to have our eye on both—on the progress, so we do not become discouraged, *and* on the magnitude of the task, so that we do not become prematurely comfortable in feminist enclaves.

Notes

1. Judges 19:25b–29, *The Oxford Annotated Bible*, ed. Herbert G. May and Bruce M. Metzger (New York: Oxford University Press, 1962), p. 320.

2. Phyllis Trible, *Texts of Terror* (Philadelphia: Fortress Press, 1984), pp. 80–81.

3. Mary D. Pellauer, "Moral Callousness and Moral Sensitivity," in *Women's Consciousness, Women's Conscience*, Barbara Hilkert Andolsen, Christine E. Gudorf, Mary D. Pellauer, eds. (Minneapolis: Winston Press, 1985), p. 42.

4. September 18, 1986 statistics, Memo to staff, Harbor Me Battered Women's Shelter, Boston, Massachusetts.

5. Pellauer, p. 43.

6. Marie M. Fortune, *Sexual Violence, The Unmentionable Sin* (New York: Pilgrim Press, 1983), p. 90.

7. Peggy Reeves Sanday, *Female Power and Male Dominance: On the Origins of Sexual Inequality* (New York: Cambridge University Press, 1981), p. 42.

8. Beryl Lieff Benderly, "Rape Free or Rape Prone," *Science* (October, 1982), p. 42.

9. Paul Dinnage, ed. *Marquis de Sade: Selections*, pp. 132-33, quoted in Fortune, p. 113.

10. Fortune, p. 116.

11. Nicholas Groth with Jean Birnbaum, *Men Who Rape* (New York: Plenum, 1979), p. 27.

12. Fortune, pp. 116-18.

13. Andrea Dworkin, *Pornography, Men Possessing Women* (New York: Perigree Books, 1979), p. 201.

14. See, for example, Margaret R. Miles, *Image as Insight, Visual Understanding in Western Christianity and Secular Culture*, Chapter 4, "Images of Women in Fourteenth-Century Tuscan Painting" (Boston: Beacon Press, 1985), pp. 63-93.

15. Tertullian, *De velandis virginibus* 5, trans. The Ante-Nicene Fathers, First Series, Vol. 4 (Buffalo: The Christian Literature Publishing Company, 1885), p. 30.

16. Lecture, Harvard Divinity School, April 1985. Another exception to standard interpretations of the Genesis 1 account of the creation of women as secondary human beings is Agrippa von Nettesheim's 1509 "Declamation on the Nobility and Excellence of the Feminine Sex." In *Opera*, vol. 2, pp. 504-7. Lyon, n.d.; photo. repr. Hildesheim, 1970.

17. See especially Elisabeth Schüssler Fiorenza, *In Memory of Her* (New York: Crossroad, 1983); see also Margaret R. Miles, "Patriarchy as Political Theology: The Establishment of North African Christianity," in *Civil Religion and Political Society*, Boston University Studies in Philosophy and Religion (Notre Dame University Press 1986), pp. 169-86; Bernadette Brooten, "Paul's Views on the Nature of Women and Female Homoeroticism," in *Immaculate and Powerful: The Female in Sacred Image and Social Reality*, ed. Atkinson et. al. (Boston: Beacon, 1986), pp. 61-87.

18. Italics mine; Augustine, *De bono conjungali* 17.20; trans. Fathers of the Church, vol. 27 (New York: Fathers of the Church, Inc. 1955), p. 34.

19. Augustine, *De civitate dei* XIX. 14; trans. Henry Bettenson, *Augustine, City of God* (New York: Penguin, 1972), p. 874.

20. James Michener, *Poland* (New York: Fawcett Crest, 1983), p. 200.

21. Tertullian, *De cultu feminarum* 1.1, trans. Ante-Nicene Fathers, vol. 4, p. 14.

22. Tertullian, *De velandus virginibus* 2, Vol. 4, p. 27.

23. Andrea Dworkin, *Woman Hating* (New York: E.P. Dutton, 1974), p. 73.

24. Jacobus de Voragine, *The Golden Legend*, trans. Granger Ryan and Helmut Ripperger (New York: Arno, 1969), p. 150.

25. Anne Hollander, in *Seeing Through Clothes* (New York: Viking, 1980), claims that naked breasts are, in any culture, "the sure conveyors of a complex delight," though cultural definitions of the norm for erotic breasts vary widely; p. 186.

26. Kathleen Cohen, *Metamorphosis of a Death Symbol: The Transi Tomb in the Late Middle Ages and the Renaissance* (Berkeley: University of California, 1973), p. 5.

27. Henri Bouget, *An Examen of Witches Drawn From Various Trials*, trans. E. Allen Ashwin, ed. Montague Summers (London: John Rodker, 1929), p. xxxiii.

28. Heinrich Kramer and James Sprenger, *The Malleus Maleficarum*, trans. Montague Summers (New York: Dover, 1971), p. xxx.

29. Elizabeth Eisenstein, "The Advent of Printing and the Protestant Revolution: A New Approach to the Disruption of Western Christendom," in *Transition and Revolution*, Robert M. Kingdon, ed. (Minneapolis, Minn.: Burgess, 1974), pp. 260ff.

30. Bryan Turner, *The Body and Society* (New York: Basil Blackwell, 1984), p. 156.

31. Pellauer, p. 49.

2

The Limits of the Appeal to Women's Experience

Sheila Greeve Davaney

In the modern period, both theology and philosophy have struggled with the collapse of the Enlightenment-inspired quest for sure founda- tions for claims of truth and the progressive erosion of the correspon- dence theory of truth. As the Enlightenment, in the name of reason, called into question appeals to the authority of revelation and ecclesiasti- cal proclamation, so the last several centuries have witnessed in turn the critique of that very reason in the name of historical consciousness. With both revelation and reason the objects of critical analysis, contemporary theology and philosophy have concerned themselves with rethinking their definitions of truth and their understandings of the norms by which competing interpretations of reality might be evaluated.

Feminist theology has been a thoroughly modern expression of this struggle insofar as its major proponents have denied that norms for adjudication and evaluation reside either in the past, in some deposit or residue of special revelation, or in a supposedly universal, neutral rea- son accessible to all.[1] Rather, women theologians, working out of a feminist perspective deeply informed by the canons of historical con- sciousness, have argued that such "elevated" norms are male products reflecting the patriarchal character of their creators and the cultural milieu within which they arose and developed. Indeed, a good deal of feminist theology has had as a central task the criticism of male-created theology for its failure to recognize the perspectival character of its visions and its propensity to universalize its claims for normativity.

Repudiating the appeal to a neutral, transhistorical reason or a male defined and controlled revelation, feminists have called for the reloca- tion of critical norms to the contemporary experience of women strug- gling for wholeness, freedom, and liberation from oppressive structures and alienating relationships. It has become axiomatic within North

American feminist theological circles that women's experience is both the source for theological reflection and the norm for evaluating the adequacy of any theological framework. Whether one has remained within the inherited traditions of Judaism and Christianity or has left these heritages for women-created communities, the appeal at least in form is the same; that is, to women's experience and feminist consciousness.

However, in recent years this appeal to "women's experience" has been challenged. In particular, women of color have noted that the proponents of such a position have been predominantly white. Therefore they have asked whose experience is meant when white feminists refer to "women's experience." They have argued that white women have made a mistake parallel to that committed by white men: the assumption of common experience and hence the false universalization of what is in fact only the experience of a particular group.[2] Further, women of color have argued that the realities of classism and racism have divided women so profoundly that to talk of either commonality or solidarity, is to fail to recognize what factors really shape the experience of women of color. Although white feminist theologians have attempted to respond to this challenge by incorporating class and race analysis within their definition and critical interpretation of patriarchy, many women of color remain skeptical about the applicability of white feminist theology to their situations.

White feminist theologians have been well aware of the critiques of reason and revelation, but less cognizant of the problematic status of the appeal to experience, especially when such an appeal assumes that experience provides a unique access to "reality" or a normative perspective having universal validity (whether for all women or all humans). Although feminist theologians have often utilized the insights of political and social theories of knowing and have appropriated, in a transformed manner, the canons of historicism in their critique of male visions of reality, they have not always applied such insights to their own appeal to women's experience and their feminist interpretations of reality.

This essay will center on North American feminists' appeal to women's experience as this appeal has been developed by leading white feminist theologians. It will explore what women's experience as theological norm has been understood to mean and the epistemological and ontological status it has been given. In particular, I will examine the often unstated presuppositions that underlie the turn to women's experience and analyze these assumptions in light of both the diversity of women's experience and a variety of theoretical issues raised by the appeal to experience. In order to focus my argument, I shall use as prototypes of this position, the claims set forth by Elisabeth Schüssler Fiorenza, Rosemary Ruether, and Mary Daly.[3]

Elisabeth Schüssler Fiorenza and Women-Church

Elisabeth Schüssler Fiorenza is a central proponent of the appeal to women's experience as source and norm for feminist theological reflection. As a biblical scholar and theologian, Schüssler Fiorenza has focused her analysis on the issue of how women should relate to their pasts, especially to that part of the past deemed authoritative within much of Judaism and Christianity, that is, the Bible. Further, from the perspective of a feminist committed to the transformation of women's lives, she has also sought to delineate those criteria in relation to which contemporary theological visions must be developed and evaluated.

Both in relation to specification of a normative standpoint for analyzing the past and in terms of critical judgment of contemporary theological options, Schüssler Fiorenza proposes the same resource and norm for evaluation, that is, women's experience as it emerges in what she terms women-church or *ekklesia*. Women-church consists, according to Schüssler Fiorenza, in the "movement of self-identified women and women-identified men."[4] This normative perspective is posited in self-conscious opposition to patriarchy which Schüssler Fiorenza defines as "a male pyramid of graded subordinations and exploitations [which] specifies women's oppression in terms of the class, race, country, or religion of the men to whom we 'belong' " (BNS, xiv).

With this turn to women-church, Schüssler Fiorenza delineates her critical point of reference in a very particular manner. For women-church does not include all women. Rather, it refers to the community of women who struggle for liberation, self-affirmation and empowerment. While potentially all women might be part of this dialogical community, in present actuality it consists of those women and men who have achieved a certain level of critical consciousness and have committed themselves to the struggle against patriarchy. Thus, while the experience of all women may provide resources for theological reflection, it is the experience and consciousness of women-identified women and women-identified men that provide the critical norm for evaluating both past and present visions of reality. While this community is only "incipiently given" even in its nascent form, it provides, according to Schüssler Fiorenza, the foundation for normative evaluation within feminist theology (BNS, xxiv).

Thus, for feminist theology, the locus of reflection is women-church;

its loyalties are not to the church, the tradition, or the Bible. Rather they are to contemporary women struggling for liberation and to the memory of foresisters who have struggled in the past. Therefore, both the visions of the past and the options of the present are to be judged according to whether they advance or impede women's struggle for "self-affirmation, power and liberation."

By arguing that the center of normative evaluations is found in women-church, Schüssler Fiorenza explicitly claims or implicitly assumes several important points. A central presupposition informing her position is that the choice of resources for theological reflection and the designation of critical criteria are socially derived. That is to say, the data upon which theology draws and the norms according to which theological options are assessed are determined not by the autonomous decisions of isolated theologians, nor by appeal to transcendent sources, or a universal, neutral reason, but emerge in the context of social life and experience.

Schüssler Fiorenza extends this claim of the social character of theological norms by stressing that all reflection and discourse including that designated theological, is value-laden and embodies the social and political interests of the knower (BNS, 62). In a world of patriarchal oppression, acknowledging the social character of theological norms leads to the recognition that these norms are tied to one's position within the patriarchal power structure. Class, race, and sexual factors all contribute to the shaping of theological methodology, content, and criteria. The result, as liberation theology has proclaimed, is that "all theology, knowingly or not, is by definition always engaged for or against the oppressed" (BNS, 45). Schüssler Fiorenza calls for the acknowledgment of the interest-laden character of theological reflection and the recognition of the advocacy stances that are embedded, though often hidden or denied, in all theological discourse.

By highlighting the social location of reflection and judgment, Schüssler Fiorenza seeks as well to account for the diversity that exists among women. Women live within numerous and heterogeneous social environments, and these social realities inform their theological analysis in distinct ways. Hence, while the norm of evaluation for women consists of liberation, affirmation and empowerment, that criterion cannot be specified in one manner applicable to all situations, but must be "specific and derived from a particular experience of oppression and liberation" (BNS, 60).[5]

Yet while stressing the concrete character of oppression, Schüssler Fiorenza also insists upon the common experience of patriarchy shared by all women.[6] It is on the basis of this commonality that women can identify across class and race lines and recognize the shared quality of their struggle (WCR, 128). Hence, while Schüssler Fiorenza recognizes the diversity of women's experience, she also posits a commonality that is a foundation for solidarity among women.

Despite emphasizing the historical and social location of theological reflection, Schüssler Fiorenza does not thereby conclude that all positions are commensurate. There are ways, she argues, to adjudicate among the diverse positions. She offers several interrelated reasons for holding that visions of reality articulated from within women-church are normative in a manner that patriarchal perspectives are not.

Most importantly, Schüssler Fiorenza contends that the experience of women struggling for liberation from patriarchy (like the experience of other oppressed groups) is grounded in and responsive to the liberating presence of God. This claim entails, first of all, the assumption that it is God's presence which engenders this transformative experience. Hence, Schüssler Fiorenza refers to the empowerment of the Holy Spirit and suggests that the struggle for liberation is itself the experience of divine grace (BNS, xiv–xv). Furthermore, she argues that in that experience God is truly made known. In her words, "the locus or place of divine revelation and grace is therefore not the Bible or the tradition of a patriarchal church but the *ekklesia* of women and the lives of women who live the 'option for our women selves' " (WCR, 128). Precisely because God is made known here, the experience of women struggling against patriarchy, it is implied, carries a normative weight that patriarchal perspectives do not; that is, its normativity rests upon divine validation and grace. According to Schüssler Fiorenza,

> The spiritual authority of women-church rests on the experience of God's sustaining grace and liberating presence in the midst of our struggles for justice, freedom and wholeness for all. It rests not simply on the 'experience of women' but on the experience of women struggling for liberation from patriarchal oppression. (BNS, xvi)

Underlying this assertion of spiritual authority is the assumption that the experience of women-church has epistemological and existential normativity because God is that cosmic reality committed to those who seek liberation, and hence is made known precisely where the oppressed struggle for new life.

In sum, while Schüssler Fiorenza rejects the notion of a value-free or neutral perspective from which truth claims can be assessed and denies patriarchal claims to have defined revelation, she does not conclude that no claims to validity or truth can be made. Instead, she appeals to a circumscribed understanding of women's experience as it emerges in the struggle against patriarchy and implies that this experience corresponds to the self-revelation of the God of liberation and thereby embodies an authority beyond simply the appeal to human experience.

Rosemary Radford Ruether and Feminist Experience

Theologian Rosemary Radford Ruether is also a proponent of the appeal to the experience of women as the source of feminist theological reflection and the norm for critical evaluation of theological options. Ruether argues that the turn to experience is not new, for theologies have always grown out of the life of communities and in turn have been evaluated in relation to such communal experience.[7] The difference in relation to feminist theology is that the appeal is self-consciously to women's lives, histories and reflection. (SG, 13)

This explicit reference to the experience of women serves to challenge traditional theological norms, arguing that they in fact represent covert appeals to male experience rather than to universal human experience or some non-socially defined criterion. By focusing upon women, Ruether claims, "Feminist theology makes the sociology of theological knowledge visible, no longer hidden behind mystifications of objectified divine and universal authority." (SG, 13)

But Ruether, like Schüssler Fiorenza, does not locate her feminist norm in women's experience in general. Rather, she argues that it is the experience that emerges from critical consciousness and the struggle for liberation that provides the criterion for analyzing the adequacy of theological visions, past and present.[8] The "fundamental principle of judgment" against which all understandings of reality are to be tested is, Ruether argues, "the affirmation of and promotion of the full humanity of women." (FI, 115). From this critical perspective, the "falsifying and alienating" experiences imposed by patriarchy are discerned and rejected, and liberating alternatives are engendered and formulated (FI, 114).

Significantly, Ruether's fundamental principle of evaluation does not have its foundation only in contemporary women's experience. According to her, this evaluative norm resonates with and extends the critical principle articulated within the prophetic traditions of Judaism and the liberating perspective embodied in Jesus' alliance with the powerless. For Ruether, such resonance with historical experience is imperative if feminist criteria are not to be simply arbitrary and self-referential. The correlation between feminist commitments and the commitments of the prophetic and liberating strand within the Hebrew and Christian religions, while not a perfect nor unproblematic correspondence, nonetheless provides a ground for locating the aspirations of women in a larger history. In Ruether's words,

> To find glimmers of this truth in submerged and alternative traditions through history is to assure oneself that one is not mad or duped. Only by finding an alternative historical community and tradition more deeply rooted than those that have become corrupted can one feel sure that in criticizing the dominant tradition, one is not just criticizing the dominant tradition, but is, rather, touching a deeper bedrock of authentic Being upon which to ground the self. One cannot wield the lever of criticism without a place to stand. (SG, 18)

Ruether's correlation of the contemporary struggle for liberation and the prophetic liberating strands of Judaism and Christianity differentiates her position from Schüssler Fiorenza's. The latter is far less certain that such a correspondence exists and while she clearly acknowledges the importance of history, she does not believe that contemporary norms emerging out of feminist experiences need historical precedents in order to claim validity. Nevertheless, like Schüssler Fiorenza, Ruether identifies the struggle for liberation with the divine. It is within the contexts of those who struggle for transformed life that God/ess is made known as the source of liberation and new being (SG, 71). Hence, the feminist norm of the full humanity of women is not for Ruether just an arbitrary criterion reflecting the social interests of women. Rather it is an evaluative principle which corresponds, if imperfectly, to the purposes of the divine matrix who is the source and goal of all life and whose presence is the animating force that empowers the oppressed to struggle (SG, 19). Conversely, patriarchal visions of reality and the norms of judgment that emerge from them do not have their source in the divine and have thereby no divine sanction for these values or purposes. In Ruether's words,

> God/ess as once and future *Shalom* of being, however, is *not* the creator, founder, or sanctioner of patriarchal-hierarchial society. This world arises in revolt against God/ess and in alienation from nature. It erects a false system of alienated dualisms modeled on its distorted and oppressive social relationships. God/ess liberates us from this false and alienated world, not by an endless continuation of the same trajectory of alienation but as a constant breakthrough that points us to new possibilities that are, at the same time, the regrounding of ourselves in the primordial matrix, the original harmony (SG, 71).

Thus, Rosemary Radford Ruether, like Schüssler Fiorenza, argues that feminist experience and norms are grounded in the encounter with the divine and that such encounter gives them a validity, a "true" quality, that the experiences and criteria of the "false and alienated" world of patriarchy do not have. For both theologians, the liberating God or God/

ess is both the foundation of women's critical experience and the source of its validation.

Ruether also shares Schüssler Fiorenza's recognition of the diverse forms the encounter with the divine can take. She speaks strongly of the social character of all human communities, including those struggling for liberation. Not only is the community the locus of transforming experience, but it is also the source of the limits of the community's experience and vision. The results of this social circumscription are several. First, the experiences of oppression and of liberation will be particular and will reflect the historical realities of individuals and groups. Moreover, the evaluative norms that develop out of the experience of critical consciousness will also have a particular cast and quality reflective of the social and historical location of their proponents. Therefore, according to Ruether, "No liberation movement can speak the universal critical word about injustice and hope for all time. It always does so within the limitations of its social location" (FI, 119). But for Ruether as for Schüssler Fiorenza, the social character of experience, while it indicates that all experience is particular, does not rule out commonality or solidarity among women. Women have deep, and sometime dividing, differences in their experiences. "Nevertheless," she declares, "patriarchy by its very nature provides enough of a common body of experiences that women, even from different cultures and religions, find commonalities" (FI, 115). Furthermore, Ruether maintains that despite the social and historical and therefore limited character of experience, legitimate knowledge of God and reality are not forfeited. It is precisely in the concrete, particular events of liberation that the liberating God/ess is encountered. The norms that emerge from feminist experience may be socially circumscribed and in need of continual revision but because of that divine foundation, they are nonetheless valid and true.

Although Ruether and Schüssler Fiorenza do not fully agree on the status of the past, they do make similar claims about women's liberating experience as both source and norm of theological reflection. Each locates her normative point of reference in the realm of feminist critical awareness and action from which patriarchy is recognized as false and actively struggled against. Further, each connects the criteria articulated within feminist theology to the experience of the divine which is the foundation for women's liberative experience and, they imply, a source of validity and authority for the feminist norm. And finally, each argues for the importance of what might be termed "the social location of experience." That is, women's experience as struggle for liberation carries a normativity that patriarchally-defined experience does not. But this is not because women, by virtue of their nature or biology, have special access to reality or to God. Rather it is because women, and other oppressed persons in their struggle against patriarchy, find themselves in the historical moment wherein the reality of the liberating God can be discerned. It is less that it is *women's* experience, in general, that is normative, than that it is the experience of women *who struggle* for liberation that is the locus of God's liberating and revelatory presence. In sum, the appeal is made to a historically derived normativity rather than to any ontological uniqueness of women.

Mary Daly and Feminist Consciousness

The work of feminist philosopher Mary Daly provides a provocative contrast with the views developed by Schüssler Fiorenza and Ruether. While Daly also turns to the experience of women as her central point of reference, her construction of the nature of such experience and its relation to "reality" and "truth" offer distinctive alternatives to feminist thought.

Like Schüssler Fiorenza and Ruether, Daly does not understand the appeal to the experience of women as a turn to women's experience in general. She too sharply circumscribes her critical point of reference, locating it in the experience of self-identified women who live out of what she terms "biophilic" or "metapatriarchal" consciousness. It is this consciousness that provides for Daly the normative perspective for developing and evaluating feminist visions of reality. Accordingly, her primary sources "are woman-identified experiences and observations."[9]

There are several elements in this position which distinguish it from Schüssler Fiorenza's and Ruether's views. First, Daly seems to delineate more sharply who is to be considered women-identified and living out of biophilic consciousness. Daly's work strongly suggests that those women who still participate in patriarchal religious traditions or still exist in primary relationships with men cannot, by and large, be understood to possess radical feminist awareness. Hence, the community of women whose experiences and consciousness are normative, for Daly, is for the most part, if not exclusively, made up of women who have stepped outside the boundaries of patriarchal traditions and for whom affiliation with males is not a central point of self-definition. Her normative point of reference is to the experience and consciousness of women forged in and embodied in separatist communities.[10]

A second central and distinctive element of Daly's position is her strong emphasis upon consciousness. Both Schüssler Fiorenza and Ruether refer to critical awareness, but they connect such awareness to the public struggle against institutions and structures. For Daly, patriarchy is first and foremost a state of mind, and therefore the struggle against it must be primarily a process of revolutionizing consciousness. In this view, patriarchal institutions and structures can only be effectively dismantled when the interpretations of reality that they embody and support are repudiated and replaced. Hence, Daly concentrates on the alternative visions of reality emerging in communities of women-identified women and envisions her own task as the creation of women-centered consciousness through the generation of new language and new myths.

Several important assumptions infuse this understanding of meta-patriarchal consciousness. First, while the emergence of biophilic consciousness is facilitated by the communal context of women-identified women, it is not primarily a product of that social setting. That is, while the social setting fosters its emergence and enhancement, what women-identified women discover is that this consciousness is part of their female nature, that it is intrinsically and naturally theirs. It is not only or primarily the by-product of historical developments, but is an expression of female essence. Over against Schüssler Fiorenza and Ruether, who tend to portray the emergence of feminist consciousness as the consequence of historical processes, Daly presents it in much more essentialist terms, tying it to a unique female nature that has existed, though often repressed, throughout history.[11]

By speaking of a form of consciousness that is female in nature, Daly does not mean to deny diversity among women. Ethnic, class, race, and cultural differences contribute to this diversity, as does the uniqueness of each woman. (PL, 26). However, while diversity is real, Daly insists that there is an underlying commonality among women that is brought to light and nourished by radical feminism (PL, 325). She states, "There is also above, beyond, beneath all this a Cosmic Commonality, a tapestry of connectedness which women as Websters/Fates are constantly weaving" (PL, 26–27). Furthermore, there exists the bond that all women are the victims of patriarchy. And finally, while Daly acknowledges that racism and classism do indeed divide women, she argues that women must remember that they are not the creators of such institutions, which are patriarchal inventions that function, among other things, to keep women divided. In her words, "None of these institutions were invented by women or have ever been under the control of women" (PL 378).

Daly's essentialist interpretation of female nature and of feminist consciousness also finds expression in her tendency to depict patriarchal males as belonging to a separate species than post-patriarchal women. Indeed, Daly suggests that the notion of human species is highly problematic when females' and males' consciousness, commitments and natures are so radically divergent. In her words, the very concept of human species, at least in its classic Aristotelian form, is contradictory in that "it would attempt to embrace creatures whose conscious behavior is wholly oriented in opposite directions" (PL 352).

Moreover, Daly argues that the form of awareness that explicitly characterizes women-identified women and potentially characterizes all women yields a different kind of knowledge and truth than does patriarchal consciousness. Within patriarchy, the world is experienced through the mediation of male interpretive schemas, resulting in the distortion and false naming of reality. That is, patriarchal consciousness yields lies and falsehoods, not truth. In contrast, the Realizing Reason of Women, which Daly often refers to as unmediated and immediate, participates in cosmic reality or Be-ing and yields true and adequate knowledge by virtue of such participation.

With this position, Daly posits her own unique version of a correspondence theory of truth, grounded in a theory of innate female faculties. Eschewing the Enlightenment model of neutral reason reflecting unchanging reality, Daly offers a vision of a dynamic reality known through radical participation. Stated succinctly, Daly proposes that women possess a distinctive nature and form of consciousness and that such consciousness has the capacity to participate in and thereby know Be-ing or Reality. This is so, she believes, because there exists a profound and natural correspondence, apparently lacking in males, between the minds of musing women and the structures of Reality. (PL 163) Women's consciousness is not neutral but value-laden and biophilic, and therefore recognizes and responds to the evaluative, biophilic dimensions of Be-ing. This process of participatory knowing is not static, nor can its truth be expressed in reified concepts or symbols. Nonetheless, Daly assumes that reality has a certain, albeit dynamic, nature that is accessible to women and that such accessibility is predicated on the nature of women's consciousness.

Limits of the Appeal to Women's Experience

The foregoing analysis has highlighted a number of presuppositions underlying central feminist theologies on the contemporary North American scene. In particular, it has argued that while the experiences of all women provide resources for feminist theology, the critical norms for such reflection arise from the experiences of a "cognitive minority." More importantly, it has suggested that the experience and consciousness of this radicalized minority are normative not only because they reflect the experience of those who have heretofore been silenced, but because they cohere in some fundamental manner with the "way things are;" that is, feminist experience and consciousness yield a more accurate rendering of reality, including the nature and purposes of what might be termed the "divine." Hence, they can claim greater ontological validity. For Ruether and Schüssler Fiorenza, such epistemological privilege is not the result of a unique female nature. Rather, women's location in the historical struggle generates knowledge both of historical processes and of the nature and purposes of the God or God/ess who participates in the struggles for liberation and empowerment. In contrast, Daly grounds her claims of epistemological privilege primarily in the assumption that women possess a distinctive nature, with innate female faculties that are capable of non-distorted, adequate, and true knowledge of Be-ing. Despite their differing rationales, all three thinkers claim a validity for feminist interpretations of reality which they refuse to grant to the visions of patriarchal males (and perhaps non-feminist women), which they label false, distorted, and perverted.

It is my conviction that all three thinkers predicate their positions on several highly problematic assumptions. Running throughout their work is the implicit, sometimes explicit assumption that there is a perspective from which we can perceive the way things really are and that feminist experience provides such a privileged location. Accompanying this underlying claim, is also, I suggest, the assumption that there is, in the words of feminist theorist Andrea Dworkin, a distinction between "truth" and "reality." Dworkin argues that reality is socially constructed, it is "whatever people at a given time believe it to be."[12] Put more forcefully, reality is the version of things that the powerful—that is, males, have imposed upon those denied power—that is, females. In contrast to this male-constructed version of reality, is truth. Truth is the way things really are, it is the ontologically accurate rendering of the universe. From the perspective of "truth," "reality" can be seen to be delusion and falsehood.

There may be strong heuristic and political reasons for referring to "truth" or to the "real" rather than simply to our various socially constructed interpretations of reality. However, the assumption, which is at least implicit in the positions being analyzed, that women, whether by virtue of historical experience or nature, have privileged access to the realm of the ontologically real is problematic for a number of reasons. First, this claim stands in tension with the assumption, shared to some degree by all three thinkers, of the social character of experience. Ruether and Schüssler Fiorenza, in particular, present the case for social location as the major determining factor in the shaping of experience. In a Marxian-like turn they argue that it is precisely the location of women in the struggle against patriarchy that provides them with an advantaged perspective for understanding historical processes. However, when the claims for the social character of experience and knowledge are pushed further, we must confront the possibility that *no* perspective offers a privileged access to the "way things really are;" all we have are alternative ways of conceiving of reality. In a thoroughly social view, we have no access to a world which is separate from our interpretations of it, nor is there a basis for claiming that one socially-derived perspective resonates and corresponds to "reality as it really is." From this perspective, Ruether's and Schüssler Fiorenza's tendency to claim not only historical adequacy but ontological validity appears as special pleading, a failure to carry through the insights of the historicism that informs so much of their work.

Daly presents a somewhat different case, for while she acknowledges the historically-circumscribed character of experience, she appeals most centrally to an innate essence of female being. Apart from problems concerning the relation of socially-derived experience and a seemingly ahistorical essence, there remains the fact that Daly, too, makes a leap from claims about female experience to assertions about the ontological nature of reality. She does so primarily on the assumption that female nature participates in and corresponds to Be-ing. The bases, however, for such a claim remain obscure and unconvincing, especially to those who interpret human existence in more social and historical terms.

The views under consideration present difficulties, as well, concerning an issue they all seek to address with utmost seriousness, that is, the diversity of women's experience. All three women acknowledge that women's lives are shaped by and within diverse social contexts, and that factors such as race and class contribute significantly to experience. Yet all three argue for a commonality, whether historically derived or naturally given, among women, and furthermore suggest that it is from the perspective of feminist experience and consciousness that such unity is discernable (FI, 115). Although perhaps unintended, the implication is that perspectives that do not recognize this commonality or assign it a peripheral status are misguided, if not distorted and false like patriarchal visions. Taking localized experience and universalizing its importance is precisely the tendency which many women of color find so objectionable. Black feminist theorist Bell Hooks argues eloquently that the appeal to commonality, made primarily by white women, not only obscures the other factors besides gender that shape women's lives but mystifies the role white women have played in the exploitation of women of color (FT, 14). Furthermore, when white women suggest that the experience and consciousness of women-identified women resonate with ontological reality and divine purpose, the message, at least covertly, is that these women, and not others, know "the way things really are" and that their visions, and not those of other women, carry the weight of divine authority. Thus, the combination of the power of white women's social location and the assumption of ontological validation result, whether intentionally or not, in the depreciation of women whose experience is different.

In an effort to avoid this depreciation, Ruether and Schüssler Fiorenza have stated that no single perspective can offer the final normative word. Rather, out of the particularity of historical struggles against oppression, a variety of critical norms will be articulated. However, underlying this claim of multiple, all apparently valid, norms is the assumption that all locations of struggle against oppression are the loci of revelation by the one God of liberation, and that all correspond to ontological reality and divine purpose. Thus, while the experience of oppression is various and the norms emerging from the struggle against it diverse, nonetheless they all can be seen to resonate. This view is reminiscent of the "perennial philosophy" notion that there exists a unity of religious experience and only the cultural forms differ. But as in the case of perennial philosophy, such an approach functions to devalue the radical differences between individuals and groups and to mask the often contradictory values and commitments of those communities. For women of color, such as Bell Hooks, who assume that white women and black women do not automatically share the same experience or commitments, the presumption of commonality is unacceptable until white women confront the barriers of racism and classism that separate women. (FT, 44).

An Alternative Proposal

The foregoing analysis has focused on the problems implicit in the appeal to women's experience and consciousness and on the assumption that such experience and consciousness have a unique access to reality, including divine reality, that supports its claims to validity. By way of conclusion, I would like to offer another model for understanding the appeal to women's experience and an alternative interpretation of the status of this experience. This view is deeply informed by a sense of the historical and social character of all human experience and consciousness and by a rejection of the claim that any human perspective has a privileged access to ontological reality. Although at points, this essay overlaps with the three positions explored in this essay, it differs from them on key points, and develops an alternative to these perspectives.

Working out of what might be termed a postmodern historicism, I concur with Ruether, Schüssler Fiorenza, and Daly that appeals to a supposedly value-free reason or a transcendently based revelation have become unacceptable. With them, and with much of modern theological thought, I affirm the turn to experience. However, just as reason has been historicized, experience must be as well. When this historicizing has taken place, no particular form of experience, including that of women, will be able to claim ontological or epistemological privilege.

This position flows out of the progressive recognition of the historical and social character of experience that has marked contemporary disciplines as diverse as philosophy and psychology, sociology and theology.[13] A variety of scholarly perspectives has increasingly emphasized that human beings do not know reality in a vacuum, or from a value-free vantage point. There is, it is widely argued, no such thing as naked, or innocent knowledge or experience. Nor is there, as Daly argues, unmediated, immediate experience. Instead, human beings, male and female alike, are culturally- and socially-defined beings who exist, act, and know within a network of historically-constructed linguistic and symbolic meanings and values. How we know and what we know are dependent upon such axiological networks which provide the "perceptual lenses," the interpretive schemas by which we know reality.

However, these perceptual grids or interpretive schemas are not products of some ahistorical structure of the mind nor, as Daly seems to assume, of female essence. Rather, they too are socially defined and determined. That is, our experience and knowledge of the world are conditioned, specified and determined by the *social a priori* that we bring to it. Socially-defined interpretive schemas, what George Lindbeck terms, "idioms for the construction of reality," are constitutive of any human encounter with reality. Several important implications are ingredient in this claim of a *social a priori*.[14]

First, by arguing that experience and knowledge are socially shaped, I am rejecting the notion that they are utterly individual and the idea that they are universal. Humanity's experience and knowledge are socially defined and socially given content. That is, the interpretive schemas through which we encounter the world are historically circumscribed and contextually defined. On the one hand, this claim acknowledges the communal aspect of experience and knowledge. That is, we humans live out of communal contexts and traditions without which no experience or knowledge is possible. The axiological grids with which we approach reality are always the product of social and historical processes, not the creation of individual minds. On the other hand, the recognition of the social character of our interpretive schemas suggests that there is no "experience in general," including the experiences of oppression and liberation. What there is, is particular, historically-circumscribed experience and knowledge.

This does not mean that similarities between groups (such as black women and white women) cannot be discerned. It does suggest, however, that rather than begin with claims of commonality and base our hopes of solidarity on this appeal we must first attend to the particularities of experience and build strategic alliances at points where values or goals might be seen to coincide. We also must confront the possibility that women's experience does not have an overriding common character and that the historical and social divisions that define our experience may be more constitutive of that experience than whatever elements we share in common. In this view, commonality and solidarity among women are historical projects, yet to be achieved, not unquestioned presuppositions.

To recognize the social foundations for human knowing and experiencing is also to recognize that they are value-defined and interest-laden. That is, our interpretive schemas are systems of values, reflections of fundamental judgments and commitments. Furthermore, the values embodied in our perceptual grids are highly dependent upon the social structure and configuration of the societal contexts in which they emerge. Put concretely, there is an intimate relationship between an individual's or a class's social status and the system of values through and by which they encounter, order, and know reality. That is, power and knowledge are inseparable in every instance. Experience is always shaped by social location and hence tied to power.[15]

To accept the social and historical character of human life and thought is to abandon the quest for a neutral Archimedean point located in reason or revelation from which to see things the "way they really are." So, too, it is to accept that no form of experience provides such a privileged access to reality. We have no access to reality separate from our value-ladened, power-infused conception of it; women's experience and knowledge therefore cannot claim, any more than can males', an ontological grounding or an epistemological superiority. Our experience and knowledge, no less than that of males, is a social product and hence is relative, ambiguous, and challengeable.

This position resonates strongly with Mary Daly's insights concerning the importance of consciousness for shaping experience. However, it is problematic to assume, as does Daly, that feminist interpretive schemas flow out of female nature and that they correspond, in contrast to those of males, to "reality as it really is." According to my historicist perspective, feminist visions of reality are rooted in specific historical locations, the products of historical processes; the most we can say is that they provide alternative but not ontologically truer interpretations of reality. With Ruether and Schüssler Fiorenza, I affirm the importance of the social location of women and others who struggle against patriarchy, for it is that location and struggle that provide the means by which patriarchy, as a world-view, as an "idiom for the construction of reality," is altered and transformed. However, it is because social location has such priority and is always circumscribed by power and historical processes, that I cannot use the language of ontology or suggest the epistemological certitude implied by Ruether and Schüssler Fiorenza as well as Daly.[16]

This understanding of feminist perspectives as alternative but not ontologically more accurate renderings of reality could lead to a nihilistic conclusion that all views, patriarchal and feminist alike, are commensurate.[17] I do not think this is necessarily the case; abandoning claims to ontological and epistemological certitude need not mean that therefore all standards and norms are arbitrary commitments. Rather, we can assess our interpretive schemas and the norms embedded in them according to the kinds of experiences such schemas and standards permit or inhibit. Such pragmatic judgments will be contextual and will necessarily reflect the commitments and power positions of those who make them. But acknowledging the relative character of our norms rather than claiming cosmic or divine sanction for them, places the issue on the only level that really matters—the level of concrete and practical consequences. It is on this level, not on the level of deciding who can claim divine authority, that the struggle against nihilism must be engaged.

To appeal to pragmatic norms rather than ontological foundations is to indicate the central importance of the community in the configuring of norms and the defining of "truth." For such decisions are always derived within social communities with particular histories. It points therefore to the necessity of fostering participation in the social conversation and the public evaluation of what should count as desirable consequences. Because there are struggles to define norms not only within but also between communities, much work still needs to be done within this perspective of neo-pragmatism concerning the possibility of conversation in a conflictual world.[18]

Abandoning the appeal to ontological grounding and recognizing the historical and often conflictual character of experience suggests that we must also forego claims to universal female experience. Women's experience is concrete and particular; presuppositions of commonality, while allowing for common action, often deflect our analysis from the exploration of the myriad and complex factors that shape women's lives. In this view, feminist analysis must focus upon such particularities rather than on universal, often abstract, claims of common oppression.

And finally, the historicist model I have proposed entails a conception of religious symbolism that differs from those implicit in the feminist theologies examined above. In this approach, religious symbols are not interpreted as referential, whether directly or indirectly, metaphorically or literally, of an assumed ontological reality. Instead they are recognized as human constructions that function to focus the worldview of which they are a part, embodying the values embedded in these interpretive schemas. That is, they mark the place of our commitments, the values for which we are willing to struggle. Their "truth," so to speak, lies not in how well they depict some ontological structure of reality, but in the forms of experience engendered by commitment to such values.

Thus although we must oppose oppressive systems, we cannot do so by appeal to either universal female experience nor to some cosmic or divine perspective. We can do so only in the name of our particular location in history and with the recognition that our Gods and Goddesses are the articulation of our values and hopes, not the foundation of certitude nor the promise of victory.

Notes

1. An underlying assumption of this article is that feminist theology, while a departure from male-constructed theology, can be seen as part of the post-Enlightenment turn to experience that has characterized liberal theology from Schleiermacher onward. A thorough analysis of feminist theology's similarities and contrasts to other empirical theologies has yet to be undertaken.

2. See Bell Hooks, *Feminist Theory: from Margin to Center* (Boston: South End Press, 1984), hereafter cited in text as FT. See also Jacquelyn Grant, "A Black Response to Feminist Theology" in *Women's Spirit Bonding*, ed. Janet Kalven and Mary I. Buckley (New York: The Pilgrim Press, 1984), pp. 117–24 and "Black Feminist Theology: Celebration in the Midst of Struggle," unpublished keynote address, Women's Inter-Seminary Conference, Denver, Colorado, 1986.

3. Although Elisabeth Schüssler Fiorenza was originally from Germany, the current primary context of her feminist work is North America. Therefore, for the purposes of this essay, she will be analyzed under the rubric of North American feminist theology.

4. Elisabeth Schüssler Fiorenza, *Bread Not Stone* (Boston: Beacon Press, 1984), p. xiv, hereafter cited in text as BNS.

5. The context of this quote concerns the evaluation of the Bible, but the claim that norms of theological judgment are context-specific is a general principle that informs much of Schüssler Fiorenza's work.

6. Schüssler Fiorenza, "The Will to Choose or to Reject: Continuing Our Critical Work" in *Feminist Interpretation of the Bible*, ed. Letty M. Russell (Philadelphia: Westminster Press, 1985), p. 127–8, hereafter cited in text as WCR.

7. Rosemary Radford Ruether, *Sexism and God-Talk* (Boston: Beacon, 1983), p. 12, hereafter cited in text as SG.

8. Ruether, "Feminist Interpretation: A Method of Correlation" in *Feminist Interpretation of the Bible*, ed. Letty M. Russell (Philadelphia: Westminster Press, 1985), p. 114, hereafter cited in text as FI.

9. Mary Daly, *Pure Lust* (Boston: Beacon Press, 1984) p. 31, hereafter cited in text as PL.

10. Daly is very careful in her discussions of feminist consciousness not to exclude explicitly any group of women. To grasp her nuanced argument, see her discussions of sisterhood and of separatism in *Pure Lust*.

11. Daly's constant reference to memory, whereby women reclaim their essential selves and cosmic connections, emphasizes this essentialist interpretation of female nature. There is, however, a tension between the essentialist approach and Daly's sense of the importance of the feminist community for the recognition and realization of this female essence. Often, Daly's treatment of female essence has a pronounced ahistorical tone, while elsewhere, especially in her analysis of community, the central importance of the historical context is stressed.

12. Andrea Dworkin, *Our Blood* (New York: Harper & Row, 1976), p. 129.

13. For examples of social scientists and philosophers who explore the repercussions of these insights, see Norma Haan et al., *Social Science as Moral Inquiry* (New York: Columbia University Press, 1983). Theologians utilizing a number of these claims include Sallie McFague, *Metaphorical Theology* (Philadelphia: Fortress Press, 1982), Gordon D. Kaufman, *The Theological Imagination* (Philadelphia: The Westminster Press, 1981), and George A. Lindbeck, *The Nature of Doctrine: Religion and Theology in a Post-Liberal Age* (Philadelphia: Westminster Press, 1984).

14. Lindbeck, p. 18.

15. The relation of power and knowledge has been a major area of exploration from the nineteenth century onward. In particular, the work of Fredrich Nietzsche and Karl Marx focused on this issue. On the contemporary scene, the work of French thinker, Michel Foucault, has been most important in relation to the analysis of power and knowledge. See especially, Foucault, *Power/Knowledge: Selected Interviews and Other Writings, 1972–1977*, ed. Colin Gordon, trans. Colin Gordon et al. (New York: Pantheon Books, 1972, 1975, 1976, 1977).

16. Arguments for epistemological privilege sometime refer to the fact that a group, such as the poor or women, are in a position to know both its own experience and that of the oppressor and hence have a more profound understanding of historical processes. While I agree to a certain extent with this claim and think that greater inclusivity of knowledge has important pragmatic repercussions, I do not think it is thereby either more objective or closer to "ontological truth."

3

Contemporary Goddess Thealogy:
A Sympathetic Critique

Emily Erwin Culpepper

"Thealogy" is a word that quite a few feminists began to create independently of each other during the 1970's. I first imagined it myself while writing one of my Th.D. General Exams at Harvard Divinity School. In the white heat of exam writing, I realized that Goddess theory of contemporary feminists was not adequately named by the conventional term theology, based as it is on the Greek *theos*, which is masculine for "god." Furthermore, most feminists interested in Goddesses are women who strongly reject western patriarchal theology. To call Goddess theory by the name *theology*, then, would erase one of the primary motivations of these women. Making a new word from the Greek feminine form, *thea*, is therefore doubly in keeping with the developing analysis of radical feminism.

After I began to speak of "thealogy," I learned from Nelle Morton that Carol Christ was also beginning to use this word. Still later, I found that Christ credits Naomi Goldenberg with coining the term.[1] These developments are a good example of a familiar phenomenon — many feminists come independently to similar ideas. This process also reflects the active oral network through which feminist thinking spreads. Many more women have heard and passed on the term "thealogy" than have read it.

The last decade has seen an immense generation of feminist interest in Goddesses. This phenomenon is widespread, multiform and continuing to grow. It is especially prominent in the United States, Mexico, and Canada, as well as western Europe and Australia. Emerging interest in Goddesses is beginning to appear in feminist networks elsewhere, especially as feminists become more in touch with each other globally. This analysis has been drawn primarily from North American developments. It is important to realize that interest in Goddesses has developed essentially in a grass-roots manner.[2] There is no one prophetess, no single thealogian, no central religious leader, no sacred book, no holy city that establishes or defines what a Goddess orientation is. Of course, this makes the phenomenon difficult to summarize.

Sources for Thealogy

I want to comment first on the sources that are important to thealogical reflection. The primary source, the continuing referent, for thealogical inspiration is one's Self, understood as the consciously reflective Self in communication with others.[3] Critical Self-awareness is the most respected and essentially present-oriented form of pursuing thealogical knowledge. Feminists often mention in this regard the ancient maxim, "Know Thyself," and are fond of noting that this tradition, so closely associated with Socrates, was spoken to him by a female oracle at Delphi.[4] Whatever is passed on through the developing feminist oral tradition or read in even the most respected books is utilized in the context of deep attention to one's own experience and one's basic responses to such Goddess information. And this is not an unpracticed ideal. By far the great majority of feminists who speak of Goddesses manifest this habit of mind and heart. The diversity of opinion and practice produced is one of the primary reasons why the exploration of Goddess spirituality continues to grow and take new forms.

There are, certainly, a number of books that are highly regarded as particularly fruitful catalysts for thealogy. Especially prominent have been the work of Helen Diner, Elizabeth Gould Davis, Mary Daly, Merlin Stone, Z. Budapest and Starhawk. In the background of these books are others, which are increasingly searched out directly by women interested in the history of Goddess theory. I have in mind here the work of Jane Ellen Harrison, Robert Graves, James Frazer, Esther Harding, Erich Neumann, Bachofen, Briffault . . . Actually this listing is literally endless. Feminists interested in Goddesses regard almost any work as a potential source of information and catalyst for insight. None of them is completely adopted; they are freely explored and experimented with. The pursuit of thealogical ideas takes some women into astrology, dream theory and holistic healing. Others (or sometimes the same women) find Goddess imagery and ritual interest them in a new way in physics or brain research, art or archaeology. As must be clear by now, thealogical orientation is an expanding universe. There are also some limiting patterns in the sources that thealogy has drawn upon. There is a predominance of interest in western Goddesses when historical materials are consulted. Greek Goddesses, for example, play entirely too large a role in Goddess lore, reflecting in part a greater availability of such sources. Certainly, examination of the history, mythology and theology of ancient western versions of patriarchy can yield vital clues for understanding large-scale patterns of technological patriarchy.[5] But the Mediterranean "cradle of civilization" theory is disturbingly ethnocentric. The focus of thealogy is narrowed by remaining insufficiently critical of such traditional patterns and biases. It can claim to produce a "universal" thealogy, while Asia, India and Africa seem to fall off the map of consciousness. Thus, there is an urgent need for an eager Self-questioning by feminists about *why* we choose to work with the sources that we do. Clearly such questioning does go on, but we need to bring a particularly concerned awareness to such problems. There also is the continuing problem that certain sources are more credible in academia, and hence become disproportionately the focus of feminist scholarship.

One of the challenges facing present feminist theory is how to raise overall observations like these without turning them into scapegoating attacks of any particular woman's work. Of course, we must criticize, and these are subjects about which passions run high. But we do not fully reach new ground if our criticisms replicate the patriarchal pattern of horizontal hostility.

As one example of pointing out an overall pattern for criticism, some Jewish feminists have criticized what Judith Plaskow has called "blaming Jews for inventing patriarchy."[6] Plaskow noted that this most often happens when attempts are made to make early Christianity look better for women than Judaism. Annette Daum has warned about a similar shortsightedness among some Goddess worshippers, which she identifies as "Blaming Jews for the Death of the Goddess."[7] In addition to the fact that patriarchy is not just a western phenomenon, placing such blame on Jews is not a new idea, but just another form of the old Christian charge of deicide.

While such parochialism and unexamined assumptions are vitally important to recognize, women *are* recognizing and raising such issues with each other. Most feminists interested in Goddesses seek to expand the focus of their interest. They are keenly aware that there have been divine females in almost all religions and are eager to widen, not narrow the scope of thealogical information.[8] Increasing interest in Yoruban African Goddesses and in Hindu Goddesses are two examples of this interest.[9]

Contemporary feminist thealogy includes Goddess imagery, myth, ritual and religion from the past, especially the ancient past. Interwoven with these materials is interest in matriarchy theory. I will not develop here the complex debate concerning matriarchy—that would be a whole article in itself.[10] Thealogy *does not depend* on matriarchy, although many women are quite interested in theories about whether pre-patriarchal history was matriarchal and/or goddess worship. Interest in such questions has become controversial, disreputable—to the point of functioning very much like an academic taboo in some disciplines, especially anthropology. Why is there a desire to close the question? After all, every wave of thinking about the scope of human history has created a vision, a story about early human social arrangements and this often includes creation myths. It is harmful to assert that feminists should not also engage in this form of theory making, constructing our own hypotheses about the ancient past. The matriarchy question is most fruitfully approached by viewing it as an open question—explosively, aggressively, thought-provokingly open. We need more theory, not less. Feminist inquiry into the matriarchy debate can help elucidate the ways in which such theory has affected the development of contemporary thealogy.

Meanings of Goddess

Thealogy is a fluid phenomenon. There is no agreement among feminists as to just what the name "Goddess" means. Carol Christ has emphasized this feature as a strength of thealogy. She writes:

> When I asked what the symbol of Goddess meant, feminist witch Starhawk replied, "It all depends on how I feel. When I feel weak, She is someone who can help and protect me. When I feel strong She is the symbol of my own power. At other times I feel her as the natural energy in my body and the world."[11]

Christ comments:

> How are we to evaluate such a statement? Theologians would call these the words of a sloppy thinker. But my deepest intuition tells me they contain a wisdom Western theological thought has lost.[12]

Starhawk practices feminist Wicce, a *religion* focused on Goddess worship. This form of Goddess religion and its autonomous coven network is growing among feminist women and some radical men. But many feminists oriented towards Goddesses do *not* see themselves as part of a religion. This larger number would characterize their interest as spiritual or psychic, but not one they seek to organize beyond occasional rituals that are often spontaneous, unconventional and irregular. What follows are some meanings and functions of "Goddess" that are major themes within this changing and shifting field. They are reference points, but not a "systematic thealogy." I do not believe that thealogy can be adequately conveyed or developed in the forms used by traditional theological discourse. Interent in its grassroots manner of creativity is the instinct to elude attempts at logical systematizing. Goddess logic includes, but is not limited by the rational; it is primarily created through a wide-ranging spiritual free-thinking.

For a great many women, "Goddess" means a spectrum of female divinity, extending from the depths of the Self to the sense of a Divine Being who creates the universe. Again, Starhawk's comments are representative.

> The Goddess is immanent; She is here; She is in us all; She is not somewhere else. She is not outside the universe; She is in every one of us; in plants, in stones, in stars, in trees, in thought, in the life-force, in the cycles of life, in the secret spiral of DNA that sleeps inside every cell and often wakens us to life; in all.[13]

"Goddess," then, often carries meanings that include both deity and soul, expressing a continuum of divinity including the divine within Self, world and beyond, extending divinity from inner to outer infinity.

For a great many other feminists, Goddess language refers primarily or even exclusively to internal realities, functioning as a name for a woman's spirit or fullest sense of Self. "The Goddess Within" is a very common phrase. Mary Daly refers to "Goddess" as "the Self-affirming be-ing in women."[14] The name "Goddess" for such meanings functions to bring honor to female Selves, so denigrated in patriarchy. Many feminists prefer to leave open (in the assertive, inquisitive way I have already described) the question of whether Goddess means an external Divine Being.[15] Connected with this view, some feminists prefer to speak in the plural of Goddesses. We will return later to this theme. Feminists of all thealogical persuasions are as much, if not more, interested in the great and growing conversations among us all about these meanings and beliefs, as we are in our differences. Goddess consciousness thrives on perceptions of interconnections amongst differences.

The Goddess and the Great Mother

As is apparent by my remarks thus far, I am in sympathy with and identify with much in thealogy. However, at this juncture, it becomes especially urgent to develop my analysis as a "sympathetic critique." I do not find myself in accord with a major, indeed almost predominant theme in thealogy, namely, its focus on *The* Goddess. Closely connected—in fact often indistinguishable—is a thealogical focus on "The Goddess" as "Mother." Many feminists who are fascinated by Goddesses understand these as aspects of "The Goddess." Sometimes "The Goddess" may be described as "the dance of being" or "the Ultimate Life Force."[16] Often intertwined with these concepts is the practice of calling The Goddess "Mother" or "The Great Mother."

I want to meet the criterion which I stated earlier, and approach Goddess consciousness through a perception of connections, as well as differences and disagreements. Therefore, I am going to turn first to examining some primary meanings that "The Goddess, The Mother" holds for her believers—and I have set for myself the challenge of doing so as appreciatively, as sympathetically, as possible. There are important insights here we should not miss or distort. Following that, I will then move to points of criticism, and the problems and dangers I see with shaping feminist thealogy around "The Goddess, The Mother."

For many feminists who regard The Goddess as a Divine Being this means The Goddess is the Creatrix of the universe. Usually The Goddess is described as the sole deity creating the world from within herself—a cosmogony of parthenogenesis. This presents a very strong image of female independence and shifts our thinking about the relationship of deity and world. The Goddess does not create the world *ex nihilo*, from nothing, She creates from within herSelf.

Quite commonly this Creatrix is imaged in the form of a Triple Goddess. The Triple Goddess's three aspects are typically named Nymph, Maiden-Mother and Crone. Greek myths of Persephene, Demeter, and Hecate are a frequent frame of reference. Each aspect is associated with particular meanings, especially: the *Nymph* as joyful, playful, exuberant girlhood; the *Maiden-Mother* as a more adult, mature persona who is Mother of us all; and *The Crone* as the wisdom of aging which includes particularly a Raging consciousness confronting injustice and understanding the meaning of death. The three stages are seen as resembling the waxing, full and waning moon. The Triple Mother Goddess is often referred to as "The Moon Goddess." Since the Mother aspect includes the meaning of creatrix of the universe, this meaning acquires special significance. The Goddess is seen as giving birth to the universe.[18] Birth becomes here the paradigm of creativity. Goddess as "Mother of the Cosmos" thus carries an ontologically prior weight, and acquires a *generic* function. "The Mother" is therefore a sort of first name, a name that uniquely stands for the whole of the Triple Goddess.

For many women and some men, this is a powerful spiritual orientation that replaces God the Father. They experience this as not just a gender change of Deity, but as a significant shift of many other meanings. Worshippers of The Goddess in this sense say that The Goddess includes men because mothers give birth to female and male children.[19]

The Mother Goddess does not abandon any of her children. She may show them many of her different faces, but her love is the paramount meaning. The two most frequently repeated maxims in oral tradition about The Goddess are that she says: "All acts of love and pleasure are my rituals," and "Do as you will but harm none." As Starhawk has noted, these principles form the basis for the ethical approach of Goddess religion.[20] For these reasons this accepting Mother Goddess is especially welcomed by those who have felt reflected and condemned by traditional theology (for not being heterosexual, for example) or who are alienated by exclusive claims and hierarchical structures and demands in established religions.

Thus, the Mother Goddess is strongly associated not just with giving birth but with *activities* of mothering; with nurturing, caring and loving; with teaching how to live; with strengthening, comforting, and consoling and with urging us onward to improve our own lives and the lives of others.

Let us now briefly focus on the Goddess as the Earth, or as it is often expressed, "the Earth as Our Mother." Sometimes, thealogical consciousness is especially focused on the Mother Goddess as meaning the Earth, implying that our planet, our home, is a living being, imaged as female. Here is a typical statement from an Earth Mother ritual:

> Since the beginning of all Times of People
> the Earth has been female; so known by
> all who walk her:
> Mother Earth
> Mother Nature
> Goddess of Change and Fecundity.[21]

A major and growing influence here is myth, art and ritual from cultures all over the world that have had Earth Mother imagery. Native American Indian teachings are especially a source of inspiration.

Feminists are deeply concerned with strengthening the sense of interconnection with nature and with constructing an activist analysis that does not see human life as alienated from and dominating nature. Many who speak of "The Goddess" as "Mother" do so initially (or even primarily) because it makes sense to them to name this connection, this interdependence with nature as "Mother." This might be called a feminist "natural thealogy," but one that looks quite different from traditional Christian and philosophical arguments for "natural theology." This natural thealogy has motivated many individuals to take up ecological and anti-nuclear activism.

Other feminists occasionally speak of the Earth as Mother, but do *not* necessarily mean that in the sense of Goddess. Rather, they understand Mother Earth as a moving metaphor for deeply held feelings. Woody Simmons has a very popular song which reflects this well:

> My life is like a feather in the wind
> Not knowing which way it will turn next
> Falling gently back to the Earth
> To seek the Mother, to sleep upon her breast.[22]

This song is a good concrete example of my own boundary relation to thealogy. I respond very deeply to this song, but I do not usually image my relation to the Earth as Mother or as Goddess. But this divergence in my own spiritual orientation does not separate me from sharing in this sensibility with other women for whom it is a more primary focus.

It is through the exploration of natural thealogy, and of the Mother Goddess understood as *all* of nature, that I see the Mother Goddess having more than simply an anthropomorphic meaning for many individuals. They see "Mother" as much in the model of seasonal changes, the cycles of plant and animal and human life, cycles of moon, sun and stars, and geological processes as in the reproductive process of human females. They see all such cycles *as metaphorically analogous with each other*, all participating in the interwoven rhythmic pulses of life.

Even though I do not share this approach, when I open myself to hearing what belief in "The Mother Goddess" means to those who worship or meditate in this way, I begin to see a new type of meaning. In this new meaning, the metaphorical links between human motherhood and natural life forces are experienced in a different, almost reverse order of comparison than we might expect. An example will help make this clear. A person might describe the ocean as Mother, a primal womb and source of life, and the human female's womb is seen as comparable to the ocean and appreciated in relation to this sense of life source as much or even *more than* the other way around.

Women's music furnishes us with a good example of this spiritual orientation, of seeing the ocean as Goddess and/or as Mother.

> In the beginning was the ocean
> The Yorubans call her yemaya
>
> Yemaya, ocean mother
> In the beginning you gave birth to the heavens
> To all the gods and goddesses
> Sister of the fishes.[23]

The Ocean Mother, The Earth Mother, The Corn Mother, The Great Mother, The Moon Mother, The Crone Mother . . . these and many other mother names are frequent names for the Goddess.

Affirming and Empowering Women

The Goddess also has meanings which affirm women's sense of Self, in ways that counteract and heal the negative conditioning of patriarchal roles. Carol Christ's essay "Why Women Need the Goddess" has especially focused on some of these meanings.[24] Christ cites four main effects of Goddess symbolism. The Godess affirms: independent female power, the female body, the female will and women's bonding and heritage. All these affirmations certainly stand in sharp contrast to the patriarchal religious record. The Goddess is often a channel for a great rethinking of a woman's Self and for the meanings of all facets of her life.

The Goddess is often a focal point, providing a language to construct rituals and celebrations. Addressing "The Goddess," celebrating "The Goddess," is often the means for creating community, for sharing commitment to particular ideals and insights, for celebrating certain forms of awareness. Quite commonly, groups of women might share the observance, for example, of seasonal celebrations, especially solstices and equinoxes, in which some or all would speak of "The Goddess." Each woman might have a different frame of reference for the ritual actions and words. These differences are usually assumed, and they may also be explicitly acknowledged and valued. What is shared is the experience of celebration, the expectation of learning from and with each other. Goddess rituals are also created to celebrate key transitions and special events in a woman's life: times of emotional and physical crisis and healing and, increasingly, to initiate and accompany organized political action. The Goddess, then, is often an organizing principle for meditation, ritual and action.

The last point in the "sympathetic" part of my analysis is related to the Goddess as catalyst for rethinking on the part of feminists. Ideas and imagery of the Goddess provide a vehicle for women to engage in the transformation of consciousness and experience. Given the important force that God as Father has had in the construction and defense of patriarchy, it is not surprising that impulses toward liberation draw women to imagery of "The Goddess, The Mother." Patriarchy has, in fact, constructed its own mythology of women as mothers, so it has been important for women to explore a symbol that values mothers.

But the vast rethinking is not only occurring in Goddess language, but also in the wide and sometimes contradictory dialogue, reactions, disagreements and response to the Goddess. As spiritual orientation toward Goddesses becomes more widespread and as individuals develop a history of change and growth of their own ideas about Goddesses, further insights are unfolding. Many women, for example, are entertaining the idea that "The Goddess as The Mother" can tend to promote the view that women are essentially mothers and/or that women are inherently more loving and nurturing than men. Adrienne Rich has warned that the equation of women with mothers is problematic:

> It can be dangerously simplistic to fix upon "nurturance" as a special strength of women, which need only be released into the larger society to create a new human. . . . [We] must reckon fully with the ambiguity of our being and with the continuum of our consciousness, the potentialities for both creative and destructive energy in each of us.[25]

It is in this spirit, recognizing the ambiguities of our being and the plurality of be-ing, that we now move to criticisms of thealogy of "The Goddess, The Mother."

Sympathetic Critique: Beyond Mother Goddess Monotheism

Some themes in feminist thealogy seem dangerous for women. Thealogy can be vital and energizing but there are also some very familiar and unliberating presences in it. Thealogy focused on The Goddess—The Mother—often reflects and is shaped by a belief in archetypes (often Jungian) that is not sufficiently examined for its explicit and implicit assumptions. Erich Neumann's book, *The Great Mother* seems to fascinate many women to a detrimental degree. For example, archetypes of "Woman" or "Femininity" or "The Mother" are too easily compatible with oppressive gender roles. Separating reality into male and female essences, however dramatically or mythically conceived, ultimately creates only a cosmic rationalization for sex role stereotyping. Archetypal theory of this sort collapses the rich diversity of living into a familiar gender dualism. When this happens, important realities in women's lives begin to fade from view.

It is understandable that Jungian archetype theory is attractive to women. Many have wanted to discover a form of scholarly work that seems to take seriously female imagery and female divine images. Unfortunately this has led some feminists to grasp at these theoretical approaches in desperation or gratitude, and with an alarming suspension of critical thought about these ideas.

Further, the academic credibility of Jungian schools of thought has a problematic and sometimes damaging influence. Since it is still difficult to gain academic credibility for radical feminist work, the discovery of a school of thought that seems to offer a language for talking about women and female images provides a foothold for feminist work in the academy. The illusion that Jungian theory is pro-female causes too many feminists (both in Women's Studies and completely outside academia) to accept this work uncritically rather than take it as food for thought.

These are difficult and slippery problems. How can we develop methods of criticizing larger patterns in feminist scholarship and popular feminist thought without appearing to launch a personal attack on particular women's choices of language and image? Because feminist ideas and scholarship involve matters women care about deeply, identifying problematic directions in other women's work is difficult to raise and hard to hear.

Feminist method often includes comment on the questions by which we have developed a particular analysis. This is part of our commitment to demystify scholarship and to write for readers outside as well as inside the academic circle. In this connection, I will describe the process by which my concerns about Goddess thealogy become clear—especially the overreliance on Jungian theory. It began with a very deep anger. When writing in my journal about my lack of enthusiasm for *The* Goddess, I discovered I felt like yelling, yelling something like, "NO! Not just THE GODDESS, not THE mother! Get out! Get out of women's minds, Jung and Neumann!"

Audre Lorde has emphasized the importance of connecting feelings to analysis, so that feelings *inform* thoughts.[26] This process of recognizing my spiritual and intellectual anger functioned to clarify my perceptions—much in the way that Mary Daly calls a "method of exorcism."[27] Through the process of recognizing and acknowledging anger, I saw that archetype theory was pervading and shaping feminist thought. This theory was an unconscious influence, a "spooking presence" of carry-overs from patriarchal ideas identified by Daly in *Gyn/Ecology*.[28] I realized further that Jungian theory was one major example of a disturbing tendency in feminist scholarship to examine assumptions inadequately, and especially to continue to think in dualistic categories.

Confronting such spooking presences, it became easier to recognize the problems and their effects. A central problem with "The Goddess" is that the symbol can function to limit perception of the realities of many women. This problem could be called *"generic erasure."* It is easy for the Goddess as generic to become not just a catalyst for insight but also a veil that covers up, erases or insufficiently differentiates important issues. When this happens, Goddess thealogy can have a flattening-out or dulling influence, giving us too pallid a picture of the richness of multiple female realities. This insight explained to me why I often found that poetry, art and ritual that focused on this generic goddess was *boring*! The archetype was receiving more attention than real women were.

Here is a typical example of this problem. The feminist journal *Heresies* announced that it would publish a special theme issue on the rapidly growing and diverse phenomenon of feminist spirituality. By the time the issue appeared it had become "The Great Goddess Issue."[29] There is much that is valuable in this issue, but it exemplifies the problem I am addressing. Gloria Orenstein's article, "The Reemergence of the Archetype of the Great Goddess in Art by Contemporary Women" illustrates this unfortunate distortion of emphasis. She says, for example, "Artists who are in touch with the archetype of the Goddess are now using the female form."[30] In her analysis, the archetype often seems *more real* than the actual women artists or their specific works. Generically generalizing all this diversity into aspects of an archetype, and validating the power of the art by seeing it as archetype, places women in a secondary status; they hold second place to an idea. *This is a familiar patriarchal position.* Ultimately it is not liberating.

When women are the second sex, our lives are molded to fit male thought. In the resulting molds, the lived realities of many women are missing. Here are some of the central distortions operating in this generic erasure:

All women are not mothers. The Great Mother is inadequate because this designation places central significance on a single potential that most women have during part of their lives. When "The Mother" is used generically for "The Goddess," who is then equated with women's deepest identity, this identification fails to discriminate among three important things: the potential ability to become a mother, the experiences that follow from actualizing that potential (by choice or not), and the power of choice about this physical possibility. Women's reproductive choice is a power that is a prime target of patriarchal attempts to control women. The blurring of these issues clouds our perceptions and serves patriarchal interest.

This blurring is also evident in Mother Goddess interpretations of Triple Goddess imagery. The Triple Goddess certainly presents one way of looking at stages in a woman's life, marked by the biological events of menarche, menstruation and fertility, and menopause. Each stage offers different choices, pressures and opportunities. It is inaccurate and damaging to name the sum of the span of these stages "Mother." In fact, women who live a long life experience all these stages whether or not they become mothers. A more accurate name for this middle stage might be "menstruant," but this name does not yet have the positive aura, the approved though sentimentalized respect that "Mother" ostensibly has in patriarchy.[31]

The way in which the Triple Mother Goddess is correlated with meditating on lunar cycles also leads to distortions. When three biological stages of female life are used to interpret lunar cycles as a symbol, this process omits naming and contemplating a fourth aspect of the moon: the dark, nonvisible phase (called the new moon, the no moon, the dark moon, the absent moon). This dark moon phase is the one most symbolically similar to death and to the hardest and often hidden stages in major transformations. To gloss over this distinct phase and combine it with the waning moon, with Crone imagery, may make contemplation of lunar cycles more comforting and more compatible with Birth Mother imagery, but it alters the reality to fit the metaphor.[32] This is like meditating on vegetation cycles and leaving out decay.

Birth is an inadequate symbol for many forms of creativity. With focus on The Goddess as The Mother, birth remains the central image for female creativity. Certainly we can understand why birth is one powerful metaphor for creativity. But when it becomes *the* metaphor, other processes of creating can too easily be viewed as substitutes and often, therefore, as less important.

This distortion is particularly harmful because pregnancy and birth are often inaccurate and misleading models. A related issue here is that an idealized model of a chosen, relatively easy conception, pregnancy and delivery is most often, though not exclusively used. This idealized model implies less activity than is often necessary to envision and support sustained, continuous, disciplined, creative activity. For example, neither the writing of this article nor the longer task of my doctoral dissertation felt like giving birth to a child.

I found it helpful during the writing of my dissertation to meditate on many different models for creativity; we do not need the inflated model that has been promoted by patriarchy as the essence of female identity.[34] It is oppressive for women to believe that giving birth and mothering are analogous to any other form of creativity. Such false assurances too easily content women with limited options. They also do not help us to value birth and mothering in themselves and hinder the development of women-defined, nonpatriarchal definitions of birth and mothering.

The Great Mother obscures the presence of lesbians and heterosexism. While there are many lesbian mothers, for most people the image of Mother does not include lesbians. A surprising number of people persist in thinking these are mutually exclusive terms. They seem so because "Mother" is primarily perceived as a heterosexual, and often nuclear family, role, and "lesbian" is perceived as a woman who hates all men and rejects the life of "real" women. Even though many Great Goddesses in the past were parthenogenetic mothers, this is *not* the sense that motherhood carries today.

This problem unfortunately limits the full power of Carol Christ's valuable article, "Why Women Need the Goddess." Christ focuses her important discussion of the affirming power of The Goddess symbol on attributes that conform to the Mother Goddess. She omits discussion of lesbians and their significant role in feminism from all four of her important points: independent women's power, the female body, the female will, and women's bonding and heritage. This is especially glaring since many of the women she quotes are lesbian feminists. The symbol of The Goddess is not functioning adequately when this name does not lead Christ to discuss the existence and contributions of lesbians as lesbians, even when she quotes them.[35]

The Great Mother inadequately challenges the model of female self-sacrifice. It might at first seem strange that so powerful a female symbol would contain debilitating models for women. However, when The Goddess is primarily The Mother, this insufficiently challenges the patriarchal pressure on mothers and all women to place others' needs before their own. The expectation that a woman is a care-giver and nurturer, often to the detriment of her own Self, has been a primary channel for patriarchal abuse. Feminists are seeking to elaborate better models, to create forms of concern for others that do not mean *submitting* to the needs of others. Such unexamined roles dull feminist consciousness when they are glorified by Goddess imagery. They lead to uncritical adoption of ideas about what it means to be sensitive, to have healthy relationships, and to work cooperatively with others. These insufficiently examined roles and assumptions too often result in conflict among feminists.

The Mother Goddess obscures the presence of single women, of spinsters. Autonomous single women, whatever their sexuality, are devalued by defining mothering as the basic image of the Goddess. Mary Daly and others have reclaimed the name "Spinster" in this regard, a name that strikes us quite differently than "Mother." I think here of my own great aunt, Miss Louise Erwin, a spinster proudly independent who struggled for respect for her choice to remain free of marriage and motherhood and for her views on racial and sexual equality—all views that were at odds with turn-of-the-century southern white femininity. It does her no honor to sum up this woman's power as an attribute of the Great Mother. To extend this personal/political insight, I think here also of my mother, Helen Erwin Culpepper. Happy and active with her work, her family and her friends, she encouraged my appreciation of diversity in women and, in particular, of my great aunt's eccentric way of being larger-than-patriarchal-life. My love for my mother does not lead me to identify female strength solely with Mother. Rather I see the sparkling independence in both these women, and their bonding.

Goddess monotheism is not new enough. Another ghost that slips into a spooking subliminal role in thealogy centered on "The Goddess, The Mother," is the ghost of the One God/Father and the mindset of monotheism. Replacement of God the Father with Goddess-the-Mother leaves images of a Divine Parent, and definitions of divine power as outside one's self inadequately examined. As Christ has written, "Symbol systems cannot be simply rejected, they must be replaced, or "the mind will revert to familiar structures at times of crisis, bafflement or defeat."[36] But we need more than simple replacements; we need a transformation of symbols and symbolizing that creates new contexts and helps generate ongoing consciousness-raising and activism.

Even when The Goddess is not construed as The Mother, it is still a reductionist term, since the *pluralism* in women's lives, symbols, and choices is an important move toward freedom. Any one concept inflated into The One God or The Goddess or The Right Way divides society into two groups: an elite that identifies with The One and an outcast group which the elite has had the power to stigmatize and define as Other, as evil, as less valued, even as sub- or non-human.

There is too much wonderful diversity, contrast and movement in the world—what de Beauvoir has called "the plurality of the concrete"—for the One to function positively as our major symbol. We need symbols for unity, but the unity of the many is very different from a collapse of all diversity into a static One. We need many models of unity too.

Starkly put, The One is basically a hostile term for feminists. It pulls together all that is valued, and separates from all that is rejected, creating "the Other" as repository for what is rejected or feared. As Marilyn Frye has noted, it also denies the positive attractions that otherness—what is strange or new or different—can often have.[37] Given these consequences, monotheism is questionable, for it inevitably creates this secondary category. Monotheism functions as a mask for a debilitating dualism, a binary hierarchy that impoverishes our imaginations and obscures the fantastic multiplicity of be-ing.

Wiccan oral tradition has a saying, "To light a candle is also to cast a shadow." This teaching expresses the realization that to set up one thing also sets up at least one other category. To see everything else only as shadow leave these realities negatively defined. They are not perceived in and for themselves, but as not-the-One. They are seen only as what they lack, they lack the quality of being the One.

Such monotheistic dualism obscures our recognition that these others are also ones. Split and hostile models of consciousness are fundamental foundations of patriarchy.[38] The One really becomes the Dominator, The Dominating One. Its distortions of women's lives are multiform. Clearly, it distorts the realities that are rejected and lumped together as the Other. What is less often noticed is that such monotheistic dualism also distorts the realities that are valued and claimed as part of the One. When the qualities identified with the One are not receiving an exaggerated, exalted emphasis, they too are often blurred together, submerged into the Dominating One itself.

Distortions in thealogy occur when a monotheistic focus on The Goddess allows imagery of this Goddess to remain predominantly envisioned by privileged groups. Early attempts to create new Goddess art frequently showed a distressing tendency to image the Goddess as an idealized nude, too much like either an air-brushed Playboy bunny or a noble Victorian heroine. This situation has been changing rapidly as more and more women insist on a variety of images for how women look.[39] Goddess imagery has been a major corrective in this regard. Interest in a variety of images has also helped to move many women to question whether a monothea-istic focus on The Goddess really makes sense. Focus on The Goddess, since it is an anthropomorphic concept, cannot conjure up enough diversity among women. Even common assurances that "The Goddess has a thousand names and a thousand faces" do not preclude serious limitations. This focus on The Goddess tends to conjure a solitary image which is therefore seriously limited in its ability to convey women-bonding.

As a final, major evidence and result of such problems:

The Goddess is too easily a white Goddess. Many Black feminists and other women of Color say that they neither see or hear themselves included in this supposedly inclusive term. A monotheistic focus can be too easily compatible with unexamined racism. Lorraine Bethel's magnificently angry poem "What chou mean *we*, white girl?" expresses this.

> Dear Ms Ann Glad Cosmic Womoon
> We're not doing that kind of work anymore
> educating white women
> teaching Colored Herstory 101.[40]

Bethel is angry at Goddess worshippers "with no libations for Black female spirits," who "pick our brain, steal our culture, style and identities." She concludes by celebrating Black women who "be lovin ourselves for real/be praisin the BLACK GODDESS."[41] Bethel must assert "Black female spirits" and "the BLACK GODDESS" because, in a white-dominated society, The Goddess does not adequately conjure up Black female images. The Goddess slides too easily into the stereotype of a dominant role.

Yvonne Flowers's poem "Black Goddesses" describes her concern not to create or fall into stereotypes. She starts with warning the reader:

> Now you can't always tell a black goddess
> by how she looks.
> She may laugh too loud or
> stand in the middle of a silence
> like my Grandma at the kitchen table
> mixing cornmeal and egg
> But you can't always tell a black goddess
> by what she cooks
> She may not
> or burns it,
> or cooks only your flesh.[42]

It is only after an insistent breaking of images that Flowers goes on to offer one image of special meaning to her:

> You can sometimes tell the black goddess
> Sometimes, by how she moves,
> dances, dances, dances.

Lest the reader miss the point, Flowers ends her poem with a lyrical incantation of many Black female names, intertwining mythic, historical and contemporary Black women.

Kate Rushin's poem "The Black Goddess" offers a further criticism.

> I am not a Black Goddess
> I am not a Black Goddess
> Look at me
> Look at me
> I do what I can

That's about it
Sometimes I make it Sometimes I don't . . .

I still get Night Terrors
And sometimes it takes me weeks to
Answer a letter or make a phone call

I am not a Black Goddess.
I am not a Black Goddess.

Once though   I was Harriet Tubman[43]

At this point in the poem she describes a time she had to rise to a dangerous occasion and talk a frightened, violent man into putting down his razor. She goes on to say that terror and bravery are both parts of herself, that she is not a Black Goddess or a Black Devil, that

I am not a picture in your mind
I am myself struggling toward myself.

It is not liberating for the women's movement to become simply the goddess movement, as some have suggested it should. The great surge of female creativity that includes thealogy as one form of thought will fail to be true to its liberating motivation if The Goddess eclipses actual women. Spirituality has an important energizing role to play in changing women's conditions. But I see thealogy at its best when it is understood as part of and rooted in the broader activities of consciousness-raising sympathetic criticism, and political activism. In this light, thealogy and Goddess imagery are more able to catalyze ongoing Self-reflection, to generate psychic energy and to challenge us to greater freedom of thought and action.

This sympathetic critique urges more attention to the processes of symbolizing and to identifying imagery of pluralism. Many women have responded strongly to symbols that carry plural meanings, and have recognized that not every woman would necessarily find all of these symbols helpful, for example, Amazons, Furies, Sisters, or Witches. Such symbols are often understood as having spiritual and political dimensions, but they are not easily fashioned into a religion. We do not worship The Great Amazon, for example, even though we know there have been Amazon Goddesses. Feminists create pantheans of symbols as one tool for recreating and changing our Selves and the World. A new sensibility is being formulated in which "the personal is political is spiritual." A pluralistic approach is less likely to erase or romanticize vital aspects of women's lives. Pluralism is more likely to help us to recognize our differences as positive and to explore what Mirtha Quintanales has called "our different primary emergencies."[44]

Developing thealogy in the direction of pluralism will give feminists safeguards against placing mythic female imagery ahead of real, living women. We must never forget that improving the condition of our sex is a primary motivation of feminism, certainly an Amazonian task and one that we cannot wait for "The Goddess" to accomplish.

Notes

1. Carol Christ, "Why Women Need the Goddess," *Heresies* 5:13, n. 11, and Naomi Goldenberg, *Changing of the Gods: Feminism and the End of Traditional Religions*, p. 96.

2. This observation has also been stressed by Merlin Stone ("The Three Faces of Goddess Spirituality," *Heresies* 5:2) and by Luisa Teish (*Jambalaya: The Natural Woman's Book of Personal Charms and Practical Rituals*, pp. ix–xii.

3. This orientation has been affirmed in virtually every conversation I have had with hundreds of feminists interested in the Goddess. This is an astounding consistency in a field of highly diverse ideas. See also: Starhawk *The Spiral Dance*, p. 12; and Christ, "Why Women Need the Goddess," pp. 8–12. (Along with some other feminists, I capitalize *Self* to stress that a deep sense of authentic woman-identified being is meant, and to distinguish this Self from the many false selves patriarchy imposes on women and which we may have internalized.)

4. Starhawk, p. 12.

5. And, as Beverly Smith has pointed out, students of a traditional academic track American education share a common exposure to what is considered western tradition. Thus, these traditions become an available mythic heritage for diverse individuals. As Smith also notes, "As a Black woman, I stand in a different relation to this material" (conversation, Fall 1981).

6. Judith Plaskow, "Blaming Jews for Inventing Patriarchy," *Lilith* 7:11.

7. Annette Daum, "Blaming Jews for the Death of the Goddess," *Lilith* 7:12.

8. See for example: Merlin Stone's *Ancient Mirrors of Womanhood*, vols. 1 and 2, which offers imaginative retelling of Goddess lore from around the World; and Barbara Walker, *The Woman's Encyclopedia of Myths and Secrets*.

9. See for example: Sabrina Sojourner, "From the House of Yemanja: The Goddess Heritage of Black Women," *The Politics of Women's Spirituality* (ed. Charlene Spretnak), pp. 57–63; Luisa Teish, *Jambalava*; and Rita M. Gross, "Hindu Female Deities as a Resource for the contemporary Rediscovery of the Goddess." *The Book of the Goddess: Past and Present*, ed. Carl Olsen, pp. 217–30.

10. "The Controversy Over Matriarchy Theory: What's At Risk" will be a chapter in my book, *The Revolt of the Symbols* (in progress), accompanying this chapter on thealogy.

11. Christ, p. 10.

12. Christ, p. 10.

13. Starhawk, "Witchcraft as a basis for Goddess Religion of the Future," *The Book of the Goddess*, ed. Ann Forfreedom and Julie Ann, p. 174.

14. Mary Daly, *Gyn/Ecology: The Metaethics of Radical Feminism*, p. 111.

15. See for example the discussion by the *WomanSpirit Magazine* Collective in "What Is This Goddess Business?" *WomanSpirit* 9:7–10.

16. Starhawk, "Ethics and Justice in Goddess Religion," in Spretnak, p. 319.

17. Stone, *The Three Faces of Goddess Spirituality*, p. xvii.

18. Starhawk, *The Spiral Dance*, p. 24.

19. Spretnak, "Introduction," *The Politics of Women's Spirituality*, p. xvii. (I am not focusing my analysis on the role of men in thealogy. But I want to note here that this explanation is problematic to me. It would be helpful for men who are interested in thealogy and who worship The Goddess to describe their understandings of this in more detail than they have so far.)

20. Starhawk, "Ethics and Justice in Goddess Religion."

21. Baba Cooper, "Mother Healing," *WomanSpirit* 14, p. 51.

22. Woody Simmons, "Feather in the Wind," *Oregon Mountains*.

23. Carolyn Brandy, "Yemaya," *Alive!*

24. Carol Christ, "Why Women Need the Goddess," *Heresies* 5:8–13.

25. Adrienne Rich, *Of Woman Born: Motherhood as Experience and Institution*, p. 283.

26. Audre Lorde, "The Erotic As Power," *Chrysalis* 9:29–31.

27. Mary Daly, *Beyond God The Father*, p. 10.

28. Daly, *Gyn/Ecology*, pp. 315–53.

29. Daly, *Heresies* 5:74.

30. Gloria Feman Orenstein, "The Reemergence of the Archetype of the Great Goddess in Art by Contemporary Women," *Heresies* 5:74.

31. Conversation with Linda Barufaldi, Fall 1980.

32. We see this problem for example in Buffie Johnson and Tracey Boyd's, "The Eternal Weaver" in *Heresies* 5:74–84.

33. My personal symbols: a house-painting job (long hours of preparation before the completing steps of actually painting are reached); a zen Koan (how to describe the current of the feminist movement when it moves on while I try to describe it); growing a plant (knowing when and where to prune); Karate study (physical and mental discipline, facing internal as well as external obstacles, shaping one's own style, exploring one's Self); making a quilt (finding patterns and pieces, deciding what to emphasize).

34. French feminists Monique Wittig and Saude Zeig have constructed a new prehistory mythology which conveys an emphatic rejection of birth as *the* model for creativity. They imagine an originally diverse and harmonious Amazon culture that becomes split by the choice of some women to base their identity in motherhood.

    Then they were struck with wonder over one of their physiological processes, childbearing. They stopped calling themselves amazons. . . . They called themselves mothers. They developed a whole "new" culture in which nothing could escape analogy to their own engenderment. They were fascinated by myths about rotundity, germination, earth and the fructification of trees. (*Lesbian Peoples*, p. 55)

35. Conversation with Linda Barufaldi, Winter 1981.

36. Christ, p. 8.

37. Marilyn Frye, "The Meaning of Difference," Feminist Theory Colloquium, Boston, Feb. 7, 1985.

38. This point is developed further in my article "Simone de Beauvoir and the Revolt of the Symbols," *Trivia: A Journal of Ideas*, 6:6–32.

39. See for example the emphasis on women's diversity throughout *Woman of Power: A Magazine of Feminism, Spirituality and Politics* (P.O. Box 827, Cambridge, Massachusetts 02238).

40. Lorraine Bethel, "What chou mean *we*, white girl?" *Conditions* 5:89. By using "Ms Ann," Bethel is bitterly, ironically updating "Miss Ann," a traditional Black name for a white woman functioning in a privileged role.

41. Bethel, p. 91.

42. Yvonne Flowers, "Black Goddesses," *Jemima* 1:10.

43. Kate Rushin, "The Black Goddess," *Home Girls: A Black Feminist Anthology*, ed. Barbara Smith, pp. 328–30.

44. Mirtha Quintanales, "I Paid Very Hard for My Immigrant Ignorance," *This Bridge Called My Back: Writing by Radical Women of Color* ed. Cherrie Moraga and Gloria Anzaldua, pp. 150–56.

4

"Some Mother's Son and Some Father's Daughter": Gender and Biblical Language in Afro-Christian Worship Tradition

Cheryl Townsend Gilkes

Feminism has illuminated the role of the Christian church in the construction of social knowledge about gender, but its light has illuminated very different kinds of shadows and of social problems. Both black and white Christian women identify problems in their churches and in society, but they define those problems differently, and they allocate their time, energies, and passions in distinctive, sometimes divergent, directions. These differing understandings of the treatment of gender in religious institutions reflect profound differences in social experience.

Feminism and Social Knowledge: Locating a Social Problem

Contemporary sociological thinking about women has moved beyond the problem of social roles to comprise several interrelated problems focusing on institutions, culture, inequality, and the sociology of knowledge. Both sociological analysis and the feminist critique of culture recognize the importance of the production of social knowledge. Multitudes of cultural materials "carry explicit and implicit suggestions regarding the appropriate social roles for women and men," writes Margaret Andersen in her examination of "sexism and the social construction of knowledge." She argues:

> The ideas about women and men that these cultural objects portray greatly influence our thinking about gender roles in society. As images, they convey an impression about the proper role of women, their sexual identity, and their self-consciousness. The ideas we hold about women and men, whether overtly sexist or more subtle in

their expression, create social definitions that we use to understand ourselves and the society we live in.[1]

The images of women projected by the media distinguish between black and white women. While the media reinforce a cultural vision of white women that is subordinating, they project for black women a profound cultural humiliation that includes black men. Since sexist images are always racially specific, and racist imagery almost always specifies gender, such images may be attributed to simple value reflection, to conscious role modeling, to organizational gender inequality, or to prevalent patriarchal interests within capitalism.[2] Andersen suggests that the exclusion of women from the pursuit and production of knowledge is the key to the problem of sexism and the social construction of knowledge.

Isolation and tokenism, as well as exclusion, are central features of women's experience in institutions of all kinds. Such social realities operate to keep women not only from contributing to the apprehension and interpretation of cultural experience, but also from a certain attachment to oppressive institutions. Their "stranger status" may produce a degree of indifference to the dominant perspective of the group. Andersen argues that while women's exclusion, isolation, and detachment hinder their effort to transform patriarchy, such detachment also "creates critical distance."[3] Thus what the powerful may take for granted, the excluded and the powerless may question and protest. Utilizing Hegel's analysis of master-slave relations, Andersen, like Angela Davis earlier, compares the world view of women to that of slaves. In relations of domination and subordination, the subordinate have a more complete or encompassing world view—their view includes themselves *and* the dominant party. The slaves' world view includes a perspective on their owners, while the owners fail to see the slaves. Women include men in their world view while men do not always "see" women. Similarly, black people may "see" white people to whom they are physically and socially invisible. Like the labor of Hegel's slaves, the work and experience of white women tends to be invisible to white men. Andersen points out that

> . . . women's labor shapes men's experience in the world (through housework and the maintenance of social and bodily relations). Women's labor makes the male mode of operation . . . possible; yet, it remains invisible to men as the dominant class.[4]

For black women, however, the situation is more complicated. They share with black men the problem of rendering all black people visible to those who control a racist society. Historically, however, black women have been visible in the black world, and their attachment to that world can be seen in many places—including the slave narratives, where the accounts of slave women's abuse, rape, and physical punishment are often vividly documented by slave men. As early as the 1860s, some black men claimed to be conscious of the errors of white men in their view of women. According to Linda Perkins' analysis of racial uplift and black women's education in the nineteenth century, "cooperative efforts between black females and males" were prevalent in the nineteenth century community, "since liberation of the race was the immediate goal of blacks, [and] the men attached great importance to the females' role in this effort." Providing an example of this black male perspective, Perkins writes:

> While sexism was not completely absent from the black community, black men became some of the earliest advocates of women's rights. In 1869 when black men formed the Colored National Labor Union, they admitted black women and elected a female to the executive committee of the group. The body voted to uphold equal rights for women and further stated that they were "profiting by the mistakes heretofore made by our white fellow citizens in omitting women."[5]

The consciousness of slaves and freedpeople of the nineteenth century was informed by the heroic status of several black women. Sojourner Truth and Harriet Tubman were two particularly prominent women whose roles within the community raised questions about every assumption concerning the capabilities of women. Furthermore, the historical separation in legal tradition between " 'incorrupt' women" who were white and imported to be wives, and slave women who were black and imported to be beasts of burden, created an historical centrality of women to the fate and future of black people as a self-conscious community.[6] In addition to heroic black women, what Angela Davis has called the "deformed equality"[7] between black women and men generated by racial oppression held distinct implications for the organization of gender roles and relations and consciousness about gender in the black cultural experience. Particularly in the black religious experience, the social problems that surround gender in the black community have not been problems of invisibility for women. The roots of the black community's sexism are not grounded in a perspective that renders women invisible or excludes them from the social world.

"Largely by Their Hands and Feet": Religious Ideas about Gender

In a church history commemorating the fiftieth anniversary of the Church of God in Christ, Bishop Ozro T. Jones wrote in 1957: "The 'proper' place of women in the church is an age-old debate and from all appearances, it seems that it perhaps will be an eternal one—for most mortals at least. This is because too often humanity has looked to the misty heights of theory rather than among the lowly foothills of practice and necessary human service."[8] Bishop Jones then argued that Christianity addressed the problems of the status of women more dramatically and positively than any other religion by insisting that they are "persons for whom Christ died." Reflecting on Galatians 3:28, Jones wrote:

> But lest we forget, this has been possible only because Christianity has defined women to be persons. In so doing, Christianity has insisted that women are not commodities or an inferior breed, or something like "factory rejects" of the human race, conceptions which held (and hold) sway wherever humanity has lived in the era of B.C. (before Christ). FOR PERSONS FOR WHOM CHRIST DIED any incidental physical condition is no longer a barrier to freedom, or dignity, or value as a person whether that physical condition be race ("Jew or Gentile"), class ("bond or free"), or sex ("male or female"). They all share one spiritual destiny and nature and value in Christ. They all are "fellow heirs" of the promise in Christ.[9]

This statement is important because it was written by a black male bishop in the mid 1950s—the time period so clearly identified with women's exclusion and oppression in the United States. Although the statement contains problematic assumptions about the history of religions and cultural universals, it prefigures by nearly two decades some of the major (and no less problematic) arguments of contemporary Christian feminists. Jones observed that the overwhelming response of women to Christianity was "grateful acknowledgement of what Christ has done." He then advanced a rhetorical but important question: "Indeed, who would dare deny that largely by their hands and feet and service has the Kingdom of our Lord moved forward?"[10] The purpose of his essay was a tribute to the Women's Department of the Church of God in Christ. It was also to express support for the women's autonomous convention under the leadership of Mother Lillian Brooks Coffey, whom Jones called "the guiding spirit and leader of this momentous army of the church."[11] Oral tradition within the Church of God in Christ indicates that Mother Coffey was a militant leader of legendary proportions who was a feminist and an energetic supporter of the black women's club movement.[12] Not only was she central to the history of the denomination—she organized the complex structure of organizations within the Women's Convention, —but also she engineered the Women's Convention's participation in larger black women's movements through her close relationship to Mary McLeod Bethune.[13] As a first-generation member of the Church of God in Christ and a former Baptist, Jones recognized the continuities of his church with the larger Afro-Christian tradition. His statement represents a central confession concerning the importance of gender to black Christians and their churches, and the centrality of women to the growth, spread, and development of the structures and traditions. Tacitly and tactfully, Bishop Jones suggests that if it were not for women, Jesus Christ would have no church.

While there are many sources of ideas and images concerning the proper roles of women and men in society, religion is the most powerful, elaborate, and historically persistent source. The dominant perspectives of contemporary feminism have criticized the role of religion and identified religious institutions as an ideological source of oppression. Indeed,

> the symbolism of religion (is) so very powerful (because) it expresses the essential facts of our human existence. That is why religious symbolism has incorporated ideas of human identity as well as of social obligation, why there is the idea of soul as well as some kind of god or spiritual force that rules the universe. And since religion symbolizes the major facts of society, it has always had to make room for social conflict in its system of symbols.[14]

Contemporary feminism's cultural critique advocates the transformation or abolition of those ideas about identity, human obligation, and social conflict that consign women to diminished human status, dependent servitude, and victimization. Many feminists recognize that patriarchal Christianity, especially in Europe and the United States, supports institutional arrangements and ideologies that control other forms of oppression and inequity. Black women, however, directly and by their absence from and ambivalence toward white feminist activities and ideologies, question whether the religious and cultural critique of contemporary feminism is adequate for assessing traditions within black congregations and denominations. Indeed, black feminist theory has explicitly affirmed that "our situation as black people necessitates that we have solidarity around the fact of race."[15] Black feminist churchwomen have not approached black religious institutions with the same level of indictment that white women have carried to theirs, in spite of the struggle over women in the pulpit. Harriet Pipes McAdoo's research suggests that contemporary black single mothers rely quite heavily on the oral tradition of the black religious experience, and that these women utilize aspects of the tradition as practical ideologies in their every day lives in order to cope with the stresses of single parenting and of economic deprivation.[16] Churched and unchurched black women persistently attest to the sustaining power of their religious tradition, irrespective of any formal relationship to it.

This paper explores the importance of women and their experiences to the construction of the African-American tradition and traditional religious knowledge. Four pillars of the Afro-Christian religious tradition are discussed—preaching, praying, singing, and testifying. The analysis aims to suggest and invite, highlighting the need for systematic investigation of gender within the context of religious roles and symbols. Several questions arise in relation to black women and their religion. Do the oral and written traditions of black churches speak about women's experience? Are women and women's experience visible within the traditions and rituals? Has the subordination of women within most, *but not all*, congregations and denominations been reflected in their role in the fashioning and maintaining of the pillars of the worship tradition? Have black women been silenced or silent about their positions in the church? If black women have been persistent and even enterprising agents of religious tradition, and if issues of gender are apprehended by the tradition (and this paper suggests that such is the case), then precisely what roles *do* women perform? What is the sociological importance of women to the entire black religious enterprise? Has black women's historical role been marginal and trivial, or central and vital? What is the relationship between the importance of black women to the social construction of black religious knowledge and the ambivalent response of black women to white feminist movements, and to those issues, for instance inclusive language, that are central to the white feminist critique of religion?

Such sociological investigation presents a methodological problem. Oral tradition tells us something about the purpose, meaning, and importance of socio-cultural events, but not much about their sequence and frequency. However, oral tradition operates as a connective tissue among aspects of the black religious experience and is therefore relevant to the problem of gender in the Afro-Christian tradition. Let me note here that I use the phrase "Afro-Christian tradition" in place of the usual "black church" because of the plurality of experiences touched upon in this discussion. We are speaking of many congregations, denominations, and settings, and when we address the issue of preaching, praying, singing, and testifying, we are focusing on phenomena that extend far beyond the walls of black churches and are passed along through the intergenerational and interactional processes that constitute tradition.

What is handed down, defended, protected, popularized, and occasionally prostituted is something that was essentially forged during slavery in a variety of settings, and it is greater than the institutional boundaries implied by the term "church." "Afro-Christian" recognizes that our African ancestors constructed a complex and dynamic tradition not only from the materials provided by the missionaries and other Europeans confronted in the nighttime of slavery, but also from the cultural imaginations of their African background, in which women were essential to cultural and religious practice. Slaves did not forget about the women priests and queen mothers in their ancestral societies.[17]

This paper is not a complete and systematic study of the problem of gender in the pillars of Afro-Christian religious tradition, nor can it answer all of the questions raised above, or all the questions such an investigation generates. My aim is to suggest new directions for sociological research on the black religious experience. Recognizing the importance of gender in the structuring of society and the content of the racist "cultural humiliation"[18] contained in social oppression, we must explore the importance of gender and the realities surrounding it in the black religious experience. I assume that such a reality cannot be properly analyzed by appropriating the white feminist critique of culture, and that scholars must first explore the black experience whose organization of gender we wish to examine.

The Pillars of Afro-Christian Tradition

Any interpretation of the Afro-Christian tradition must take into account the centrality within it of the English Bible. The African imagination, in its criticism of white oppression, valued the vivid depictions of liberation within the Hebrew Scriptures and their New Testament connections. The Afro-American religious imagination is a biblical imagination. Generations of black Christians who endured slavery, reconstruction, Jim (and Jane) Crow, urban migration, and the civil rights era constructed and fashioned their songs, prayers, testimonies, and sermons with the English (King James Version) Bible as a resource for the interpretation of past and present sequences of events, and for the envisioning of futures and of strategies to achieve those futures. The suggestion that black people and their preachers do religion with the Bible in one hand and the newspaper in the other reflects this tradition. The title of Zora Neale Hurston's great work, *Their Eyes Were Watching God*, also captures the interpretive principle governing the everyday life and wisdom of black people in the segregated South. In the context of racial oppression, Hurston's observation, "They seemed to be staring at the dark, but their eyes were watching God,"[19] underscores the fact that the Afro-American cultural and political imagination is at its foundations a theological imagination. After reflection on their own experience, the most important critical tool used by black people has been the Bible.

Sermons, prayers, songs, and testimonies utilize the English Bible as a mediator between individual experience and the community. Since slave owners attempted to appropriate the Bible for ideological purposes, black people made it their business to de-ideologize their "blessed book." Anyone who could read it was valuable to the community, and the learning ethic "each one teach one" became a reality in some slave communities.[20] The early recruitment of women as teachers helped to establish their inclusion among the ranks of "educators," a status claimed by male preachers. Later those educators comprised the preachers and teachers who constituted the earliest free leadership class.[21] Their role as educators provided black women with access to leadership in other fields, especially in the area of business. Maggie Lena Walker, Ida Wells Barnett, Myrtle Foster Cook, Lucy Campbell, and Mary McLeod Bethune are famous examples.[22] Carter Woodson argued that the faith of black washerwomen, evidenced in their willingness to invest in black-owned business ventures, fostered substantial social and economic development.[23] All of this activity took place in the context of religious tradition. Reading meant reading the Bible, and most black leaders of the time left some record indicating that a biblical imagination shaped their admonitions and ideas. According to Paula Giddings, Maria Stewart was the first woman of any race to give a public lecture. As early as the 1830s, Stewart defended herself against critics by appealing to the role of women in the Bible, especially as carriers of the Gospel message.[24] Recent investigations of slavery and its aftermath suggest that black women were central to the development of individual spirituality as well as institutions and ideologies.[25] Black women were important actors in the historical process from which black religious experience grew.

Although black churches, with the exception of the African Methodist Episcopal Zion Church, did not support women's ordination, during the eighteenth and nineteenth centuries women did participate in the deliberative assemblies (religious and secular) that took place in church buildings.[26] Black women were rarely forced to justify their presence in any setting involving the welfare or future of black people. Since issues of social change were framed in religious terms, and religious perspectives focused on social change, black women participated in religious discourse even in settings where their right to preach was not affirmed.

Often, they could only be "teachers." The opening lines of Lucy Camp-bell's famous hymn, "Something Within," indicate the extent of these teachers' participation. She wrote,

> Preachers and teachers would make their appeal,
> Fighting as soldiers on great battlefields,
> When to their pleadings my poor heart did yield,
> All I could say, there is something within.[27]

Black women were also "troublers" or prophetic critics in their community and the larger society. Sojourner Truth, a powerful preacher with a feminist hermeneutic and liberating ethic, once confronted Frederick Douglass in one of his more cynical moments, asking the question, "Is God dead?" In a similar manner, many black women worked to maintain the link between questions of faith and questions of social change.[28]

By World War I, black women were performing the central roles that fostered the growth and development of black churches. As missionaries they led devotions and preached Women's Days. As evangelists within the Sanctified Church (black-founded Holiness and Pentecostal denominations and congregations), they preached revivals and "dug out" churches. In those denominations that still do not fully ordain women as pastors, their historical role as organizers and builders of churches fuels the persistent conflicts surrounding the discrimination they experience. Sometimes black women left churches and organized new congregations and denominations where they could participate in every aspect of church leadership. Small denominations such as the Mt. Sinai Holy Church of America, and the House of God Which Is the Church of the Living God, the Pillar and Ground of the Truth, Inc. were organized in this way. In other denominations such as the Fire Baptized Holiness Church of God of the Americas and the Church of the Living God, Christian Workers for Fellowship, women pastored churches and shared more equitably in the work. Usually they were forced simply to develop strong Women's Departments which were essential infrastructures to the life and expansion of congregations and denominations.

Subordination and subservience were evident problems, but not silence, isolation, and exclusion. Not only did black church women fashion important and necessary roles for themselves, they also had a powerful effect on religious discourse. When we examine preaching, prayer, testimony, and song, it is clear that women's experiences and church activities are reflected in the stories presented, the images of God, and the pattern of biblical usage. Phyllis Trible has identified the stories of Hagar, Tamar, Jephtha's daughter, and the Levite's concubine as neglected aspects of the church's concern and she calls these biblical stories "texts of terror."[29] Within the Afro-Christian tradition, these women's stories are familiar, and they are preached. They illustrate the way in which both biblical imagination and women's experience are important sources for the interpretation of the black experience. Traditionally male and female preachers (and "speakers" or "teachers") have presented Hagar as the archetype of the slave woman (and by extension of all suffering black women with children), raped and abandoned by her owner and " 'buked, scorned, tossed, and driven" by his jealous and selfish wife. Ishmael is often described with the black cultural term "outside child."[30] Langston Hughes's "Aunt Hagar" and E. Franklin Frazier's essay on "Hagar and Her Children" reflect secular appropriations of the Afro-Christian tradition's use of the experience of Hagar.[31] Not only do women in the Order of Eastern Star utilize Jephthah's daughter as a central character in their rituals and a role model for faithful behavior, but black women's organizations and benevolent societies have appropriated women in the Bible for their autonomous rituals.[32] Even the rape of Tamar and the tragedy of the Levite's concubine are familiar sermon topics. Vashti, the queen whom Esther replaced, receives a highly favorable response in the naming of baby girls, in black women's preaching, and in the poetry of Frances Ella Watkins Harper.[33] Biblical material pertinent to women's experience, while neglected in the European and white American churches, has been woven into the biblical imagination that undergirds the Afro-Christian tradition. Women are active in the process of producing religious knowledge, and the effect of their activities can be found in the kind of attention that the biblical material has received within the context of preaching and the other aspects of worship tradition.

The Eagle Stirreth Her Nest: Black Preaching

The tradition for which the Sunday service is noted is its preaching. In spite of racism, white people have often recognized the special talent evident in the preaching of black churches. Within black congregations, bad preaching is the unforgivable sin. Preaching is the most masculine aspect of black religious ritual. In spite of the progress of women in ministry, preaching remains overwhelmingly a form of male discourse. Within this male discourse, however, one finds evidence of the centrality of women to the evolution of religious tradition.[34] Black preaching, even in its most androcentric, masculinist, and sexist expressions, is forced to make some reasonable connection with the community at which it is aimed — primarily a community of women.

Black preaching depends upon its connections with the congregations' experiences and their visible assent, their response to the call. Interdependence is an essential condition for effective preaching. The question "will it preach?" is not simply one of form and exegesis; it is also the question, "will the congregation respond in a visible, audible, and meaningful way?" Those preachers who utilize the community's perspectives and biblical imagination as presented in prayer, testimony, and song are probably most successful in making the connections with their congregations that are perceived as successful preaching. When preachers use these other pillars of tradition in their sermons, they enhance the inclusive potential of the preaching tradition, in spite of its masculinist character.

Prayer often frames the preaching event and provides a general charge for the preacher. James Weldon Johnson noted that the black preachers who inspired his work *God's Trombones* were often preceded by a special prayer, and that prayer was often delivered by a woman. Preachers usually acknowledge their dependence upon the prayers of the people for God's arrival in the form of "my Help." They actively and sometimes repeatedly call upon "my Help" and welcome its arrival during the sermon.[35] Historically, new members of churches were trained in the art of public prayer and of raising a song on the assumption that it was a skill that every church member should have.[36] Women are visible participants in the prayer tradition and therefore in framing and shaping the preaching event. Often their "words of prayer" can be found in the words of the preacher. The missionary who begins her prayer by thanking God for waking her "clothed in my right mind" may hear those words come back as a declaration about the God who "wakes me up clothed in my right mind."[37]

The musical tradition is another vital resource for preaching. Music functions in several ways within the context of preaching. In some churches the traditional pre-sermon prayer has been replaced by the pre-sermon solo, and like prayer, it often frames the preaching event. Like the prayer, it functions to provide a pathway for the Spirit, thus actualizing the oft-stated belief that "the Spirit comes on the wings of a song." Since the restriction of women in the music tradition is unheard of, the church soloist is often "she."

The music tradition is also a resource for the actual sermon. Familiar songs illustrate and reinforce aspects of sermons. It is not unusual for a sermon to build toward a dramatic conclusion based on a hymn, spiritual, or gospel song. Some preachers use the song lyrics as a form of meditation at the beginning of their sermons. Black congregations underscore the importance of the music tradition through their preference for the preacher who sings, and some of these preachers have been known to use a talent for song to compensate for homiletical weakness.[38] Songs often fix important theological and biblical images in the congregation's and in the larger community's consciousness. Ideas about God and Jesus are often carried in very familiar terms by song lyrics. Furthermore, images of heaven, models for prayer, and responses to suffering are carried along in the songs. Music tradition is an important tool for the preacher in making a sermon memorable and connected to the community's experience.

Testimonies are priceless resources for sermons. Not only do examples of church members' testimonies provide cogent sermon illustrations, but also such testimonies provide connections between the situations of biblical characters and contemporary problems and experiences. Testimonies provide believable examples of faith that may motivate others to try a particular strategy for confronting and coping with problems. For black congregations whose troubles are disproportionately numerous, effective coping is an important aspect of spiritual well-being. Overwhelmingly, it is women who provide the testimony from which preachers are able to draw illustrations. Women lead many testimony services, especially in Pentecostal congregations, and are particularly effective at encouraging their sisters to speak out. It is this value of testimony for preaching that increases the significance and visibility of women in the shaping of Afro-Christian tradition. The appropriation of their testimonies for sermon illustrations is quite common and extensive.

The late Rev. Clarence LaVaughn Franklin may serve as an illustration for the appropriation of women's testimony for biblical preaching. Not only is he important because of his classic style, but his influence was wide-ranging within and beyond his denomination. To illustrate the importance of steadfast hope (a theme that characterized most of his preaching), Rev. Franklin used the testimony of two women who sent their sons off to war. One of the mothers had five sons, all of whom she accompanied to the train station. In her testimony, the first mother claimed to have asked the Lord, "if it be His will, to bring all of my sons safely home." Franklin claimed that she testified, "the Lord heard my cry" and brought her sons safely back home. The second woman, who had three sons, prayed the same prayer and lost all of her sons and yet she got up to "thank the Lord also . . . because He gave me the strength to get through my situation," and because "the Lord is still watching over, . . . opening doors, . . . and making a way for me" and, therefore, consistent with the central theme of Franklin's sermon, "nothing shall separate me from the love of God."[39]

The manner in which Franklin and many other preachers use such testimony is instructive for our understanding of the consciousness of gender in black churches. First of all, Franklin had just been talking about Job. He used the testimony of the women to connect the problem of Job with the problem of contemporary experience. Beyond that, he transferred a biblical story centered on male experience to the experience of contemporary black women.[40] Secondly, Franklin and others often locate the problems of black suffering, through the direct or the indirect use of women's discourse and testimony, to the actual experience of suffering shared by black women. In other words, by reflecting women's testimony back to the community in the sermon, the black preacher affirms for black women that they have suffered, and unreasonably so. Finally, the black preacher not only contextualizes black women's suffering with reference to a document and canon that focuses largely on males, but also conveys the entire text to women as an appropriate possession for black women as they negotiate their purpose and meaning in a racist and sexist society. Women are encouraged to use the Bible as a resource for their own spiritual well-being. Unless one understands the active role of black women as the community to which the preacher is connected, and the centrality of a shared understanding of the biblical text, one cannot begin to understand the tenacity with which black women cling to the King James Version of the English Bible. Women who defend its use in church settings often argue their affection for this text on the basis of its literary style and its importance to tradition, not on the basis of its providing infallible revelation. A vivid example of this view is found in the Bible Study manual of the Church of God in Christ. This manual is taught largely by missionaries throughout the denomination. It emphasizes the details of the translation process for the King James Version, so that the laity are admonished to recognize that they possess a translation of the Bible.[41]

Male preachers manage to include women in their sermons in other ways. One strategy is to draw illustrations from female biblical characters and to place in the mouths of these biblical women an ordinary discourse that is recognizable as that of contemporary black women. To highlight the necessity of suffering for the maturation of the Christian, C.L. Franklin used the example of the mother of James and John. Portraying this woman in a sympathetic light, he attributed to her all of the concerns and care about the future of her children associated with an heroic perception of the role of black women in their families.[42] Another strategy involves calling women's names when the sermon rhetoric includes a roll call of characters of a specific type. In one sermon where "the grave" attested to its role as "landlord of the universe," the preacher included in his list of inhabitants great women church officers and community leaders in a roll call of deceased.

Finally, black male preachers occasionally provide androgynous or feminine imagery in the context of a sermon. Some of them are masters of the androgynous sermon. Such a sermon is grounded in imagery of God that transcends specifically male or female attributes and occasionally manages to dispense with human reference altogether. One sermon, called "Who," was preached by an elderly Boston preacher notorious for his refusal to approve or affirm women preachers. At a regional convention, however, he preached his sermon as an answer to the question, which he happened to ponder in his study one day, "Who did all this?" The entire sermon was a long epic poem about "Who" and focused entirely on God's biblical activity without referring to God with a personal pronoun. God remained "Who" for the entire sermon. It is not unusual for preachers to transcend human attributes in the inspired endings or sermon conclusions characteristic of the black preaching style. Such endings, if they do not transcend specifically human attributes, draw upon the images of God as nurturer and combine these with other metaphors to disengage gender from divinity.[43]

One of the most vivid examples of the tendency to emphasize God as mother in black preaching is Franklin's sermon, "The Eagle Stirreth Her Nest." It is his most popular and, perhaps, most often-borrowed sermon. Within that sermon, Franklin goes to great lengths to stress that the Bible speaks of God through a variety of images. He then proceeds to describe in deep and lively detail the ways in which God operates in our lives as a mother eagle. It is a masterful sermon that stresses the ways in which God's eagle nature is representative of *his* majesty, and then, continuing in masculine language, insists that people must not confuse the "puny" kings of the earth with God. Although the masculine language surrounding the pronouns attached to God remains through the sermon, the admonition against patriarchal idolatry is very clearly present. Franklin then discusses the problem of suffering with reference to God's role as a mother eagle. Franklin points out that the mother eagle makes a nest in high places where she feeds and cares for the baby eagles. However, as they begin to outgrow the nest, she begins to pull the soft feathers out of the nest so that they are less comfortable and want to go out on their own. Such imagery is consistent with his view of human suffering as a way of creating a mature Christian. Finally, Franklin develops indirectly the themes of godly benevolence and providence in his description of the mother eagle's flying lessons for the baby eagles. She takes them out of the nest and drops them, and continues to catch them up on her wings until they finally learn to fly on their own.[44] The sermon is a masterpiece of feminine imagery set in the framework of male discourse. When one hears that sermon, one is able to hear Franklin's glancing references elsewhere to the motherly nature of God. In other sermons such as "The Lord Is Good," one can experience God as the heavenly keeper of the human nursery.[45]

Preaching, as one of the pillars of Afro-Christian worship, is most prominent in the central ritual event—the church service. It is also the most masculine of the pillars. While systematic study of sermons, through such strategies as content analysis and in-depth studies of influential preachers, is needed, it is important to note that this male tradition is connected in recognizable and important ways to black women's experience. The other three pillars of tradition are even more directly tied to women's experience and more directly responsible for black women's sense of ownership of their churches and their traditions.

Women Warriors: The Prayer Tradition

The song, "If I Could Hear My Mother Pray Again," highlights the centrality of women to the prayer tradition. Most black Christians have been taught to pray by their mothers. The poet Joanne Braxton has stated that her goal in life is to write poetry the way her grandmother prayed. Another writer and literary critic remembers the impact of her grandmother's morning prayer on her entire household. Harold Carter in his reflection on the "prayer tradition of black people" cites the importance of women to the vitality and sustenance of the tradition.[46] It is an area of the black experience within which women have never been silent. In his study of socialization in the slave quarters community, Webber attributes the deep spirituality of the slaves to their early exposure to prayers for freedom among mothers and aunts in the cabins.[47]

The label "prayer warrior" runs deep in black tradition. Mamie Garvin Fields relates the story of the events surrounding the purchase of a church from whites by freedmen and freedwomen in Charleston, South Carolina a year after the Civil War ended. She tells the story she heard growing up in the parsonage of that church. She said:

> The money had to be to the bank by twelve noon, sharp. So a small boat was hired to row out to the ship and unload the gold, while the warriors of the church prayed and prayed for the money to get to the appointed place at the appointed time. The staunchest in the congregation were praying very hard, because they had given up the monies that they had buried in cans, savings for their funerals. Anyway, this little boat went out and back, the men "rowing for life," as the story goes. When they got back to the wharf, the drayman was waiting with the best horses he could find,

and the drayman whipped those horses through the streets of Charleston. All this time the prayer warriors kept on.[48]

When describing the outcome, Mrs. Fields stated simply, "The Lord brought us the rest of the way." In the black tradition, church mothers who have a mighty gift of prayer are called "warriors." Men with such gifts are usually Deacons.

Thus when preachers say "some old warrior," the referent is usually "she." In a sermon that laments the waning of certain worship traditions, Jasper Williams demonstrates the manner and the style of these "old warriors":

> They had those old time covenant meetings; they had those red hot covenant testifying services. People would get up and talk about how good God had been to them. . . . You'd see some old warrior, when time came for her to testify, she'd get up and come down the aisle and lock her arms back behind her back. And she'd cry a while; and then walk a while. And just stand before the altar and say, "Rev., I'm sorry but it's all over me, it's all in me, it's all under me." And she'd stand there and shout a while. And finally when she would regain her composure, she'd tell the church: "You all remember last month I stood here and asked you to pray for my son. . . . I'm happy to report to you this month that God has heard our prayer."[49]

The importance of these women to the church tradition is attested in black literature as well. James Baldwin's character, Praying Mother Washington, is such an example.[50] Langston Hughes incorporates the prayer warrior tradition into his novel *Not Without Laughter* in the character of Aunt Hagar.[51] The link between black women and the prayer tradition is firm and well recognized in letters and folklore.

Rosemary Ruether argues that one of the principal means by which women are subordinated within the religious tradition is through enforced silence.[52] The prayer tradition is a blatant contradiction to this tendency. Whatever the various interpretations of Paul's admonition to women to be silent in dominant culture churches, black denominations have interpreted this to mean "from the floor." Thus it is not unusual to see, in churches that do not permit women to preach or otherwise use the pulpit, women (missionaries and evangelists) leading worship services and praying from lecterns placed below or near the pulpit. Thus while black women may not pray from the pulpit, their "silence" speaks loudly in the literary, oral, and preaching traditions of the black experience.

A Mother to the Motherless: The Musical Tradition

Women are most prominent and visible in the area of music. While this is true in any Christian communion, black women are largely responsible for shaping what is distinctive and defining in the black sacred music tradition. The crystallization of the image of God as "a Mother to the motherless and a Father to the fatherless" is but one important indication of their importance. Music has been the most powerful vehicle for this dramatic and well-articulated litany of deity that reflects both genders. This description of God is so entrenched within Afro-Christian tradition that the average church member is able to recite it and use it. The song, "Surely Our God Is Able," written by a man in collaboration with a woman and popularized by women requires consideration.[53]

Popularized by Clara Ward and the Ward singers, the song was written by the Rev. Herbert Brewster. Brewster believed that "a gospel song was a sermon set to music. It must have sentiment and doctrine, rhetorical beauty and splendor."[54] The singers for whom Brewster wrote were primarily women. As a result, this gospel composer often used inclusive language in his songs. Popularized by Mahalia Jackson, Brewster's hit song, "Move on Up a Little Higher," states, "All God's sons and daughters,/ Will be drinking that healing water. . . . "[55] In Brewster's song "Surely," the characteristics of God combine masculine and feminine attributes. As part of an extended chorus to the song, singers sang:

> Don't you know God is able, He's able;
> God is able, Yes, he's able.
> Clouds may gather all around you
> So dark and sable.
> He'll be your mother, when you're motherless;
> He's your father, when you're fatherless;
> He's your sister, when you're sisterless;
> He's a brother, when you're brotherless.
> He's a doctor, in the sick room;
> He's your lawyer, in the courtroom;
> When you go down to the Jordan,
> He will be there to bear your burden.
> He will step out before you;
> And my God will know you.
> Surely, surely, God's able to carry you through.[56]

The words of the chorus, with their theological affirmations, are probably older than "Surely." However, "Surely" fixed the images of God as a mother to the motherless in popular language and culture. The words of the chorus are heard, consequently, throughout the prayer and the preaching traditions, and they appear in the testimonies of prayer meetings. The words are also heard beyond the walls of the church.

Although such examples do not resolve the very real crisis of exclusive and inclusive language, they remind us of the importance of the gospel music tradition to the imagery black people share concerning God and other theological subjects. Visions of heaven, understandings of the role of Jesus, and a host of other concerns have been conveyed by gospel music. Popular religious music assigned a role flexibility to God and Jesus that went beyond dominant social conventions concerning gender. The gospel songs have also fixed in the oral tradition the importance of such characters as the woman at the well, or Mary and Martha.[57]

Within the music tradition women are often the principal insiders in the production of religious knowledge. They not only sang men's compositions, they wrote their own. Mahalia Jackson, Roberta Martin, Beatrice Brown, B. Alma Androzzo ("If I Can Help Somebody"), and Mattie Moss Clark are a few names in a very large pantheon of women who both sang and composed gospel music. Clark not only composes but heads the music department of the Church of God in Christ, participating in the relationship between canon and black community. Women are also prominent and powerful members—and occasionally, chairs—of hymnal committees. For some women, gospel singing became an alternative to preaching; some women achieved fame as "evangelists" within this musical movement. Mother Willie Mae Ford Smith and Shirley Caesar are the most prominent examples. Because of these and many other singers, music is the most widespread and popular aspect of the Afro-Christian tradition. It has crossed racial boundaries and represents a central characterization of black religion—to some minds, too central. Women are its most prominent and responsible agents, fashioning and communicating this critical category of religious knowledge. Two major publishing houses of Gospel music were founded and owned by women, Sallie Martin and Roberta Martin, and within the annals of gospel musicology, women are cited as agents of style. The centrality of music to the black religious tradition is well known, and women are central to that tradition; the tradition explicitly includes them and their consciousness in both the production and the product.

This Joy I Have: The Testimony Tradition

The importance of testimony to the process of preaching has already been stated. However, it is important to examine testimony with reference to the black community itself. The shared nature of the experiences to which black religion speaks depends upon testimony. Testimony transforms the collection of worshippers into a community. Oppression and suffering make testimony important for psychological survival. Testimony does not resolve black problems but does transform them from the private troubles of distressed individuals into the public issues of a covenant community. Testimony is one of the important antecedents to movements for social change. Black women are the best testifiers in the community. They carry forward the slaves' determination to "tell God how you treat me one of these days." The women's testimony affirms their determination "to run on and see what the end is going to be" and contributes to their determination to survive. It is not unreasonable to attribute black women's relatively low suicide rate to the survival value of testimony. It is not surprising that testimony figures prominently in the success of secular self-help groups such as Alcoholics Anonymous, and in the consciousness-raising groups of contemporary feminists.

For women, testimony can be a form of protest against some of the constraints of being female and a means of lament over the brokeness in their relationships with men. Occasionally one can hear testimony that includes these lines:

> This joy I have, man didn't give it to me;
> This peace I have, man didn't give it to me;
> This love I have, man didn't give it to me;
> Man didn't give it and man can't take it away.

Not only do such manipulations of the androcentric dimensions of the King James text occur, but the generic "man" is subverted into a usable women's perspective—a protest perspective. Women will rise up and testify about their struggles as women alone. In any pre-revival devotional session, one can hear a litany of the social problems affecting black women: abandonment, assaults, aging, poverty, violent crime, single-parenthood, and their children's futures. Testimony may also be responsible for the ideology of sisterhood among black women. It sometimes serves as an instrument of reconciliation. For his reflection on church tradition, Williams' sermon is again helpful:

> When he (the old preacher) got through, some old mother would get up and say, "Brother pastor! I'm sorry to cut across you but I've got to say this! I can't go another (step) further. I've got this grudge I've been carrying around in my heart against Mother Jones. And I can't sleep at night. I can't even pray. And I promised God I wasn't going to leave here until I got things settled. And here we are getting ready to take the Lord's supper. And I can't eat of my God's body, drink of His blood with what I've got in my heart against Mother Jones." And right there in front of everybody, she'd walk over to Mother Jones and give Mother Jones her hand and say,

"Mother Jones, if I have hurt you or wronged you in any fashion, I want you to forgive me. Charge it to my head and not my heart."[58]

Because of the fragmented and fragmenting nature of life in black communities, this integrative dimension should not be overlooked. The potential for debilitating bitterness on the part of many black women is reduced while the potential for community and for collective action is enhanced. Since the feminist movement strives to develop sisterhood, black women's activity in this tradition represents an important resource.[59]

Some Mother's Son and Some Father's Daughter: The Creative Tension

Historically, black preachers often substituted the phrase, "some mother's son and some father's daughter" for the terms "man," "somebody," or "someone." This traditional public rhetoric symbolizes the creative tension surrounding the imagery of gender that exists within the Afro-Christian tradition. Preaching, prayer, song, and testimony are historically derived pillars of the Afro-Christian tradition that transcend congregational and denominational boundaries. They are vehicles for women to construct meaning and imagery that become part of the religious experience women and men share. These pillars also reflect images of humans and of the Deity in ways that expand and relativize the androcentrism of the Bible, making it possible for women to appropriate and to own the Bible and the church tradition for their spiritual and psychological survival. Women participate in the production of the social knowledge contained in the Afro-Christian tradition, and their experience is, therefore, explicitly included. While not inclusive by contemporary feminist standards, there exists an important foundation for change and inclusion. This inclusive potential influences roles and rhetoric. It can contribute to arguments for more egalitarian approaches to religious practice that may revise some of the existing strengths of the community while constructively criticizing some possible political excesses.

For instance, one problem that developed in the late 1960s was the impact of a more exclusive political rhetoric within a growing black power movement, when the problem of "the Negro" became the problem of "the black man." The transition from "Negro" to "black" was a necessary phase in the public politics of race relations and in both black and white cultural consciousness and awareness, but an element of gender inclusiveness was lost in the process. Black women had always felt included in the term "Negro." Since one of the important themes of black preaching in all denominations was the problem of racial oppression, the rhetorical switch from "Negro" to "black man" at precisely the moment that gender and women's rights became one of the most central issues of public politics may have been one of the most unfortunate contradictions of black liberation. Preaching and other forms of public male discourse that had been more or less inclusive of women and women's experience became more exclusive. I think it is reasonable to argue that this shift invited a problematic departure from tradition that must be assessed in our reflections on the intersection of gender and race-ethnicity, particularly in the area of consciousness.

Pauli Murray reminds us that the experience of racial oppression has incorporated both Jim Crow and Jane Crow. She criticized the social implications of this rhetoric, observing that the rhetoric of black power sounded as if it were merely a movement for black males to share power with white males. She links this new language to the ideological consequences of the Moynihan Report. Pointing to the failures of the black family by exaggerating the insubordination of black women, the report engendered a sense of shame concerning black women's putative achievements in the political, economic, and cultural life of the black community. Murray's criticisms suggest that the black power movement was a successful masculinist movement within the black community.[60] The particular expressions of racism against black men generated conditions for the movement's success. Such an irruption is intelligible in a patriarchy that sought explicitly and particularly to destroy all black male claims to manhood. Such specialized destruction existed to negate, violently if need be, all claims of black females to womanhood. The more important result of this dual process was the negation of the peoplehood and humanity of all black people. Thus it does become necessary to criticize a definition of humanity that rests solely upon "black manhood." The preaching tradition did indeed generate that criticism.

C. L. Franklin addressed this problem when he complained about the members of his church and his community walking around boasting "I'm a man!"[61] His complaint was then followed by the admonition that every Christian should boast about how much of a "child" in the kingdom of God he was. In other words, black "manhood" was not an important or positive concept in Christian community.[62] In his sermon, "The Meaning of Black Power," Franklin addressed this masculinist tendency. After castigating black power advocates for their violation of Christian ethics in their bid for separatism, he concluded:

> If there is any meaning at all to black power, . . . we must know that we are God's children. Proud black men and women—creative, resourceful, productive, working

for unity among ourselves, with a new sense of political, social, and economic responsibility. . . . We must control our own destiny.[63]

When one reflects on the evangelistic inclusiveness that undergirded the phrase, "some mother's son and some father's daughter," one can observe an intergenerational and inter-gender basis for unity, a foundation for creative tension in the area of gender and sacred imagery. The dynamics of gender organization and of religious discourse in black churches operate at some times and under some conditions to include women and their experience under the umbrella of racial oppression and as a context illustrative of God's activity on behalf of people. Although the overall reality of the black church is *not* egalitarian, it does address the experience of women, and it does generate a subliminal level of consciousness that is integrative. It links men's issues and women's issues in the community's consciousness.

The phrase, "some mother's son and some father's daughter," represents an intergenerational and cross-gender linkage in people's consciousness and implies a common interest surrounding racial oppression in the lives of black women and men. Historically, it was "mother's sons" who wrote the slave narratives and preached the sermons that described the special terrors of black women such as Hagar and her children. At the same time, it was "fathers' daughters" such as Ida B. Wells Barnett and Mary McLeod Bethune who struggled within the women's club movement with the problem of lynching, and who moved to positions of intellectual leadership at the height of the struggle against Jim (and Jane) Crow. An interesting social dilemma is created when the settings for women's discourse concerning men's issues exist outside of the black church pulpits, while men's ritual re-telling of women's terrors and troubles occur largely within those pulpits. The relative absence of men from church audiences implies that female leadership may be critically important for the re-inclusion and re-integration of men among the laity. Furthermore, the tales of black female hostility to women preachers become intelligible (although not excusable) in this context.

An additional and unstated aspect of the black religious ritual emerges in the form of aging congregations of mothers hearing assurances from their sons that they will carry forward their cherished traditions. Although currently dormant and under some stress, this intergenerational and inter-gender integration has in the past given rise to amazing levels of solidarity within the Afro-Christian tradition. The Civil Rights movement is one example.[63] Historical accounts of the slave church suggest that its egalitarianism of necessity also created such a context.[64]

An examination of the wellsprings of Afro-American religious tradition must conclude that women are not outsiders to its social production. While the black religious experience is clearly patriarchal in most of its expression, and decidedly masculinist in much of its preaching, the cultural maxim, "If it wasn't for the women, you wouldn't have a church," rises up against male attempts to exclude, ignore, trivialize, or marginalize women in a number of capacities.

The biblical scholar Krister Stendahl commented, "I have come to think of heaven as the place where one can discuss one issue at a time."[65] For a scholar concerned with the intersection of gender and race in the problems of this society, this observation rings particularly true. The problems confronting members of our society cut across lines of race, ethnicity, and gender to such an extent that we must begin to think pluralistically about concrete expressions of racial oppression and gender inequity. In the face of such complexity, the study of the black religious experience as a vital aspect of social organization in the context of survival, rebellion, and cultural tradition comprises a number of tasks. The work of thorough description and explanation of the experience and its organization and interpretation of gender must precede the tasks of restructuring, of redress, and of recasting a tradition that has, in the words of testimony and song, "brought us from a mighty long way." Critical and creative thinking about the Afro-Christian tradition must reflect upon those historically derived strengths and potentials while it articulates a vision of change that fosters wholeness.

Acknowledgments

Earlier versions of this paper were presented to the Society for the Study of Black Religion and to the Center for Research on Women, Memphis State University. I wish to acknowledge the support of Boston University Department of Sociology and of the Summer Visiting Scholar Program of the Center for Research on Women, Memphis State University, for their contributions at various stages of the research and writing.

Notes

1. Margaret Andersen, *Thinking about Women: Sociological and Feminist Perspectives* (New York: Macmillan, 1983), p. 208.

2. Ibid., pp. 219–23.

3. Ibid., p. 227. Her use of Hegel parallels a similar and earlier usage by Angela Davis in her important work, "Reflections on the Black Woman's Role in the Community of Slaves," *Black Scholar* 3 (December 1971), pp. 2–15.

4. Andersen, pp. 231-32.

5. Linda M. Perkins, "Black Women and Racial 'Uplift' Prior to Emancipation," in *The Black Woman Cross-Culturally*, ed. Filomena Chioma Steady (Cambridge, Mass.: Schenkman Publishing Company, 1981), p. 321.

6. Paula Giddings, *When and Where I Enter: The Impact of Black Women on Race and Sex in America* (New York: William Morrow, 1984).

7. Angela Davis, p. 8. Davis reworks and expands some of this analysis in her book, *Women, Race, and Class* (New York: Random House, 1981), especially in the first chapter "The Legacy of Slavery: Standards for a New Womanhood."

8. Bishop Charles Pleas, *Fifty Years Achievement (History): Church of God in Christ* (Memphis: Church of God in Christ Publishing House, n.d., *ca.* 1957), p. 35.

9. Ibid., p. 36.

10. Ibid.

11. Ibid., p. 37.

12. Ibid., pp. 38-39. Lucille Cornelius, *The Pioneer History of the Church of God in Christ* (Memphis: Church of God in Christ Publishing House, 1975), pp. 38-39.

13. Jualynne E. Dodson and Cheryl Townsend Gilkes, "Something Within: Social Change and Collective Endurance in the Sacred World of Black Christian Women," in *Women and Religion in America: Volume 3: 1900-1968*, eds. Rosemary Radford Ruether and Rosemary Skinner Keller (San Francisco: Harper & Row, 1986), pp. 107-12.

14. Randall Collins, *Sociological Insight: An Introduction to Nonobvious Sociology* (New York: Oxford University Press, 1982), p. 37.

15. The Combahee River Collective, "A Black Feminist Statement," in *But Some of Us Are Brave*, eds., Gloria T. Hull, Patricia Bell Scott, and Barbara Smith (Old Westbury, New York: The Feminist Press, 1982), p. 16.

16. Harriet Pipes McAdoo, Editor, *Black Families* (Beverly Hills, California: Sage Publications, 1981). McAdoo discussed her subjects' use of the spirituals as practical ideologies in a discussion following a paper she presented at the American Sociological Association annual meeting (New York, 1984).

17. Cheryl Townsend Gilkes, "The Roles of Church and Community Mothers; Ambivalent American Sexism or Fragmented African Familyhood?" *Journal of Feminist Studies in Religion* 2 (Spring 1986), pp. 41-59.

18. James Cone uses the phrase "cultural humiliation" to characterize one of the unique features of racism in the culture of the United States and the experience of black people. See *For My People* (Maryknoll, New York; Orbis Books, 1982).

19. Zora Neale Hurston, *Their Eyes Were Watching God* (New York: J. B. Lippincott, 1937), p. 236.

20. Mamie Garvin Fields with Karen Fields, *Lemon Swamp and Other Places: A Carolina Memoir* (New York: The Free Press, 1983). References to practices during slavery abound throughout the narrative.

21. Cheryl Townsend Gilkes, "Together and in Harness: Women's Traditions in the Sanctified Church" *Signs: Journal of Women in Culture and Society* 10 (Summer 1985), pp. 687-89.

22. Dodson and Gilkes, pp. 93–96. See also Paula Giddings for more extended discussions of these and many other women.

23. Carter G. Woodson, "The Negro Washerwoman" *The Journal of Negro History* 15, no. 3 (1930), pp. 269–77.

24. Giddings, p. 52.

25. Thomas Webber, *Deep like the Rivers: Education in the Slave Quarter Community, 1830–1865* (New York: W.W. Norton, 1978); Deborah Gray White, *Ar'n't I A Woman: Female Slaves in the Plantation South* (New York: W.W. Norton, 1985); Giddings, *When and Where I Enter*; Dorothy Sterling, *We Are Your Sisters: Black Women in the Nineteenth Century* (New York: W. W. Norton, 1984).

26. Vincent Harding, *There Is a River: The Black Struggle for Freedom in America* (New York: Harcourt, Brace, and Jovanovich, 1981).

27. Campbell's hymn is reprinted in Dodson and Gilkes's article in Rosemary Ruether and Rosemary Keller, *Women and Religion in America*, pp. 93–94.

28. Saunders Redding, *The Lonesome Road: A Narrative History of the Black American Experience* (Garden City, New York: Anchor Press/Doubleday, 1973), pp. 66–68.

29. Phyllis Trible, *Texts of Terror: Literary-Feminist Readings of Biblical Narratives* (Philadelphia: Fortress Press, 1984).

30. In a sermon entitled "What Ails You?" (Princeton University, 1982), Rev. Dr. Arlene Church made particularly effective use of this term, "as mother used to call it, this 'outside child'," in paralleling the experience of Hagar with black women generally, and with black women ministers particularly.

31. Langston Hughes, *Not Without Laughter* (New York: Collier Books, 1969); E. Franklin Frazier, *The Negro Family in the United States* (Chicago: University of Chicago Press, 1939).

32. From a feminist perspective, Jephthah's daughter is a highly problematic role model; she is a willing accomplice in her own destruction. Year after year, thousands of women in the Order of the Eastern Star celebrate this woman as an example of faithfulness. Since most feminists are not members of Eastern Star, they fail to perceive the depth to which this woman is revered in one of the most patriarchal and explicitly and exclusively patrilineal organizations to which Anglo-American and Afro-American women belong.

33. Suzan D. Johnson, "God's Woman," in Ella Pearson Mitchell, ed., *Those Preachin' Women: Sermons by Black Women Preachers* (Valley Forge, Pennsylvania: Judson Press, 1985), pp. 119–26; Frances Ella Watkins Harper, "Vashti," in Erlene Stetson, ed. *Black Sister: Poetry by Black American Women, 1746–1980* (Bloomington: Indiana University Press, 1981), pp. 27–29.

34. Records are helpful in that they represent what is popular and accessible. They do not provide a full range of what is representative. Few women pastors command the resources and institutional supports to enter the market of recorded sermons. Recorded sermons, however, do provide excellent examples of the use of tradition.

35. Virginia Ramey Mollenkott's discussion of "God Our Ezer" in *The Divine Feminine: The Biblical Imagery of God as Female* (New York: Crossroad Publishing Company, 1983) enables one to comprehend the irony of patriarchal and masculinist male preachers calling on God as a female.

36. Howard Thurman describes this phenomenon in his autobiography, *With Head and Heart: The Autobiography of Howard Thurman* (New York: Harcourt, Brace, Jovanovich, 1979).

37. C. L. Franklin, "The 100th Psalm (The Lord Is Good)" (Englewood, New Jersey: Chess Records, Sermon No. 62).

38. Wyatt Tee Walker, *Somebody's Calling My Name: Black Sacred Music and Social Change* (Valley Forge, Pennsylvania: Judson Press, 1979).

39. C. L. Franklin, "Nothing Shall Separate Me From the Lord" (Englewood, New Jersey: Chess Records, Sermon No. 16).

40. The war referred to in the sermon is most likely the Viet Nam War.

41. Bishop P. A. Brooks and Charles Hawthorne, *Understanding Bible Doctrine as Taught in the Church of God in Christ* (Detroit, Michigan: Church of God in Christ, First Jurisdiction, Michigan, 1981). It is important to realize that missionaries in the Church of God in Christ would be considered ministers and preachers in other denominations; as of this writing the Church of God in Christ still does not officially ordain women to the titles pastor, elder, or bishop.

42. Franklin, "Nothing Shall Separate Me."

43. Jasper Williams, Jr., "He's the Best I've Ever Seen (Jesus' Trial)" (Atlanta, Georgia: Church Door Records, 1984).

44. C. L. Franklin, "The Eagle Stirreth Her Nest" (Englewood, New Jersey: Chess Records, Sermon No. 21).

45. C. L. Franklin, "The Lord Is Good"

46. Harold Carter, *The Prayer Tradition of Black People* (Valley Forge, Pennsylvania: Judson Press, 1976).

47. Webber, *Deep like the Rivers*, see, for example, pp. 43-58, 80-90, 157-79, 191-206.

48. Fields, *Lemon Swamp*, p. 36.

49. Jasper Williams, Jr., "Didn't It Rain? (Mount Carmel)" (Atlanta, Georgia: Church Door Records, 1980).

50. James Baldwin, *Go Tell It on the Mountain* (New York: Dell Publishing Company, 1965; Dial Press, 1953).

51. Hughes, *Not Without Laughter.*

52. Rosemary Radford Ruether, *Sexism and God-Talk: Toward a Feminist Theology* (Boston: Beacon Press, 1983), p. 74.

53. W. Herbert Brewster, "Our God Is Able" in *Golden Gospel Songs: Volume 1* (Chicago: Martin Morris Music, Inc., 1975), p. 1 (1949). The arranger for Brewster was Virginia Davis. According to the late Olden "Pop" Jones of Memphis, Tennessee, Brewster also collaborated with Isabella Jones on some of his songs (Interview with Herbert Plummer Jones, July 18, 1986). It is not unreasonable to think that Brewster's relationships with women had some bearing on the appeal of his songs to female singers and the inclusive nature of the language and imagery.

54. Anthony Heilbut, *The Gospel Sound: Good News and Bad Times* (New York: Simon and Schuster, 1975), p. 98.

55. Ibid., p. 100.

56. Ibid., p. 252. Additional words have also been transcribed from "Surely God Is Able," The Young Hearts, Alabama State University, The National Black College Gospel Workshop (Nashville, Tennessee: Reed Records, Nashboro Record Company, 1978).

57. Extended discussions of the importance of gospel music for the overall religious tradition can be found in Heilbut, *The Gospel Sound*; Walker, *Somebody's Calling My Name*.

58. Williams, "Didn't It Rain?"

59. See Bonnie Thornton Dill's article on the importance of sisterhood among black women and its importance for feminist theory. Bonnie Thornton Dill, " 'On the Hem of Life': Race, Class, and the Prospects for Sisterhood," in Amy Swerdlow and Hanna Lessinger, Ed., *Class, Race, and Sex: The Dynamics of Control* (Boston: G. K. Hall, 1983), pp. 173–188.

60. Pauli Murray, "The Liberation of Black Women," in *Voices of the New Feminism*, ed., Mary L. Thompson (Boston: Beacon Press, 1970), pp. 354–55; "Jim Crow and Jane Crow," in *Black Women in White America*, ed. Gerda Lerner, (New York: Random House, 1972), pp. 592–99.

61. C. L. Franklin, "The Meaning of Black Power" (Englewood, New Jersey: Chess Records, Sermon No. 45).

62. Ibid.

63. Harding, *There Is a River*.

64. Webber, *Deep Like the Rivers*; Mechal Sobel, *Travelin' On: The Slaves' Journey to an Afro-Baptist Faith* (Westport, Connecticut: Greenwood Press, 1979); Albert Raboteau, *Slave Religion: The Invisible Institution in the AnteBellum South* (New York: Oxford University Press, 1978).

65. Krister Stendahl, *The Bible and the Role of Women: A Case Study in Hermeneutics* (Philadelphia: Fortress Press, 1966), p. 2.

5

"A Loving League of Sisters": Class, Race, Gender, and Religion in Louisa May Alcott's *Work*

Amy Schrager Lang

The difficulties that beset feminist theology, like those of feminism more broadly, might be said to be etymological and thus original. They begin, feminist theologians quite reasonably claim, in the beginning, with the masculine *theos*. In framing this discussion of Louisa May Alcott's *Work*, a novel both feminist and Christian, I would like to propose that the problem, indeed, the beginning, may lie in the other half of the term, that is, in *logos*. It may seem odd to begin a literary critical treatment of a mid-nineteenth-century text with a consideration of modern feminist theology. But the problem of monotheism—philosophical and theological—or, conversely, the problem of difference is central both to Alcott's novel and to modern feminist thinking and central, moreover, to our understanding of the intersection of race, class, and gender.

To replace *theology* with *thealogy*, as some feminist theologians have done, leaves the word and, more importantly, the Word intact. In fact, it has the paradoxical (and surely unintentional) effect of recalling us to the normative *theos*; it highlights the feminine as variation, or even deviation. But *theology* posits not just a masculine God but a single, unifying, and transcendent Truth: it posits monotheism. Yet even as feminist theologians acknowledge that monotheism—whether it is understood as the invocation of a static and indivisible One or, alternatively, as the covert enunciation of a disabling dualism—disadvantages women by its insistence on unity, they nonetheless tend to refuse the substitution of *logoi* for *logos*. This refusal makes sense, of course, for what is lost in *logoi* is precisely the possibility of transcendence; when the Word becomes words, Western religion itself is jeopardized. It is not, in other words, merely a private longing for "synthesis, harmony, integration" but the central imperative of Western religious faith that returns the feminist theologian to monotheism.

Having deconstructed the theological text, the feminist theologian, necessarily it would seem, hastens to the task of reconstruction. Struggling to reconcile transcendence and difference, she turns more often than not to pluralism, to the idea of the one in the many, to a multitudinous but no less ultimate reality. But pluralism, while it may offer a new and more expansive definition of Truth, only changes the face of things. For insofar as transcendence requires (and effects) the resolution of the unique and the all-representative into one, it proposes an ultimate reality superceding all others, and even pluralism returns us to unity.

This tendency to turn from radical deconstruction to the reconstruction of a new version of an all-encompassing orthodoxy at the very moment when deconstruction threatens to succeed irreparably in exposing the lie at the heart of myth, does not, of course, belong to feminist theologians alone. In fact, as Myra Jehlen has argued, the assertion of a new Truth follows the disassembling of the old in Roland Barthes no less than in Frederick Jameson, in Marxism no less than in feminism.[1] The radical critic, Jehlen explains, invokes a new Truth as the ground for action, even the action of displacing the old one. But in religion, perhaps more profoundly than elsewhere, the abandonment of an ideal of human wholeness, as Jehlen calls it, threatens the very enterprise. For without the resolution of difference—without unity—transcendence becomes an empty term. Western religion, that is, requires synthesis not merely as a ground for action but as a condition of its existence.

Alcott's *Work* is, first of all, a novel that poses gender as the unifying category, as the common ground on which women of all ages, colors, and classes may come together as one, as sisters in Christ and in struggle. In these terms, it stands as a dramatic demonstration of the capacity of gender to deny difference even as it invokes it. But *Work* also formulates a "natural" and pluralistic Christianity, a Christianity whose God may be imaged either as male or female, a socially responsible and politically engaged Christianity. Pluralism—in its familiar American guise as well as its feminist Christian one—is explicitly offered as the answer to monotheism. Yet even as Alcott describes this ideal faith, she recounts the loss of particularity entailed by transcendence and the inevitable disadvantaging of women by monotheism. In fact, *Work* offers a pluralistic ideal so all-embracing as to write difference—even the crucial gender difference with which Alcott begins—out of both the social and the religious scheme of things. In the broadest sense, then, *Work* describes the inevitable return of pluralism to monotheism, the retreat from *logoi* to *logos*. And in this same sense, it stands as a peculiarly instructive tale for modern feminists.

The Gendered Plot

Work: A Story of Experience (1873)[2] is that anomaly in nineteenth-century popular American fiction: an explicitly feminist novel. It tells the story of an orphan named Christy Devon who, at twenty-one, rebels at the limited prospects of rural life—household drudgery in a loveless marriage, embittered spinsterhood as a district-school teacher, or suicide—and travels to the city to seek her fortune. Rejecting both the grasping materialism of the uncle who raised her and the voluntary servitude of his kind but ineffectual wife, she is "hungry for love and a larger, nobler life" (W,12) than theirs. "Discontented, proud and ambitious," she does not intend "to sit and wait for any man to give [her] independence, if [she] can earn it [herself]" (W,8).

Willing and able to work, Christy abandons the farm for the urban world of waged labor only to discover that she has traded the stultifying dullness of the country for the alienation of the city. The life of the single working woman turns out to be one not of romance and adventure, as she had imagined, but of anonymity and humiliation. Independence implies either isolation or competition not equality; personal relationships are founded on self-interest; and dilettantism and frivolity reign at one end of the social scale, while a pitiable ignorance characterizes all too many of Christy's fellow workers. After experimenting with a variety of jobs ranging from domestic servant to actress to seamstress, Christy finds herself unemployed, unloved, and ill.

Plunged into despair, Christy is rescued from suicide by the joint efforts of a laundress and a "fallen woman" whom she has befriended. They deliver her into the care of one Reverend Mr. Power who offers her the solace of a socially-conscious Christianity and introduces her to her future husband, a man as committed as she to independence and sexual equality. Married on the very brink of the Civil War, Christy returns from service as an army nurse widowed and pregnant. At the novel's end, Christy, now forty years old, is happily established in an exclusively female household comprised of her late husband's mother and sister and her small daughter. Having successfully managed her husband's nursery business and continued as well his efforts on behalf of working girls, she is financially independent, politically committed, and spiritually reborn. Newly launched as a leader in the movement for women's emancipation, she has, she announces at the novel's end, "found independence, education, happiness, and religion" (W,442) in labor.

Amid the lachrymose tales of pious self-denial and voluntary submission produced in such abundance by popular novelists of the mid-nineteenth century, *Work* comes as a surprise: the subtext has surfaced, and women's aspirations, rather than the pain of their accommodation, become the explicit subject. In fact, when Christy declares early in the novel that she "shan't cry but act," a whole class of women's writing—one might even argue, a whole version of womanhood—is cast aside. Rightly, then, literary critics have regarded *Work* as "a deliberate unsettling of convention and expectation."[3]

Patterned on, but surpassing in its social vision the male *Bildungsroman*, *Work* affirms "what *Little Women* ultimately has to deny . . . the possibility of growth in female community."[4] *Little Women* replaces a community of sisters with a gathering of spouses, parents, and children. The March girls, at first so varied in temperament and aspirations, are, by the end of the novel, all women, that is, wives and mothers. The differences between them, now reflected largely in the different fortunes and characters of their husbands, are overridden by their common maternity. But if *Little Women* moves inexorably away from sisterhood and toward marriage and maternity, *Work* as decidedly reverses that progress. It begins with a repudiation of conventional marriage, of dependence and of domesticity and ends with a "loving league of sisters, old and young, black and white, rich and poor, each ready to do her part in the coming of the happy end" (W,442)—both the Christian millennium and the new era of sexual equality. The deferential hierarchy of the traditional family is supplanted by the perfect equality of the new, a "family" linked not by kinship but by the common religious and political values of women. *Work* closes with an extraordinary final vision of a community of women in which age, class, and race are superceded by gender.

But the problem of Alcott's novel is how to get from here to there, from woman's traditional "place" to a new place in which women can use their peculiar strength to remake the world. Inverting the conventional female plot—a plot in which marriage and faith reward the girl who struggles to subdue a rebellious natural self—*Work* begins by ratifying rebellion and ends with the prospect of liberty. Without the girl's plot, however, Alcott is left with the boy's. Initially, then, Christy is cast in the role of a Robin Molineux or a Redburn, in the role of the boy whose rebellion against his father's authority must culminate in the discovery of his own autonomy because it replicates the rebellion of young America against the political fathers of England. But gender, of course, matters, and in this role Christy must fail, for she could achieve the individualistic success of her male counterparts only by forfeiting the set of specifically female values—values which are, ultimately, indistinguishable from those of an ideal Christianity—that empower the new community of women. The political and the religious values of the novel's ending—the values of community and of women—are, then, at odds with this first plot, a plot politically and historically committed to recording the individual successes and failures of men. But the alternative plot, the girl's plot that ratifies the communal and maternal values of Christian women, remands our heroine back to the domestic sphere.

As striking as it is for its feminist politics, *Work* is equally striking as a novel that struggles with what might be called an ideological convention of the nineteenth-century novel, a convention that represents man and woman in complementary relation, as two sides of what Margaret Fuller called the "radical dualism of Nature," as two halves of a whole. Beginning with what seems an ideal "singleness," with independence, self-reliance, individualism, *Work* necessarily begins with a boy's plot and a man's world, the "real" and ugly world of a marketplace characterized by greed, oppression, and heartless self-interest. But precisely for the sake of its feminist ending, Alcott's novel must return at last to relation, to "doubleness," and to the allegorized world of women.

Millenial Expectations

Not surprisingly, *Work* begins by positing for women an alternative to the domestic sphere. Caught in an endless round of household chores, Christy yearns to find her "place, wherever it is" (W,2). Though it is decidedly elsewhere, the nature of that place is unclear not only to her aunt and uncle but to Christy herself. She imagines herself "rich" at one moment, famous and philanthropic—"a Florence Nightingale" (W,6)—at the next, and "a beautiful example . . . to help one other woman" (W,9) at yet a third. The range of her imaginings captures Christy's all too familiar ambivalence about leaving home—both her uncle's house and, more generally, woman's sphere. At one extreme, she wants the material success and the public acclaim sought by the youthful heroes of "boy's books"; she wants heroism and adventure as well as romance. At the other extreme, she wants, more modestly and less specifically, only "to be a useful, happy woman" (W,9). These alternatives, though not mutually exclusive, make reference to two different versions of *novelistic* success, one male and public, the other female and inevitably private.

It is interesting in this connection that Alcott, who began *Work* in 1861 and completed it for Henry Ward Beecher's *The Christian Union* in

1873, changed the novel's title from *Success* to *Work* just before its publication.[5] The ambiguity of the original title would have neatly bridged the novelistic gender gap. *Success* might be taken to suggest that the conventional boy's plot moves to its cheerful end regardless of the sex of the protagonist, or conversely it could be understood to refer to the less tangible victories of the heroines of works like *The Wide, Wide World, The Lamplighter,* or *Tempest and Sunshine.* It might, that is, have either invalidated gender as a term in the novel or conventionalized it. Rejecting both implications, Alcott turned instead to *Work* for her title just as Christy turns to "work I can put my heart into" as the best description of her aspirations. *Work,* then, is a solution in one sense. It highlights the problem of the novel—that is, "women's work"—and it reminds the reader of the exertion of energy necessary to overcome the recalcitrance of the world, whether material or social. But in another sense, *Work* is obviously a problem, for the work into which Christy can put her "heart" must be work which allows for the expression of the ideal in woman. Christy is, after all, not only named Christy—an allusion to woman sacrificed on the cross of male capitalism—but she is as well a representative "New England girl," embodying the best of a culture in which "a brave and cheerful spirit, rich in self-knowledge, self-control, and self-trust" are woman's "best success' (W,11).

Nonetheless, the "idea . . . full of enchantment" to Christy is "to break loose from this narrow life, go out into the world and see what she could do for herself" (W,13). "Aunt Betsey," she announces in the first line of the novel, "there's going to be a new Declaration of Independence" (W,1). This announcement is layered with meaning. Most immediately, it reflects Christy's naive insistence that, in the words of one critic, "the principles of the American Revolution be applied to women" (W,xxxvii) as well as to men. It calls on America to enact the values it not only espouses but enshrines as the values of a New World. Moreover, it claims a traditional boy's plot for girls. Had she been a boy, Christy points out to her aunt, she would have been regarded as "old enough to take care of [herself]" long before she reached her twenty-first birthday. The significance of that birthday, too, is incorporated into Christy's declaration of independence. Legally independent and without moral obligation to her aunt and uncle—in fact, a "burden" to them, in her view—she declares herself free of their world, a world made old not merely by analogy to England but by its rural character.

That the world Christy proposes to leave is, definitively, an old world is made evident in another and more important way. In deference to her aunt and uncle, Christy is willing to belittle her desire for independence by calling it a "discontented fit" of the kind that "young folks always have," but it is clear that she means to distance herself from the life of her mercenary uncle and, more crucially, from that of her aunt, the farmer's drudge. She is no more willing to exchange "her girlish aspirations for a man whose soul was in his pocket" (W,8) as Aunt Betsey did than she is to "hev a good cry, and forgit all about it" (W,10) as Betsey advises. Fond as she is of her aunt, Christy wants no part of Betsey's "old-fashioned and dutiful awe of her lord and master" (W,10). Christy's declaration of independence alludes, then, to a new revolution, to the rhetoric of Seneca Falls and women's rights. The story of Youth's rebellion against Age, of America's revolution, is translated into a story of woman's revolt against patriarchy.

Despite the defiant ring of Christy's pronouncement, however, no one opposes her plans. Her aunt claims "no right to keep" her while her uncle thinks it "the best thing [she] could do" and likes her "good sense in pupposin' on 't" (W,3,5). They are willing to see her go not because they begrudge her a home, but because they dimly sense that she belongs to some other world. To put it bluntly, they, like Christy, recognize her as their better. Kind Aunt Betsey, "loth to lose the one youthful element in her quiet life," is anxious to accommodate her superiority; she hopes to keep Christy at home by lightening her work and leaving her "more time for . . . books and things" (W,6). But Uncle Enos quite reasonably resents Christy's disdain for his way of life and dismisses her "hifalutin notions" about "independence and self-culture" as "poor capital to start a fortin' on" (W,8). Depending on the world of work to provide the "breakin' in" she needs, he ends the discussion of Christy's plans by remarking sarcastically to his wife, "We can't understand the wants of her higher nater, as Christy calls it, and we've had enough lecterin' for one night" (W,10).

Of course, Enos is right: they cannot understand Christy, who, although with them, is not of them. The daughter of an impoverished gentleman and a restless country girl who, like herself, could not bear "the commonplace life," Christy has inherited her father's "refined tastes" along with his library. As her earnestness and her perfect diction suggest, hers is, in fact, a higher nature, one which finds "nothing to attract her in the society of the commonplace and often coarse people about her" (W,12). In fact, just as the declaration of women's independence is Christy's by right as a woman, so the Declaration of Independence is also hers by right as a member of the middle class whose revolution the Revolution was.

As a prosperous farmer, Enos is likewise a member of that middle class, but Alcott draws a crucial distinction between his version of middle-classness and Christy's, a distinction indicated by their different speech and confirmed by their gender. Enos is part of the coarse and commonplace middle class for whom "the one idea is eat, drink, and get rich" (W,2). Rude, uneducated, and tightfisted, his life is without beauty or love or usefulness. Christy, on the contrary, is, like other New England girls, endowed with "romance and enthusiasm and the spirit which can rise to heroism when the great moment comes." But in addition to being energetic and enthusiastic, she is "cultivated," a "gentlewoman" by nature. Filled with a "native refinement," Christy is "a woman who never 'forgot the modesty of nature' " (w,46,48). She is, in fact, nothing if not genteel. Enos, then, typifies the worst of the middle class—its grasping, ungenerous, intolerant face—while Christy exemplifies its ideal. From the start, the moral gradations of class are expressed as gender.

But to say that Christy embodies a middle-class ideal is to suggest that the cynical Enos is right in another respect, too, for the world of the novel is anything but ideal. On the contrary, it is a world full of Enoses, all of them with their "souls in their pockets" and their hearts hardened to stone. Christy's "capital"—her sensibility and her refinement, her modesty and her enthusiasm—is indeed worth less in that world than the "little suthing" her uncle gives her as she departs. If Enos reminds Christy of the hard realities of the marketplace, however, Betsey likewise dampens Christy's optimism by recalling her to her nature as woman.

In the kitchen, kneading bread dough "as if it was her destiny, and she was shaping it to suit herself" (W,2), Christy explains her decision to leave the farm. She and her aunt, she explains, are differently constituted: "There was more yeast put into my composition . . . and, after standing quiet in a warm corner so long, I begin to ferment, and ought to be kneaded up . . . so that I may turn out a wholesome loaf." Betsey is willing to allow that Christy may be "better riz" than she, but, good cook that she is, she insists nonetheless that "too much emptins makes bread poor stuff, like baker's trash; and too much workin' up makes it hard and dry" (W,3). The ingredients of a wholesome loaf are not infinitely variable any more than dough is infinitely malleable. If she is not to end up "baker's trash," Christy must remember that she is a woman, and, being a woman, seek not excitement or fame or wealth but "contentedness."

But these lessons in contented domesticity and the value of a dollar are the lessons of an old world, an agrarian culture in which traditional religious and social forms are observed, and Christy, setting out for the city in quest of independence, is headed for a new one. Determined eventually to find "a place among cultivated people" (W,26) she is, in the meantime, willing to "begin at the beginning, and work [her] way up" (W,16)—in fact, it is crucial to her emergence as a ideal member of the ideal middle class in an ideally democratic nation that she do just that— and crucial to the feminist politics of the novel that she fail. Thus when her lack of accomplishment in the "ornamental" branches of education— French, music, and drawing—unexpectedly disqualifies her as a governess, Christy joins the ranks of immigrants and " 'smart' American" women seeking employment at "that purgatory of the poor, the intelligence office." (W,16).

The "beginning" turns out to be domestic service in the household of a wealthy, artistically-inclined, and thoroughly pretentious woman whose first act on engaging Christy is to take away her name. "Too long," she declares peremptorily, "I should prefer to call you Jane as I am accustomed to the name" (W,19). Right from the start, the world of work shows itself not merely impersonal but quite literally depersonalizing. Reduced to a cipher, one in a long line of "Janes," Christy is required to trade her name for the independence of a wage.

It is not just personal identity that the woman worker must sacrifice for a wage but also gender identity. Nonplussed by Mrs. Stuart's insistence that she be called Jane, Christy is enraged at her husband's demand that she remove and clean his boots. "It isn't the work; it's the degradation," she angrily explains to the black cook Hepsey, "and I won't submit to it" (W,22). Christy's indignation has nothing to do with her ability to clean boots or with her willingness to labor at menial tasks; it has, rather, to do with her understanding of woman's work. What is degrading is that she is expected to do work ordinarily (and in her opinion, rightfully) done by a boy. Hepsey agrees—"I'se shore I'd never ask it of any woman if I was a man" (W,22)—but, in the process of offering to black the boots herself, she introduces another factor into the equation. Pointing out that Christy is at least paid for her labor, she mildly suggests that the degradation of blacking boots for a wage is perhaps less severe than the degradation of slavery. "Dis ain't no deggy-dation to me now," she explains, "I's a free woman" (W,22).

The very mention of slavery, "the greatest of all wrongs," brings Christy to her senses and reduces the degradation of boot-blacking to a "small injury" (W,23). Waged labor, however distasteful or humiliating, is, after all, better than slave labor. Hepsey's allusion to her enslavement thus reconciles Christy to her menial position—a position in which gender is not a factor in the distribution of chores—and makes her ashamed of her indignation. But further, it "bring[s] home to her a sense of obligation so forcibly that she [begins] at once to pay a little part of the great debt which the white race owes the black" (W,29). Ironically the same contrast between the conditions of slave and free labor that makes Christy grateful for her relatively luxurious position as a paid servant in a well-appointed household also heightens her consciousness of the social extremes of the Stuart household. The slavery that has kept Hepsey illiterate stands in sharp contrast to the wealth that brings the literati to Mrs. Stuart's soirees.

Yearning for the cultivated society to which her paternity entitles her, Christy is drawn to the "polite world" of the Stuarts. Through a crack in the parlor door, she studies the rich and the famous, "laugh[s] at the wits, stare[s] at the lions, hear[s] the music, [is] impressed by the wisdom, and much edified by the gentility of the whole affair" (W,27). But she is only briefly smitten with the "trained canaries" who attend the Stuart's "evenings." Their "elegant sameness" bores her and their "twaddle" about "art, and music, and poetry, and cosmos" quickly comes to seem artificial. In a city full of "appeals for help for the poor, and reforms of all kinds, and splendid works" (W,28), their "dillettante-ism" is trivial, and the false gentility that prevents them from mentioning, much less addressing, the pressing social issues of the day is morally abhorrent. By contrast, Hepsey's tales of slavery are "bitterly real." So real, in fact, that fictions of all kinds and novels in particular lose their charm: filled with moral indignation, Christy repudiates Art in favor of Truth. Devoting her spare time to Hepsey's education and her excess wages to the purchase of Hepsey's enslaved mother, Christy seals her alliance with the poor, the black, the downtrodden.

As servant to the Stuarts, Christy discovers the other side of that land of opportunity in which one need only "begin at the beginning" in order to work one's way up. She discovers, that is, class and race. But she discovers these inequalities of society from the vantage point of her own superiority, a superiority that Alcott bases in gender and thus proposes as the basis for a new equality. Better educated and more sophisticated than the black cook, Christy becomes Hepsey's mentor, teaching her to read "with an energy and skill she had never known before" and cheering her on with "happy prophecies of success" in freeing " 'ole mammy' " (W,30). And promising "all the help that in her lay" to free Hepsey's mother, Christy keeps her word "religiously."

In class terms, Christy is Hepsey's "better" because she is literate; in the terms of race, because she is white. But from the vantage point of gender, they are equals. Just as Christy's feminine sympathy leads her to make Hepsey's cause her own, so the motherly ex-slave sympathizes with Christy's injuries as a woman. Their common identity as women, then, measures the distance imposed by race and class. Knowing themselves to be oppressed as women, they see more clearly and sympathize more keenly with the oppression of others. But insofar as their identity as women also bridges that distance, it distracts our attention from issues of race and class. Asked to attend to their perfect equality as women, we are, in effect, asked to forget that Hepsey is nonetheless poor and black while Christy is white and well-born.[4]

The ready sympathy, the generosity, and the sense of moral obligation with which Christy greets Hepsey's account of her mother's plight instantly distinguishes her from the Stuarts and their friends. Their insignificant twaddle, their self-importance, their gossip, and their "prinking"—the rattle of "canaries" in their "gilded cage"—exposes their enervated gentility. Earnest, industrious, sensible of the injuries of others, "religiously" faithful both to mistress and friend, Christy is not a lady like Mrs. Stuart but a woman with a woman's heart, capable of sympathy and affection. Her inferior status only highlights her altogether superior virtue. In fact, Christy is dismissed from the Stuart household precisely because, in an unguarded moment, Mrs. Stuart forgets her dignity and, "scold[ing] like any shrew," reveals the inferiority of the lady to the woman who is her servant.

This first phase of Christy's working life predicts what will follow. As she moves from one job to another, the forms of humiliation she must suffer for her wage multiply. And with every additional proof of her superior nature, Christy's isolation increases. As an actress, she must contend with the covert sexual advances—the "impertinent 'my dear,' " if not the " 'love' and 'darling' " and kisses—of the stage managers. Seduced by the "sound of applause," she experiences "an ever-increasing forgetfulness of any higher aspiration than dramatic fame" (W,49). She is, she realizes, "a fine actress," but worries about "how good a woman" (W,51). Her success is an obstacle to friendship and her heroic and heartfelt scenes but a "poor counterfeit" of the noble life she once imagined for herself. Just when Christy has determined to exchange her "better self" for theatrical success, however, this "mimic life" is redeemed by an act of true heroism and self-sacrifice. With one "impulsive spring" Christy saves her fellow actress from a falling prop, thus winning "heartier applause than [she] had ever received for her best rendering of more heroic deeds" (W,55).

Abandoning the "counterfeit" life of the stage, she becomes a governess only to be wooed by the fashionable brother of her employer who tries to blackmail her into marriage by threatening to expose her history as an actress. Hired next to care for a young woman suffering from hereditary insanity, she is lavishly paid and satisfied that she is "doing good, as women best love to do it," but, a menial employee, she is not entrusted with the facts of her patient's illness.

Nevertheless, having dutifully begun at the beginning, each of Christy's positions, up to this point, improves on the one before. But when her melancholy charge commits suicide, Christy takes a job as a seamstress in a mantua-making establishment. As a servant, Christy finds affection in Hepsey and a womanly satisfaction in caring for the Stuarts' "handsome rooms." As an actress, she is gratified by her success even as she is appalled at its cost to her modesty. As a governess, she is flattered by Mr. Fletcher's romantic attentions and, as a companion, her feminine sympathy has free rein and is rewarded with gratitude as well as money. But as a seamstress, Christy is reduced to "a sort of sewing-machine" (W, 130).

Employed at the laborious and repetitious task of assembling garments, Christy finds nothing to interest her either in her work or, with one exception, in her fellow workers, "well-meaning girls, but full of . . . frivolous purposes and pleasures" (W, 129). Her life is brightened only by her friendship with the "fallen woman," Rachel, a "creature sadder and more solitary than herself" on whom she can "[lavish] the affection of her generous nature" (W, 132). But that affection is sorely tested when the forewoman of the shop discovers Rachel's dark past and insists that she be dismissed. Speaking on behalf of her friend, Christy appeals to the owner of the establishment to "think of [her] own daughters" and be charitable. Concerned though she is about the "character of [her] rooms," the motherly Mrs. King is about to relent and "pity . . . to win the day" when "prudence" in the shape of the forewoman, a "spiteful spinster," intervenes. Threatening to leave herself, if the disreputable Rachel does not, she recalls Mrs. King from sympathy to self-interest. Rachel is fired and Christy, required by the all too respectable Mrs. King to abandon her friend if she would keep her job, leaves as well.

At this moment, the boy's plot fails, thus proving the virtue of the girl. Christy, who has convincingly played an Amazon in her "mimic life" on the stage, is, it seems, no woman warrior after all nor even an eager young worker with an eye to the main chance. Choosing friendship over employment, heart over head, right over expedience, she is instead a new and socially-conscious version of the devout domestic heroine in the making. But her impulsive deed—a testament to her womanly heart—attests as well to her privileged position. In need of work, Christy is nonetheless "no pauper." In fact, the "poverty" from which she suffers after Rachel leaves to find her place in the world is a poverty of the heart not the belly. With a little money put by, Christy works with "desperate industry" not in order to eat but in order to "buy a little happiness for herself" by giving to the poor. Womanly virtue and middle-class privilege thus stand in a reciprocal relation to one another even as the language of gender absorbs that of class. Christy's middle-classness makes possible the expression of feminine virtue which, in turn, identifies her as an ideal member both of her class and her gender.

Christy's experiences as a working woman constitute an indictment of an urban wage system in which self-interest holds sway and charity has no place. That system, as we have seen, puts the worker wholly at the mercy of the employer to suffer whatever humiliation or injustice is meted out. But the inhuman and depersonalizing effects of the market have their impact as well on the employer whose generous impulses must be suppressed in the name of material gain or, less directly, in the name of that false gentility on which material success depends. If the worker exchanges her dignity for a wage, the employer cashes in her heart for profit.

But reprehensible as the wage system is in general, it is particularly odious in its effect on women, and even more so in its impact on those "poor gentlewomen" who are "unable to bear the contact with coarser natures which makes labor seem degrading, or to endure the hard struggle for the bare necessities of life when life has lost all that makes it beautiful" (W,149). Unlike men, women must sacrifice their *natural* virtues—virtues most fully developed in those best protected from the market, that is, in gentlewomen—in order to participate successfully in the wage system. The very qualities that assure us of Christy's "higher nature"—her modesty, her honesty, her sympathy and her sensibility—are devalued, or even jeopardized, in the world of work. In that world, the status-seeking Mrs. Stuart dismisses her servant precisely because she is too virtuous, and the charitable instincts of the maternal Mrs. King are necessarily overridden by the appeal to self-interest of the "spiteful spinster."

There can be, one scholar has observed, "no true women in [the] scenes of genteel family life" because "as husbands and fathers participated in the "freedom" of a competitive and speculative marketplace, they needed wives and daughters who could maneuver in the social marketplace to [their] advantage" (W,xxix). Even more clearly, there can be none in the workshops owned by women who are themselves engaged in the free competition of the market. Women's participation or complicity in the market world, in other words, calls their very womanhood into question. It is only appropriate, then, that the climactic scene in the sewing room pits a "mother" against a "spinster." Deprived of the most essential experience of woman, motherhood, the unmarried Miss Cotton is also, unlike Christy, without the maternal sympathy which is woman's most essential quality. She is, in fact, a perfect example of Aunt Betsey's "baker's trash." Dried and hardened into spitefulness, she has sold her soul for a wage. Neither man nor, in the terms of the novel, recognizably woman, she is neither a competitor in the market nor its victim, but worse, its lackey. Thus when the motherly Mrs. King yields to Miss Cotton, the individualism of the marketplace is finally condemned as heartless, as antithetical to all that is naturally female. But as we will see, the same heartless wage system that makes women suffer also gives scope to the woman reformer.

Ironically, but not surprisingly, the evils of the wage system recall Christy to the virtues of home and hearth. With Rachel's departure, Christy reaches the nadir of her working career. Unemployed and friendless, she begins to dream "of a home in the country somewhere, with cows and flowers, clothes bleaching on green grass . . . and the smell of new-mown hay" (W,129). This dream of something "fresh and free" is, paradoxically, a dream of the world she has left. It is the world of Aunt Betsey and Uncle Enos, complete with laundry. But that world is, as we know, neither fresh nor free but commonplace and stifling. If domesticity is to become a viable alternative to the working world of the city, it must be reconstituted. In fact, its terms must be reversed. The "home in the country" must be characterized not by drudgery, dependence, or unnecessary frugality, but by work a woman can put her heart into. In short, the Enoses must be ousted and the Christys take charge.

It is precisely this revolution that the second half of the novel undertakes to accomplish. The first half of *Work* traces Christy's increasing disillusionment with her new world; the second returns us to the old world made new, to an ideal, reconstituted domesticity. Inevitably, the intermediate and transformative term in this pattern is Christianity. Inevitably, because the failure of the social world, whether rural and domestic or urban and waged, leaves Christy nowhere else to turn, and more importantly, because the womanly virtues which will, ultimately, allow Christy to construct a third possibility for women out of the two the world seems to offer must be authorized as ideal virtues. The socially conservative character of Christy's dreams of a rural home prepares us, then, for the pivotal chapter of the novel, a chapter recounting her crisis of faith aptly called "Through the Mist."

Christy's sojourn in the working world is designed to expose the evils of the wage system but it also enacts a spiritual journey. The marketplace, even as it devalues Christy's "higher nature," becomes a proving ground for her virtues. In fact, *The Pilgrim's Progress*, the acknowledged subtext of *Little Women*, can be seen as shaping *Work* as well. Like Christian whose name she shares, Christy passes through The Valley of the Shadow of Death, overcomes the temptations of By-Ends and Mr. Worldly-Wiseman, visits Doubting Castle and Vanity Fair, and falls, at last, into the hands of Giant Despair. Just as Christian flees home and family in the City of Destruction crying "Life, life, eternal life," so Christy has taken flight from her rural home crying "Life." What she must learn in order to fulfill her name is that it is *eternal* life that woman must seek. To avoid the fate of Miss Cotton, to remain a woman, Christy must become a Christian.

But this is no easy matter, for the same vices that afflict the marketplace also afflict institutional religion. Looking for God, Christy attends "many churches, studies many creeds." But the religion she finds there is either "cold and narrow," "theatrical and superficial," or "stern and terrible." Lest we miss the overlapping relevance of these terms to the marketplace and the church, we are told that Christy finds "too much *machinery* . . . between the Father and His children," "too much fear, too little love . . . too little faith in the instincts of the soul" (W,147). In the grip of despair with neither work nor faith nor friend, dunned by her landlady, Mrs. Flint, and unwilling to turn to her uncle or to a generous former employer for help, Christy wanders the city streets coming to rest, exhausted and ill, on a wharf by the river. Transfixed by the water, she imagines herself drowned: "So plainly did she see it, so peaceful was the white face, so full of rest the folded hands, so strangely like and yet unlike herself, that she seemed to lose her identity." (W,158)

Lost in the hallucination of her lost self, Christy discovers what we have known ever since Mrs. Stuart took away her name: that for women, the world of work entails a loss of identity, that she herself is in danger of being lost "for want of a home" (W,162). With this revelation, Christy lets go of the pillar to which she is clinging. But just as she is about to fall, a woman's hand seizes her and she is "herself again." Not, it turns out, the self brought to despair by her quest for independence but the truer self, desperately in need of being "taken care of."

The woman is, of course, Rachel who has, since last we saw her, found her salvation and her life's work "groping in the mire to save lost souls" (W,162). Her remedy for Christy's despair is to take her home, not to her own home or to the "flinty" Mrs. Flint's, but to the "humble but happy" home of C. Wilkins, Clear-Starcher. Mrs. Wilkins provides Christy with "a woman's three best comforters,—kind words, a baby, and a cup of tea." But what Christy needs more than these—or rather what these motherly comforts intimate—is a religion of the heart, a "natural religion which has no name but godliness, whose creed is boundless and benignant as the sunshine, whose faith is as the tender trust of little children in their mother's love" (W,147). In short, a religion founded on feminine values.

This religion Christy finds in the church of the Reverend Mr. Power.

A quiet man of "inward force and true inspiration," Mr. Power shepherds a flock composed of "rich and poor, black and white, young and old" (W,206). "Gentle as a lamb" himself, he earnestly preaches a religion of democracy and social justice. In his heartfelt sermons, his listeners find "their own vague instincts . . . confirmed and nobly uttered" and are left "eager to do something to redeem the country and the world" (W,208). Even while denouncing slavery and the "modern money-changers," Power speaks as if in "quiet talk with God . . . confiding all things trustfully to the 'dear father and mother of souls' " (W,207).

With the invocation of a natural and socially-conscious Christianity, all the elements necessary to Christy's recovery of her self and to the reconstitution of the domestic world are in place. Finding, at last, a "mother's love" in a "paternal friend," Christy returns to family and to dependence, but with a difference. Although she does not yet count herself among the converted, the "stronger faith" and "more submissive spirit" that characterize Christy as she emerges from the "mist" both spiritualizes and idealizes her gender. In fact—in yet another instance of the appropriation of the language of class by that of gender—we are told that women like Christy are driven to "desperate deaths" not by "want, insanity or sin" but rather by

> a dreadful loneliness of heart, a hunger for home and friends, worse than starvation, a bitter sense of wrong in being denied the tender ties, the pleasant duties, the sweet rewards that can make the humblest life happy; a rebellious protest against God who, when they cry for bread, seems to offer them a stone. (W,150)

The loneliness worse than starvation, the poverty of the single life, is the cross of the gentlewoman. And to those gentlewomen-by-nature, like Christy, whose "good deed[s] shine in a naughty world" (W,150), natural religion naturally belongs. For these women—the best of women—wage labor entails a soul sacrifice, a loss of self. The illusory and debilitating independence of a wage must be abandoned for the real and empowering independence of Christianity. The pun is Alcott's: Mr. Power transforms religion into "a power that [Christy] could grasp and feel and take into her life and make her daily bread" (W,213).

But the influence of Mr. Power is not only spiritual; through his agency, Christy is placed in a new job and, right from the start, we understand that this job is unlike any Christy has had before. It is not, in fact, a job at all. She is to go, "not as a servant" but as a "helper," to live with "a dear old lady" named Mrs. Sterling in her "pleasant little nest" (W,211) just outside of town. Delivered from Flint to Sterling by Power, Christy's fortunes are clearly on the mend. And with her recovery of her true self — her self as woman and, thus, as Christian — the language of the novel shifts toward allegory. Christy is, as the chapter title reminds us, "Beginning Again." And metaphorically, if not yet spiritually, reborn, she begins this time convinced of the value of home.

The intersection of values at once female, middle class, and Christian reverses the direction of the novel away from the market world and back toward home. And at precisely that intersection stands the "old-fashioned cottage" of the Sterlings, mother and son. Positioned midway between the city and the rural backwater of Enos and Betsey, the Sterling cottage shares equally in the advantages of society and those of undefiled Nature. Occupying a middle ground geographically, it represents a golden mean socially. It avoids the pretensions of the Stuarts, and likewise the chaos of the Wilkins'. No gilded cage, neither is the Sterling house filled with rambunctious children and steaming laundry coppers. Instead it is pervaded with a "fragrant shining cleanliness." And just as grace and simplicity, not "style," characterize its "old-fashioned table" and its cozy furnishings, so honesty and kindness typify its inhabitants.

But if the "old-fashioned" domestic arrangements of the Sterling household answer the superficiality of the wealthy, the disorder of the poor, and the vacuousness of a money-grubbing middle class, its economic arrangements answer the evils of the marketplace. David Sterling supports the household as a nurseryman, a form of work which not only renders him independent of the corrupt relationships of the marketplace — his greenhouses are, literally, at home — but one which allies him symbolically with the natural world. The flowers he grows are "not merely valued . . . as merchandise," but are known and loved as "friends" (W,236). And friends — in particular, the many desperate young women who, like Christy, take refuge at the Sterlings — are tended as carefully as the most delicate blossom. Between them, the Quaker Mrs. Sterling and her son, a disciple of Mr. Power, introduce Christy to the best of middle-class, suburban domesticity.

Ensconced in a room "as plain and white and still as a nun's cell" (W,221), Christy finds her perfect setting in the Sterling cottage but she has yet to find her ideal role. Proving her fitness for this "pleasant place" by recalling all "the good old-fashioned arts" of Aunt Betsey, she is still committed to a newfangled equation of singleness with independence. She quickly learns the value of old-fashioned domesticity, but she understandably resists old-fashioned marriage. In the flowery language that dominates her evolving romance with David Sterling, she prefers single carnations to the "untidy" double ones, having yet to learn that they are "seldom perfect, and look . . . incomplete" (W,255).

If Christy is to achieve womanly perfection, she must leave her "nun's cell" and marry; but unless we are to return simply to a refined version of Uncle Enos and Aunt Betsey, her marriage must not be an "old-fashioned" one. Love, it is true, lends charm to domesticity, and Christy wishes, on occasion, that David would be more "masterful," more ambitious, more heroic. But when, after considerable confusion and misunderstanding, they finally marry, their marriage is an act of completion, not submission. David is not Christy's "lord and master," nor Christy his household drudge; they are instead two halves of a whole. As if to ensure this point, immediately upon marrying, they leave their peaceful little cottage to join the "rich and poor" who have proved "that they [love] their liberty better than their money or their lives" (W,359) by enlisting in the Union army. "Shoulder to shoulder," the "faithful comrades," David and Christy, march off to the Civil War. Still no Amazon, Christy is, better, an army nurse, like Alcott herself. Having "always wanted to live in stirring times, to have a part in great deeds, to sacrifice and suffer something for a principle or a person" (W,376), Christy gets romance and adventure, marriage and heroism, all at once.

But marriage and the Civil War are themselves only a transitional stage along the way to Christy's final apotheosis as mother, Christian and feminist. When David dies rescuing a bereaved slave mother, Christy returns, pregnant and inconsolable, to Mrs. Sterling and her daughter, the long-lost Rachel, in the "cottage in the lane." But now the "stern discipline of grief" brings the still-rebellious Christy to true "submission." Forgiving God "for robbing [David] of . . . his honors" and her of her happiness, Christy leaves bitterness behind and, converted at last, takes up the sacred duties of motherhood. Finding both consolation and new purpose in her daughter, she takes "garden and green-house into her own hands" with several young women to help her, and life in the cottage is reorganized along communitarian lines. As she explains to elderly Uncle Enos, who is considering the disposition of his "hoard," the three women "don't make bargains" but instead "work for one another and share everything together" (W,419). To which Enos, of course, grumbles, "So like women!" (W,419).

But not, as we know, like all women. The fashionable Mrs. Stuart, the mercenary Mrs. King, the merciless Miss Cotton, are as corrupted by the marketplace as the male "money changers." The selflessness that characterizes female community belongs to women whose natural virtues have been tried in the world and perfected by marriage, domesticity, maternity, and Christian faith. Thus when Christy finally finds "the task [her] life has been fitting [her] for" in the cause of female emancipation she proves herself a "genuine woman." But more than that, she fulfills the world of the Sterlings—a self-sufficient, middle-class suburban world that mediates between the old and the new, the urban and the rural, the luxurious and the laborious, the independent and the interdependent. In keeping with that world, the Christian Christy becomes, like Christ, a "mediator." And well she might, for she is in every respect "fitted to act as interpreter between the two classes" of women whose united action alone can end the oppression of working women and bring the new day of sexual equality: "From the gentleman her father she had inherited the fine instincts, gracious manners, and unblemished name of an old and honorable race; from the farmer's daughter, her mother, came the equally valuable dower of practical virtues, a sturdy love of independence, and great respect for the skill and courage that can win it" (W,430). But in addition to these inherited virtues, Christy brings the "power of voice" of an actress and the experience of a laborer. A paragon of female virtue, she must be "a radical, and a reformer" (W,437). And having begun with the Declaration of Independence, we are not surprised to discover that Christy is as well a "pioneer," one of that "loving league of sisters, old and young, black and white, rich and poor" who promise "that the coming generation of women will not only receive but deserve their liberty, by learning that the greatest of God's gifts to us is the privilege of sharing His great work" (W,443).

But if *Work* identifies the ideal woman with radical reform, it also associates ideal reform with Christianity. At the close of the novel, the women—Christy, Hepsey, Mrs. Sterling, Rachel—gather before a painting of Bunyan's Mr. Greatheart, a child in his arms, leading Mercy and Christiana away from the City of Destruction. They comment on the "hint of Davy" in Greatheart's face, on the fact that the "women oughter bin black," on the resemblance of the child to Christy's daughter. The allegory reveals its doctrinal lesson, as it must, but it also allegorizes Christy's life. Christy, who earlier repudiated art in favor of truth, can now embrace art *as* truth, for David not only saved the slave women from literal destruction by the Confederate army but, like Greatheart, saved Christy herself from spiritual destruction. In life, he "completed" her, and in death converted her. Woman's ideality and her independence are, finally, enabled by Man, though not by marriage. *Work*, in other words, has it both ways: David's death brings Christy to a new life, in both social and spiritual terms, but at the very center of that new life stands David as husband, son, father, brother, as champion, as political hero and as spiritual mentor. Even in his absence, he is present. Thus it is peculiarly appropriate that the final illustration in the first edition of *Work* represents the league of sisters, hands clasped together, seated around a table beneath a shrine to David. His portrait encircled by a laurel wreath, his crossed swords, and his cap look down on them as they announce the coming of the new age of women's liberty in the Christian millenium.

Monotheism and Difference

What the utopian conclusion of *Work* proposes is not, then, as one scholar has suggested, an "alternative . . . to the dominant society's values," (W,xxxiii) but instead the realization of its ideals. *Work* repudiates individualism and with it the choice for women of "entrance into the waged world or . . . acceptance of the compensatory separate sphere," but what it offers instead is gender identification as an answer to distinctions of class and race, and Christianity as the route to social reform. The perfect community of women – perfect because exclusively female – will, by reconstituting domestic Christian values as political ones, recall America to its highest ideals. That the voices of dissent should call for the achievement of a cultural ideal is not, of course, in itself unusual, particularly in the United States where the "American" values of freedom and democracy are routinely invoked by those demanding social change. In *Work*, however, the ideal invoked by dissent is one which actively denies both the possibility of and the necessity for any alternative to the dominant ideology. *Work* supplants class and race with gender at the same time that it depends on gender to provoke, by analogy, the awareness of distinctions of class and race that will prompt women to political action. Acknowledging their oppression as women, women will identify with the oppression of others: political consciousness, that is, begins in gender consciousness.

But it ends there as well. For *Work* asserts the moral and political primacy of a set of values as identifiably middle-class as they are female and as thoroughly Christian as they are genteel. Christian faith is not only intimately tied to gender but monotheistic religion represents a way of surpassing gender and returning to an ideal of human wholeness. The capacity for faith is disproportionately attributed to women in Alcott's novel but insofar as the work a woman can put her heart into turns out to be the work of social reform which is, in turn, God's work, it is not exclusively female. The apparently female values celebrated by *Work* are values which, in their Christian guise, were embraced by white middle-class America.

The radicalism we ascribe to *Work* – and more broadly to women's fiction of the nineteenth century – is the radicalism of an ideal, not an alternative politics. This is not the case because of an inescapable conservatism on the part of women writers. Nor does it indicate a failure of imagination, intellect, or nerve. Rather it suggests the importance of texts like *Work* which direct our attention once again to the reciprocal relationship between the understanding of gender and the dominant politics of a particular cultural moment. The very construction of gender in the mid-nineteenth century—even the construction of gender by feminists like Margaret Fuller and, more especially, the construction of gender in the novel[7]—grows out of a concept of human wholeness which casts Woman, variously, as Man's unacknowledged other half or as his equal but never as his alternative. It is, then, perhaps inevitable that the maternal and communitarian values of Alcott's "family" of women perfectly mirror an ideal and monotheistic Christianity embraced rhetorically, if not actually, by the white middle class in this period. But further, and more importantly, *Work* reminds us that the use of gender to banish distinctions of class and race denies us access to these latter terms—terms which, if used, would force a far more radical analysis of, among other things, the politics of gender. In Alcott's novel, gender, by appropriating race and class, asserts a new, pluralistic social unity while Christianity resolves gender itself into Oneness. Defining itself vis-a-vis the ideals of even a socially-conscious Christianity, gender carries us away from class and race and back toward the conservatism of its original term.

Notes

1. I am grateful to Myra Jehlen for the opportunity to read her unpublished essay "Against Human Wholeness: A Suggestion for a Feminist Epistemology."

2. Louisa May Alcott, *Work: A Story of Experience* (New York: Schocken, 1977). All subsequent references to this edition will be cited in the text and identified by the abbreviation W.

3. *The Voyage In: Fictions of Female Development*, ed. Elizabeth Abel, Marianne Hirsch, Elizabeth Langland (Hanover: University Press of New England, 1983), p. 114.

4. *The Voyage In*, p. 116.

5. In an 1872 journal entry commenting on the salvific effects of work, Alcott writes that she "Got out the old manuscript of 'Success,' and called it 'Work.' " (*Louisa May Alcott: Her Life, Letters and Journals*, ed. Ednah D. Cheney (Boston: Roberts Brothers, 1890), p. 267.

6. Of course, the complications of a character like Hepsey go much further than this, for here as in *Uncle Tom's Cabin*, for example, the tragedy of the black woman is taken to be that she cannot, like her white counterpart, simply be woman. In fact, the tension between blackness and femaleness is imbedded in her exchange with Christy over the bootblacking. On the one hand, Hepsey sympathizes with the slight to Christy's

womanhood. On the other hand, however, she explains her offer to black the boots by pointing out that "blackin' can't do these ole hands no hurt"—they are, after all, black already. Insofar as *Work* moves toward establishing a reciprocal relationship between femaleness and middle-classness, the problem of the black female character is intensified.

7. The relation of gender to fictional form has interested a wide range of feminist literary scholars. See, for example, Nina Baym, "Melodramas of Beset Manhood: How Theories of American Fiction Exclude Women Authors," Nancy K. Miller, "Emphasis Added: Plots and Plausibilities in Women's Fiction," Rosalind Coward, "Are Women's Novel's Feminist Novels" in *The New Feminist Criticism: Essays on Women, Literature and Theory*, ed. Elaine Showalter (New York: Pantheon, 1985); Myra Jehlen, "Archimedes and the Paradox of Feminist Criticism," *Signs*, vol. 6, no. 4 (1981); and less directly, Jane Tompkins, *Sensational Designs: The Cultural Work of American Fiction, 1790–1860* (New York: Oxford University Press, 1985).

6

The Power to Heal:
Reflections on Women, Religion, and Medicine

Karen McCarthy Brown

Women's difficulties in relation to western medicine, including psychoanalysis, are well documented in feminist literature. The relationships between particular sexist ideologies and medical perceptions, diagnoses, and treatments have been uncovered.[1] Women's difficulties in breaking into the medical profession are equally well known.[2] When women have sought access to the power to heal by becoming doctors, they have met resistance in one form or another in every place and every period of the history of Western scientific medicine.

The root metaphors of Western civilization are more visible in medicine than in many areas of life. On the most basic level, cultures are shaped by their root metaphors. These are the unarticulated yet deeply formative images that direct the flow of thought and action in any given culture. As in any operational thought system, there is a time lag between the root metaphors and current theory of Western medicine. There is a naive empiricism still deep in the medical ethos even though it has been set aside to some extent in medical textbooks. Feminist research, or research in general for that matter, has yet to reveal all the ramifications of Western medicine's intense physicalization of disease or of its view of healing as something done by an heroic actor who "possesses" power to an essentially passive, physical body that has no personal identity, social context, or history.

In Western medicine, healing power, like diseases and patients, is controlled by defining it as a piece of property. The power to heal is understood to reside in things—medical implements, drugs, and machines—whose use is restricted to those who possess other things—diplomas, licenses, and white coats—that indicate their ownership of a particular body of knowledge. It is the view of healing power as material property which can be owned and used by an elite few that I wish to explore in this essay. Seeing healing power as property, subject to all the dynamics of a capitalist system, is one of the most significant root metaphors of Western medicine and one of the most damaging to women.

It is extremely difficult to become conscious of the root metaphors of one's own people and place. Once grasped, they are even harder to hold on to and pursue through the complex layers of daily life and collective history. It is precisely because they operate below consciousness that these metaphors are so efficient in the processes of culture formation and maintenance. If our root metaphors were available to us easily, if every day we could accept, reject or amend them, there would be no shared culture. Yet to see them as essential to communal life and to see their elusive character as integral to their functioning is not to conclude that they should not be tampered with. Change of the magnitude feminists call for requires that we pursue them. Yet this is not easy. One way to crack open the Western medical system to its root metaphors is to place it in relation to a healing system from another culture which is strikingly different. This is what I propose to do here.

The heart of this essay is a case study of healing in Haitian Vodou, the African-Catholic religion that grew up on the slave plantations of the eighteenth-century French sugar colony then called Saint Domingue. This case, drawn from a New York-based Haitian healer, will be preceded by a discussion of women healers in Haiti in which I will attempt to uncover the reasons for women's relatively easy access to this power domain and also show something of the women's style, as distinct from the men's, of using power within it. The actual case study will be followed by some analytical comments about healing in the Vodou system which will be used to locate and describe a healing power that cannot be privately owned and tightly controlled. The conclusion will address western scientific medicine and particularly the feminist critique of it. This section will include suggestions that feminists ought to focus on understanding the oppressive nature of power in Western medicine and on clarifying our own tendency to think of power as property.

Women Healers in Haiti

While in some parts of rural Haiti women can gain recognition and prestige as *manbo* (priestesses) and they can be herbalists and *fèm saj* (midwives) throughout the island, nowhere in the countryside do they effectively challenge the hegemony of the male in the healing sphere. This is not so in the cities where there are probably as many women as men doing healing work. The urban Vodou context is the heritage of Alourdes, the woman healer who will be described in the case study which is the focus of this paper. This relatively recent phenomenon of large numbers of women heading Vodou temples is due in part to chance.

Haiti is a poor country with an extremely depressed economy where the agricultural productivity which once made it the "Pearl of the Antilles" is now long gone. The reasons are long-term political corruption, overpopulation, and soil erosion. The large, patriarchal extended family dominated in Haiti's past, and this is still thought of as the ideal family. Even moderately successful men in the countryside can enter into multiple *plasaj* (common-law) unions with women. Each of these women is then set up in a house of her own in which she raises the children born of their union. Having her own household gives the rural woman limited autonomy, and her freedom and responsibility are increased by the fact that it is women who run the markets.[3] In the markets, women sell such things as baskets, candies, and bread along with the family farm produce. A market woman learns selling skills and money management through this work. The small profits she makes from the things she has produced with her own hands are hers to keep as insurance against natural and social catastrophe. These monies are often the only thing that prevents her children from starving.

As more and more young people have been forced off the family land, away from the rural extended families and toward the greater autonomy of city life, women have generally fared better than men. Their adaptable, small-scale market skills are one reason. The preference of piece-work factories for women, who are thought to be steadier workers and less likely to cause problems, is another. Women have become breadwinners and their relationships with men, many of whom have significantly less earning power, have become more unstable as a result. Women in the cities have thus found themselves the heads of their own houses, as they were to some extent in the country, but with no supporting (and confining) extended family to back up that household unit.

Urban Vodou is, at its core, an attempt to recreate the security gained from the extended families of the countryside. In the cities, it is the Vodou temple and the fictive kinship network it provides that compensate for the loss of the large rural family. The head of the temple is called "mother" or "father" and the initiates are addressed as "children of the house." The Vodou initiate owes service and loyalty to his or her Vodou parent after the pattern of filial piety owed all parents by their children in Haiti. In turn, Vodou parents like actual ones, owe their children protection, care, and help in times of trouble. In certain circumstances this help is of a very tangible sort: food, a place to sleep, assistance in finding work.

In rural Haiti the patriarch has unquestioned control, a control that extends to his role as priest when the family serves the Vodou spirits. But in urban Haiti, women's increased autonomy and access to money have made it possible for them to become heads of Vodou "families." Furthermore, I believe that certain aspects of healing and priestcraft have changed as a result of women's greater participation. I do not wish to overstate this conclusion, yet neither do I want to dismiss it simply because it is based on impressions. Starting when I first went to Haiti in 1973 and long before I considered undergoing initiation myself, many male and female friends offered this advice: "If you *kouche* [undergo initiation], do it in a woman's temple. The men will want to use you."

The urban Vodou temples run by men tend to mimic the patriarchal structure of the rural extended families. The authority of the priest is absolute. Also, the urban priest is notorious for fathering many children and recruiting desirable young women to be among his *hunsi* (brides of the gods), the ritual chorus and general workforce of a Vodou temple.[4] He thus creates for himself a highly visible father role which he then extends to all those who serve the spirits under his tutelage. While the priestess who heads a temple is not necessarily more democratic in all of her relationships with those who serve in her house, she does tend to be so in the ways that a mother's role with her children is normally less inflexibly hierarchical than that of a father. For example, some temples headed by women function as day-care centers for the working mothers associated with them. The woman-headed temple tends to reiterate the tone and atmosphere inside the individual home, a place where women have usually been in charge. This is an atmosphere that allows the priestess more flexibility and play in human relationships than the priest who acts out of the more public, and therefore more static and controlled, role of the patriarch.

Thus it has been social change that has created a chink in the patriarchal armor. Women have slipped through and, in urban temples, created "families" of their own modeled partially on the patriarchal family but with important modifications. Women's healing style is subtly but significantly different due to the age-old roles they have played in child rearing and barter marketing. Haitian market women, like many North American Black women who support their families, probably have a greater sense of being effective in the world than do the white, middle-class, North American women whose voices dominate in feminist scholarship. This self-assurance is the firm base on which their flexibility operates. Furthermore, the greater flexibility and play of women's roles as compared to those of men have meshed with central attitudes in the larger culture, specifically attitudes toward healing. This meshing has taken place in such a way that key aspects of the character of the people as a whole have been enhanced under the leadership of women. The following study of a woman healer at work will support these observations.

The Soldier Who Was Hungry for Family

Late in March of 1984, I went to visit Alourdes[5] at her home in the Fort Greene section of Brooklyn. Alourdes is a Vodou priestess and healer. In this African-American spiritual system, the terms priest or priestess and healer are synonymous. Mama Lola, as Alourdes is sometimes called, ministers to the many needs of a substantial immigrant community of taxi drivers, dishwashers, gas station attendants, nurses' aides, telephone operators and the chronically unemployed. She reads cards, practices herbal medicine, manufactures charms and talismans, uses her considerable intuitive powers ("the gift of eyes"), and the well-honed empathy of a strong woman of fifty who is now a homeowner and head of a sizeable household, yet spent the first half of her life in Haiti where at times she was driven to prostitute herself to feed her children. In addition to her personal skills and strengths, Mama Lola also provides her healing clients with access to the wisdom and power of the Vodou spirits, a configuration of African spirit entities loosely identified with Catholic saints, each of whom presides over a particular life domain such as child-bearing and rearing, family roots, anger and assertion, humor, and death. (Humor and death necessarily go together in the Haitian view of things.) Alourdes gains access to the spirits through dreams and through possession-trance, which is central in Vodou. In treatment sessions, she will frequently "call" the spirits for diagnosis, insight or specific instructions as to what is to be done to bring about healing.

I have known Alourdes for nearly ten years. She presided over my initiation into Vodou and now calls me her "daughter." We have been working together on a book about her life for the past eight years. I have an easy familiarity in her home. So when we sat at her kitchen table in March of 1984, it was not unusual for her to tell me what was currently going on in her healing practice. Alourdes can be discreet if that is what is called for; however, if there is nothing about a client's problem that needs protecting, she sometimes teaches by sharing the details of cases. "I got somebody," she said. "I'm doing some work for him. He is in the army. Oh boy, Karen! That man so big! When he go downstairs, he got to go like this." With her usual refusal to reduce a story to words, Alourdes' stout and squat body sprang up from her chair and hobbled across the kitchen imitating a tall man in fear of hitting his head on the ceiling. Mama Lola continued:

> He from Virginia, but his mother in New York. She live in Brooklyn. But when he come he don't stay with her. He stay in hotel. I say to him, "Why you don't stay with your mother? Let her take care of you." He say, "Not me. I not dependent on nobody. What I need that for? The army is my family. I love the army and I going to stay in it until I die . . . er . . . until I retire." That what he say. I look at him and I think, "That funny!", because I never meet nobody . . . that's the *first* person I meet who say, "I love the army." So you know what I think? I think he just hungry for family.

As is the custom, the lieutenant had presented himself to Alourdes with an introduction from a mutual friend and a non-specific problem. He had "no luck." Although she sometimes knows what is wrong with clients as soon as she meets them, Mama Lola told me she always performs the expected diagnostic card reading so they will not be intimidated by her. She did such a reading for the lieutenant.

As she told me the story I could imagine the two of them in her cramped altar room tucked away in one corner of the basement, the one tiny window blocked by a heavy curtain, bunches of odorous herbs and a collection of baskets hanging from the ceiling, smoke-darkened color lithographs of the Catholic saints attached to the walls above altar tables dense with tiny flickering flames, smooth dark stones sitting in oil baths, bottles of rum, vodka and perfume, herbal brews and sweet syrups. She would have sat in the big armchair with the stuffing coming out of one arm, her broad mocha face lighted from underneath by a candle stub that burned on one corner of the small table in front of her. I smiled to think of the big army officer hunched on the tiny bench opposite her where clients always sit.

After a preliminary sign of the cross, Alourdes would have shuffled the cards and offered them to him to cut. When they were spread in front of her in four rows of eight, she would already have been in a withdrawn, concentrated state of mind. After some minutes of silence, Alourdes would have begun to tap the cards ("heat them up") in an order determined by her inner vision and ask him questions, such as "You have some trouble in your house? You fight?"

At this stage of the divination process, the healer faces a large number of choices as to the direction of questions. Just as a healer such as Mama Lola is a combination medical doctor, psychotherapist, social worker, and priest, so the "problems" or "bad luck" she is faced with may manifest across a spectrum ranging from the physical to the social to the spiritual. No matter how the bad luck is eventually defined, it will always be diagnosed as ultimately due to a disruption in relationships, whether these are relationships with the living, the dead, or the spirits. The presenting symptom, though carefully articulated and then attended to by the healer, is to some extent arbitrary. In other words, trouble with one's father could equally well result in stomach pains or difficulty on the job. Haitians thus see the person as defined by a relational matrix and disturbance at any point in that matrix can create problems anywhere else.

During diagnostic card readings, the client is free to answer yes or no to the healer's probing questions without prejudice. Thus the client is active in the diagnosis yet does not dictate the description of the problem. When the questions and answers have gone on for some time, a joint definition of the problem will usually emerge. Most clients would acknowledge a significant difference between the problem they thought they came with and the one that was defined through divination. The outsized lieutenant from Virginia was no exception, although it took him awhile to realize this.

After many questions and many negative responses from the lieutenant, it finally came out during his first session with Alourdes that he wanted a promotion to a higher rank in the army and thought one of his superiors was standing in his way. Alourdes was not sure.

> I read card for him, but I don't see nothing. You know some people, they really got bad luck and you just see it. But with him, I don't see nothing like that . . . little thing maybe, but no real big thing in his path . . . nobody at work want to stop him. So I say to him, "How long you feel you got bad luck?" He think . . . he think . . . he think and he say, "Since I was a little boy." I say, "You can't have bad luck since you little boy!" Then I say, "What happened when you was a little boy?" Oh sweetheart, he tell me a story that was so sad . . . so awful.

The lieutenant had grown up in poverty in the Bahamas. A key event happened when he was no more than six or seven. One day his mother had nothing to give her children to eat. Neither did she have money to buy food. "He was so hungry . . . so hungry," Alourdes said. The enterprising and desperate young boy went, without his mother's permission or knowledge, to the factory where his father worked to ask for money for food. The man, shamed in front of his co-workers, turned on the boy with a terrible, hurtful truth that had been hidden until that moment. "Why you calling me Daddy?", he snapped. "I'm not your father." The young boy hid his hurt in anger and retaliated in a way that reveals much about the ideology of male power in Caribbean societies.

He yelled at the man he had always thought to be his father: "You going to be sorry. Someday I going to be rich and I going to support you. I not going to be a hungry man like you!" Then, Alourdes said, he went home and cried. But he never said anything to his mother about the incident.

A few years later the boy found out by chance who his real father was. There was a woman who lived not far from his house whom the child had always addressed as Auntie without knowing if she really was an aunt or only a friend given the honorary title as is common in the islands. One day as he walked by her house, a young blonde woman sitting on the porch called him over, took his chin in her hand, lifted his face for careful inspection and said to Auntie: "That brother of yours can't deny this one. Oh no!" Alourdes reported that Auntie then told the boy, "That your daddy's new wife. He marry her in Germany. She come to visit me." That afternoon, for the first time, the boy heard the name of his biological father.

As a young adult already showing signs of promise in an army career, he went to Germany with the intention of looking up his father. But he procrastinated and left the country without making contact. According to Alourdes, her client explained his actions by saying: "What I need to find that man for? He not my father . . . not really."

Alourdes began her treatment, in pace with her client, by addressing the problem the lieutenant had acknowledged: his failure to get promoted. I was temporarily living in Massachusetts, working on Alourdes' biography, so I did not stay in close touch with the details of his case. It is likely that Alourdes gave him a "good luck bath"—herbal infusions and perfume mixed with fresh basil leaves (a general prophylactic) and water—which was spread upward, in small handfuls, over his body. After such a "bath" he would be instructed not to bathe with soap and water for three days.[6] She probably made one or more good luck charms for him as well. Surely she made an herb-doctored cologne that he could wear every day to enhance his luck. If she chose to take his story about the ill will of the senior officer seriously, she may also have manufactured a charm to "tie" or "bind" the supposed enemy. Making these charms is an interesting process for it requires exhausting amounts of concentration on the part of the client. The lieutenant may well have been given a container of straight pins and told to count out two piles of 101 pins each and then count the piles again, and then again. Once absolutely certain that he had the exact number he would have been instructed to push each one (it takes effort) into a thick wax candle, while repeating aloud his desire that the man get out of his way and doing so in the name of the appropriate saint at each thrust of metal into wax. Among other things, this would have helped the lieutenant get clear as to whether it was his superior officer who was the source of his problems.

Some months after our first conversation about the soldier, Alourdes reported that deeper problems had been uncovered in the course of a subsequent card reading and they were now starting to work on those. It seems the woman known as Auntie had quarrelled with the boy's mother[7] not long after the chance meeting in which he learned the name of his father. The now grown man had a dim memory of the boy witnessing an act of magic, the placement of a charm. The boy remembered seeing Auntie write his name several times on a piece of paper and bury it along with a tiny oil lamp beneath one of the trees in her courtyard. Alourdes had to work on a larger canvas now. There were relational problems within the extended family and, since the charm was buried under a tree which everyone knew was the dwelling place of a spirit, the spirits themselves were now involved. This would take time.

Again, I was not in New York and did not observe any of the particulars of the army officer's treatment. But it is unthinkable that it would have gone on without Alourdes calling Papa Gède, Master of the Cemetery, one of the two main Vodou spirits with whom she works. Once this spirit had struggled with and displaced Alourdes' *gro bonanj*, big guardian angel, an aspect of the human soul that is roughly equal to consciousness and/or personality, he would have begun to speak and act through Alourdes' body, slugging down herb- and pepper-laced rum (Alourdes herself drinks little and then only sweet wine or liqueur) and searching about for his bowler hat and his dark glasses with one lens missing.[8] Some say Gède's glasses have only one lens because the penis has only one eye. Others take a metaphysical approach and suggest that Papa Gède sees between the worlds of the living and the dead and that this sense of disjuncture accounts for his randy behavior and merciless joking. Gède delights in going after straight-laced people like the lieutenant who exercise strong control over themselves and their lives. It is likely that Gède teased him relentlessly, though not without point or lesson.

Ezili Dantò[9], the fearsome dark-skinned spirit associated with the Catholic Madonna known as Mater Salvatoris, may also have made a visit to Alourdes' tiny altar chamber while the lieutenant squatted on the low red wooden stool. If she did, she did not mince words with a man who neglected his mother and rejected invitations to sleep in her house and eat her food. Ezili Dantò can deliver frightening diatribes.

Whatever its specifics, the treatment went on for some months, with hiatuses when the lieutenant was not able to be away from the base in

Virginia. In the course of things, Alourdes got to know her client well and when he came for treatments, she offered him coffee and they sat at the upstairs kitchen table before descending to the basement where the proud soldier had to hunch and squat in order to squeeze himself into the presence of the healing spirits. I asked about him in one of the regular phone calls that went from Cambridge to Brooklyn during the summer of 1984. Alourdes reported a recent conversation she had had with him:

> I talk to him real good. Oh sweetheart, I talk to him. I tell him to forgive his mother. She lie to him and tell him that other man his father. But she say that cause she ashame. So he got to forgive his mother and forgive that man who tell him, "I am not your father." Forgive him, cause he hurt and angry. I tell him, "Even he angry at you and your mother, that not your fault. You was just a child. No child responsible for that. Maybe at first your mother lie to him too. Maybe she say 'I'm pregnant for you,' when it really not his baby. But . . . maybe she hungry. Maybe she got to do that so he could feed her all that time she pregnant. Maybe he not know you was not his baby til after you born and then he hurt and angry. Don't judge her. Women got to do all kind of thing." I know . . . cause when I got Robert [the third of Alourdes' four children and the last one born in Haiti] I tell somebody "I pregnant for you," but it not true. What I going to do? I got to eat or that baby going to die! I tell him, "You got to love your mother . . . do everything to see she happy before she dead . . . she an old lady now . . . send her money . . . go see her." But you know who I hate, Karen? Who the bum? That man who go to England! He the bum! Cause maybe he find out she pregnant and maybe he think that going to be expensive. So he just run away. And you know what? He a racist. He got to go marry a white woman. Black woman not good enough. Ehh!

The course of treatment had been decided on. Healing, forgiveness, and reconnection were the desired ends (as well as disconnection and moral censure for the biological father and his family) and, undoubtedly, Alourdes worked on these goals through her usual combination of prayers and charms and visits from the spirits who would variously tease, empathize, and deliver stern lectures.

To ask whether this clarification of the nature of the problem, when it finally did come, or the cure itself, when that finally was effected, should be credited to Alourdes or to the spirits is to ask a confusing question from the Vodou point of view. Those who serve the spirits do not make such neat distinctions between the person and the *lwa* (spirit) who resides "in" or "around the head" all the time and who "rides" the back of the neck during possession.[10]

Nearly a year later the name of Alourdes' sad and ungainly soldier friend came up in a conversation. "What ever happened to him?", I asked. "Did he get his promotion?" Alourdes responded in a vague and distracted fashion. She thought he did get it. She was not sure. Maybe he did not. "But," and here she brightened up and turned her full attention to me, "when he in New York now, he stay with his mother. His mother the only family he got. That man who raise him dead long time. He don't come to see me no more but he okay now. Don't you worry, sweetheart."

Heating Up: Healing in Haitian Vodou

The word "power" (*pouvwa* in Haitian Creole) is rarely used to refer to the ability to heal. In fact it would hint of associations with malevolent magic if someone were to say of Alourdes, "li genyen pouvwa," she has power. Yet many do say of her, "li genyen konesans," she has knowledge. In Vodou circles *konesans* refers to sacred knowledge, the knowledge of how to heal. It is a word with a wide referential field including complex information about herbs, arcane teachings (including what we might call theology), and, most importantly, open channels of communication with the ancestors and the spirits which provide information as to what is going on at the deepest levels of a person or even what will happen in the future.

"Heating up" is another term used in relation to healing. It is always used in an active mode, as in the following example: "The spirits will not come to help us until the ceremony is *byen echofe*," well heated up. It is only when the singers, dancers, and drummers at a Vodou ceremony have moved beyond the fatigue and preoccupations of their difficult lives and are performing enthusiastically, drawing on a spiritual energy reserve tank[11], that the spirits will be enticed to "ride" one of the faithful. Yet it is not only large groups that are able to heat things up sufficiently to bring about transformation. Alourdes' own energy can be similarly raised and heated by gazing into a candle flame when she wishes to call one of the spirits for help in performing a treatment. And if charms are expected to work over time, they also must be periodically "heated up" by being focused on and prayed over. Often a candle is lighted by the charm or "point" as part of this process.

With the concepts of "knowledge" and "heating up" we move close to the root metaphors that shape the Haitian understanding of healing power. *Konesans* is a wide-ranging and mostly non-specific thing. Even those few priests and priestesses who have "the gift of eyes," highly developed intuitive powers, know that this knowledge, like the energy that enables a manual laborer to dance all night, comes from sources beyond themselves and is not something to be counted on in every situation. Thus a Vodou healer can never really be said to "own" such knowledge. Furthermore heat, even though its presence in the body is a basic life sign and its transformative presence in the hearth makes cooking, eating, and therefore survival possible, is also an evanescent thing. It must be sought again and again, rekindled and recycled. Waxing and waning is part of the nature of heat and so, if healing is accomplished through heating, then it is never appropriate to think of the healer as "having" healing power in the way one can "have" a piece of property. The most that can be said of a Vodou priestess such as Alourdes is that she has mastered some techniques for enticing the heat to rise. In working with the soldier, Alourdes' initial problem was to heat him up enough for the real sources of pain and blockage to rise to the surface.

In Vodou, heat is life energy and it is intimately connected to death, humor, and sexuality. I do not have the leisure here to support these connections by teasing them out of the intricate details of ritual, although this can be done and presents the most convincing case since there is no scriptural canon or written doctrine in Vodou. I can make a few general comments, however, which will show the connections on a broad scale. The easiest place to begin is with Gède. This spirit is guardian of the cemetery; he is a trickster, and the dance performed for him is a mime of sexual intercourse. During the long and taxing rituals for the Vodou spirits, Gède appears in the interstices, between dramatic and somber possessions that touch deep emotional chords in those gathered to "serve the spirits." His role is not unlike that of a cheerleader who entertains the crowd and gets it revved up for the second half of the game. He also appears at the end of ceremonies, in the early morning hours, when the social and personal wounds cauterized during the long night of spirit contact must be covered with the soothing salve of humor so the participants can return protected to jobs and family. Gède was the humorous but effective medicine most likely applied early in the soldier's cure. Its purpose was to soothe him, but also to energize him, to shake him up.

The word *balanse*, to balance, has special meanings in Vodou circles. It refers to an active balancing as when something or someone is swung equally far between two poles. When sacred objects are taken off the Vodou altars and introduced into the ritual action, they must first be "heated up." To do this the ritual assistant is directed to *balanse*, dance, with the object in a side to side swinging motion. The word is also used in wider contexts. A Vodou priest once told me about the death of a mutual friend and, in commenting on the grieving family, he said "Gède, Master of the Cemetery, came to the house and balanced it," i.e. sent the household reeling.

Energy is what is sought in Vodou healing ceremonies, but like electricity this energy can be constructive or destructive. It all depends on how it is used.[12] The analogy of electricity is useful and yet, from another perspective, it hides something of the wisdom of the system. Those who serve the spirits do not understand the life energy they work with as morally indifferent so much as they see it as actually created from clash and contradiction. And death is the biggest contradiction of all.

Death and sexuality work together to raise life energy. Without death, there would be no point to sex and birthing. Death and humor go together because humor is the only appropriate and strong response to what is both dreadful and inevitable. Gède's is not an easy dismissive humor based on a false sense of superiority, but one that arises when a person hits rock bottom and rebounds because, put simply, there is nothing else to do. As a result of their cruel history of slavery, oppression, and poverty (Haiti is the poorest country in the western hemisphere), Haitians individually and collectively have repeatedly hit rock bottom. The humor and energetic creativity that characterize their culture, and particularly the Vodou dimensions of it, come from acceptance of the conditions of life. "Moun fèt pou mouri," people are born to die, Haitians are fond of saying with a shrug of the shoulders.

Vodou is based on an open-eyed acceptance of the fact of death and, in a related way, all attempts at healing in Vodou begin with the recognition that there are limits to what human knowledge, effort, and will can accomplish. For example, the first determination that a healer makes is whether a problem is "from god" or "from the spirits." God, Bondye, is the distant and omnipotent creator. The spirits are god's "angels" or emissaries in the world. Healers cannot change the mood or will of god. If a problem is discovered to be from god, the healer simply leaves it alone. But healers can feed the spirits, coax and cajole them into being more gentle and forgiving with one of their "children." In the second stage of the soldier's treatment, this is what Alourdes had to do with the spirit whose ill will had been set in motion by the charm "Auntie" buried under the tree in her courtyard.

The Vodou understanding of the multiple dimensions of the human soul parallels the limits the healer faces in problems from god. In addition to several other facets of soul (including the *gro bonanj* that is displaced during possession) there is also *zetwal*, star, a person's fate. At birth, the larger outline of a human life is already determined from beginning to end. All maneuvering, whether it is that of a Vodou healer such as Alourdes or of an ordinary individual, is done within the confines of what is fated to be. Each client is thus a given, someone unique who simply is what he or she is. Clients of Vodou healing do not lose personal history or social identity, and this may partially explain why, at all stages of the cure, the patient is an active participant. The lieutenant from Virginia helped define his problem through his responses to questions during the card reading; he participated in the manufacture of the baths and charms designed to prompt healing; and he engaged in conversation with Alourdes as well as with the Vodou spirits who were called in the course of his healing.

Modern Vodou healers acknowledge other limits to their powers. While most are skilled and effective herbalists, when certain symptoms are present, Alourdes and the hundreds of others like her who serve urban communities where there are scientific medical resources available will recommend that a patient see a medical doctor for x-rays or antibiotics.

Because Mama Lola operates out of a healing system based on an acceptance of limits, she is able to handle the power to heal in a flexible way that is neither grasping nor controlling. In curing the soldier, Alourdes employed a range of powers. She used "the gift of eyes," what I have been calling intuition, for her diagnosis of his problem. She used personal experience and empathy to understand the situation. She drew on community norms for judgment against the irresponsible biological father. She used herbs and charms. She also called on the spirits. Spirit possession when combined with her other skills provided range and flexibility in the postures she could take in relation to her client. At one time she could be a friend whose own experience of having a child in the womb and no man willing to take responsibility for it became the resource for wise counsel and deep compassion for the soldier. At another time she could be an awesome spirit, such as Ezili Dantò, censuring behavior and dictating the terms on which help would be given. This fluidity of roles means that any power a Vodou healer such as Alourdes exercises over a client is applied in a specific place and time, for a specific purpose. Her power as a healer does not adhere to her as a permanent attribute nor does it generalize itself to all her social relations.

Furthermore, because healing power in Vodou cannot be controlled and owned, neither can the object of that power be confined and controlled. Physical problems are taken seriously (and they are treated), but problems are not reduced to their physical manifestations. In Vodou there is a flow between the material and the non-material, the inside and the outside, the intrapsychic and the person, society, and history. Charms of the sort described in the story of the soldier's cure are examples of the internal externalized, of the temporary concretizing of a problem in order that it can be addressed directly. The "good luck bath" is an example of the reverse where an olfactory statement about how things *should* be is manufactured, administered, and breathed in by a patient for a period of three days.

In sum, healing power, the process of applying that power, and the problems to which it is applied are all characterized by fluidity and flexibility. And, as I have argued above, the power can be held so lightly because those who orchestrate this power are neither denying their own or another's ultimate vulnerability, nor are they pretending there are no limits to their skills. Facing and accepting (though not surrendering in front of) the givens of the human condition and the limitations on one's own power is the source of the Vodou power to heal, just as death is the source of Gède's humor and drive to propagate life. Acceptance of the rules of the game, the clash of opposites that is life, enhances life energy, heats things up, and heals.

Conclusions

The point of these thoughts is, of course, not to convince anyone to throw over Western scientific medicine and attempt to introduce traditional Vodou healing into the mainstream of North American culture. The purpose of the exercise lies in using the stark contrast with Haitian Vodou to unearth the property metaphor deep in western medicine (and western civilization in general) and to examine the tendencies to parcel out, fence in, control, and defend which are fostered in the medical arena by this root metaphor. In Western medicine, unlike Vodou healing, the patient's body is fenced off from his or her identity, history, and social context. We have separate healers to deal with each piece of territory. The physical-psychological-social-historical-spiritual disease cycle is similarly broken apart and parceled out among the experts with few persons paying attention to the interrelations. Within medicine, those specialties which of necessity deal with the interrelations have the least prestige. Think of environmental studies, nutrition, public health, and preventive medicine in general. Furthermore, as a result of being divided, conquered, and colonized, the patient is rendered passive in the curing process.

None of these points is new, nor is it news that women have been especially strongly controlled within such a control-oriented system. If Friedrich Engels was right in connecting the rise of women's oppression with the development of the notion of property[13], then we can appreciate why women have had so much trouble with western scientific medicine. This comparative exercise may make a modest addition to the feminist critique of medicine in demonstrating that otherwise diffuse insights into the nature of western medicine are knit together by the hidden cultural metaphor that defines patients and diseases as pieces of property subject to ownership, use, and alteration.

The more substantial contribution may come in realizing that, unlike the fluid and flexible "heat" in Haitian Vodou, the power to heal in western medicine is also treated like a piece of prime real estate. Doctors own their power as if it were a thing and control access to it through the medical fraternities. One result of this unarticulated assumption about the nature of healing power is that it leaves doctors with a prestigious but rigid and greatly diminished human role. Doctors are required to deny significant portions of their humanity in order to function according to accepted standards. Doctors cannot bring their broader life experiences, their humor, or their own embodiedness into the healing process except as "bedside manner," and that is stage management having nothing directly to do with curing. Furthermore, the role of the western medical doctor, once defined and controlled, becomes the possession of the person with the diploma, a permanent attribute of that person. This in turn causes the power of the doctor while actually doctoring—a situation in which he or she has awesome power over the vulnerable patient—to generalize itself to other areas of life where it manifests as class status and economic bounty. Along this line, it is interesting that Alourdes strictly follows the unwritten rule of Vodou healing that the healer should never take undue profit from curative work.

Western medical consciousness is carefully controlled like the role of the doctor. Medicine is a science and science enshrines reason, a focused and consistent use of the mind that eschews wider and deeper though less controllable ways of knowing. The supposed universal claim of the well-reasoned argument, its ability to detach itself from the specificity of the person who thought it and function in an equally powerful way no matter where it is applied, is another attempt to reify a power and establish control over it. Western civilization as a whole therefore fears so-called altered states of consciousness (altered from what norm?) of the sort that are central to Vodou possession-trance. For example, while there are substantive reasons for our wariness of "recreational drugs" and alcohol, it is also clear that we fear them because they make people inconsistent and unreasonable. We even apologize when we have a cold for "not being ourselves today." It may well be that one of the reasons Vodou has attracted so many negative stereotypes in this culture is that, in heating things up, it brings out the many and not always consistent persona that inhabit each of us. Yet when trance and other altered states of consciousness are discussed in the academic and scientific communities, the question that seems to need answering is why some have chosen to spend time and effort exploring them. Rarely does anyone turn the question around and ask why we, in the western world, have narrowed our consciousness to such a pure and unflickering beam of light. Erika Bourguignon's work seems to indicate that most groups at most times and in most places have utilized altered states in ways central to their societies.[14] It would seem that our passion for consistent and controlled knowing is more anomalous in the larger human picture than is Alourdes' ability to move in and out of trance states in which spirit entities speak and act through her.

In Vodou healing, the power is not so controlled. Healing power is an evanescent thing raised for the moment through the humor and strength that lie on the other side of an honest facing of death and one's own more short-range limitations. This sense of limits is exactly what we do not have in western medicine where the doctor is a superhero and every disease is an enemy just about to be conquered, if it has not already submitted to the power of medicine to enforce change. In discussions about abortion and euthanasia as well as in such celebrated cases as that of Baby Jane Doe (an infant born with serious physical deformities), western culture reveals itself struggling but largely unable to integrate death into life or to acknowledge limits to the power of medicine.

Western civilization has generated a great deal of power and property. This has given us the opportunity to create the illusion that we can avoid the harsh limits that have become the source of strength and healing in places like Haiti. Such a statement is not intended to glorify Haitians, who are as human as any other group, but rather to point to the need for a kind of wisdom in our medical establishments that, among third-world liberation communities, has been called the "epistemological privilege of the oppressed."

One of the reasons it is so difficult for Western medical doctors to face and accept such major limits as death is that we have cut the healing arts off from spirituality, which would provide the only framework large enough and safe enough to make the confrontation possible. When religion and healing are separated, both appear to lose. The humorless, de-sexed, and death-denying monotheism that we currently pursue in western culture may well have parallels with the lonely beacon of reason that we follow in scientific thought. But I will leave that connection for others to explore.

Feminists who have found this comparison of healing in Vodou and in western medicine helpful may wish to ponder the formative powers of the property metaphor at greater length. When we fight the medical establishment for "control of our bodies" or for "control of reproduction," when we identify "our bodies" with "our selves," even when we address a misogynist society by declaring our intention to "take back the night," we sound more as if we are battling over property than changing the terms of the debate. Changing root metaphors is not easy, but we might begin the task by taking a clue from Alourdes and attempting an act of radical empathy with those who wield the power that damages us. It seems to me that it is time for feminists to examine the ways in which we demonize men and male behavior. For a while we have needed to do that to gather strength and reach clarity, but the easy caricaturing of men which passes for humor in some (certainly not all) feminist circles is a thin and brittle humor far removed from the richness of Gède's laugh. If we could look at one male-controlled institution, the medical establishment for example, and see through the heroic antics and controlling ethos to the genuine human hunger for life and life energy from which they spring, then we might be able to do what Alourdes did. She treated the lieutenant from Virginia by exposing his hunger for prestige, power, and independence as what it truly was, a hunger for human connection.

Notes

1. Among the best examples of this work are G. J. Barker-Benfield, *The Horrors of the Half-Known Life: Male Attitudes Toward Women and Sexuality in Nineteenth-Century America* (New York: Harper and Row, 1976) and Barbara Ehrenreich and Deirdre English, *For Her Own Good: 150 years of the Experts' Advice to Women* (New York: Doubleday, 1978).

2. See for example, Barbara Ehrenreich and Deirdre English, *Witches, Midwives and Nurses: A History of Women Healers* (New York: The Feminist Press, 1973).

3. For further insight into market women see Sidney W. Mintz, "The Employment of Capital by Market Women in Haiti," in *Capital, Saving and Credit in Peasant Societies*, edited by Raymond Firth and B. S. Yamey (Chicago: Aldine Publishing Company, 1964).

4. This point needs to be qualified by recognition of the large numbers of homosexual priests who have genuine power and prestige within Vodou. This is somewhat surprising given the homophobia observable in the larger Haitian culture. However this is only a partial qualification since many of these same priests would be more precisely called bisexual. They father children and have traditional families over which they exercise more or less traditional forms of power.

5. Alourdes is not yet certain if she wishes her full name to be known. I hope no one will see my use of only her first name in this article as a sign of disrespect.

6. A "bath" is applied in an upward direction, starting at the feet and ending with the head, when it is designed to enhance good luck and in a downward direction when it is supposed to remove bad luck. Leaving the bath on the skin for three days is in my view (I have taken many "baths" myself) a powerful form of aroma therapy. All are pungent. One lives with the smells, waking and sleeping, for a long enough period of time for them to address the deep self, more technically, the limbic mind where the sense of smell is located.

7. Punitive magic, something not nearly as central to Vodou as its image in North

America would lead us to believe, is most often carried out between families or groups. But its target, intentional or de facto, is often the youngest and most vulnerable member of that family. This explains Auntie's charm being directed against the boy even though the quarrel had been between herself and the boy's mother.

8. Possession in Haitian Vodou is not a matter of putting on an act or assuming a ritual posture. It is a deep trance state which most often leaves the one possessed unable to remember anything that happened while being ridden by the spirit. It is a fascinating state from a psychological perspective because the spirit will often contradict and even, at times, severely chastise the very person being ridden.

9. Ezili Dantò is the woman who bears children. Her iconography and possession-performance work through all the permutations of mother-child relations from the most fiercely defensive to the most fiercely rejecting. Dantò is a member of the Petro pantheon of spirits, one of two major groups recognized in urban Vodou. Petro spirits are not evil but they are recognized as having "hot" temperaments and uncompromising standards.

10. The question as to whether persons and spirits are truly separate and distinct is answered in paradoxical ways in Vodou. Beliefs surrounding possession trance and the struggle of the *gro bonanj* with the possessing spirit point to a separation. Yet initiation rituals simultaneously "feed the spirits in the head" of the person and establish a repository for them outside the person. Also, when the ceremony is performed for an ancestor that calls his or her spirit "up from the water" and establishes it on the family altar, that entity is called both by the name of the ancestor and by the name of the chief Vodou spirit with whom he or she worked. Thus reference may be made to "Marie's Dantò" or to "Pierre's Gède."

11. Although the terminology is mine, the notion of a spiritual energy reserve tank is one that is actually quite developed in Vodou. In Vodou belief, one of the dimensions of the human soul is called the *ti bonanj*, little guardian angel. For a long time I had trouble understanding what this was. Then Alourdes gave me the following example of how it works: "When you walking a long way or you carrying something very heavy . . . and you know you not going to make it . . . then the *ti bonanj* take over so you can do what you got to do."

12. The notion that power has no moral direction of its own and thus can be used either constructively or destructively may account in part for the bad reputation that Vodou has in North America. There are instances of punitive magic being carried out by Vodou priests and priestesses but there is also a strong belief in the overall interconnectedness of things and events which makes them rare. The use of the will to damage another necessarily produces an equally damaging counter-effect on the one manufacturing the charm unless that person is either righteous beyond a doubt or very well protected.

13. F. Engels, *The Origin of the Family, Private Property and the State* (New York: Pathfinder Press, 1972).

14. I believe this to be a fair conclusion to draw from Erika Bourguignon's research even if it must by necessity be an impressionistic one. The reader should know that Bourguignon herself is far too cautious a statistician and researcher to claim to have actually proven anything as sweeping as this statement. See Erika Bourguignon, *Possession* (San Francisco: Chandler and Sharp, 1976) and "World Distribution and Patterns of Possession States," in *Trance and Possession States*, edited by Raymond Prince (Montreal: R. M. Bucke Memorial Society, 1968).

7

Ferraro, the Bishops, and the 1984 Election

Mary C. Segers

A major concern of contemporary feminists and political scientists is the underrepresentation of women in American politics generally and the virtually complete exclusion of women from high public office at the national level. Traditional research has tended to emphasize sex-role socialization, and thus to point to women's own attitudes to explain their relative absence from the political arena. According to this view, male politicians did not recruit women as candidates and women themselves did not aspire to public office because women and men alike believed that "politics is a man's world." Any woman who defied convention and did stand for public office had to contend not only with outright sex discrimination, but also with popular attitudes among voters reflective of such stereotypical views.

More recently, political scientists have emphasized systemic limitations in the structure of political opportunity as explanations of the dearth of women in public office. Rather than blame women for internalizing the attitudes of a sexist society, they have pointed to external barriers to women's entry into the league of public leadership.[1] Factors such as access to financial resources, previous elective officeholding experience, and the advantage of incumbency have been used to explain the low numbers of women officeholders.

We can test these explanations of women's relative invisibility in politics by looking at the first attempt in American history to run a female candidate on a major party ticket for high national office. Probably the truth in these matters can be found on both sides of the debate; that is, despite slow but steady progress over the last fifteen years, women still remain largely invisible in American politics because there are structural impediments to full political participation and because women and men have internalized the notion that politics is an unnatural practice for women. This essay examines the candidacy of Geraldine Ferraro for vice president in 1984 and concludes that Ferraro encountered outright sex discrimination related to the persistence of myths, and of the belief that politics is indeed a man's world where women don't belong. What is interesting and perhaps surprising in the case of Ferraro's candidacy is that these attitudes were expressed most forcefully by prominent Catholic churchmen. Indeed, the statements and conduct of leading American Catholic bishops during the 1984 election campaign carry ominous implications for the future of American Catholicism in general and for American Catholic women in particular.

American Catholic history may fruitfully be characterized as the story of a people alternately accused of being subversively un-American or excessively patriotic. Throughout much of the colonial period and the great immigration of the nineteenth century, Catholics were viewed as poor, ignorant foreigners who owed primary allegiance to the Roman papacy and were unable to accommodate themselves to the requirements of democratic citizenship and the customs of a free people. In the first half of the twentieth century, by contrast, Catholics' general support of American involvement in two World Wars, the New Deal, McCarthyism, and the Korean War often caused the Catholic community to be blamed for an excess rather than a deficiency of patriotism. In 1965, the uncritical support of the war in Vietnam by Francis Cardinal Spellman, Archbishop of New York,[2] served to confirm the worst fears of those who thought that American Catholics were devoted to the flag at the expense of the cross.

It is tempting to say that the events of the 1960s rendered obsolete this caricature of the American Catholic community. The election of John F. Kennedy in 1960 as the first Catholic president seemed to signal the end of anti-Catholicism in American politics. The emergence in the late 1960s of a Catholic Left opposition to the Vietnamese War appeared to confirm the prophetic potential of Catholic Christianity in the United States. The reign of Pope John XXIII (1959–63) and the reforms of the Second Vatican Council, which met in Rome from 1962 to 1965, seemed to represent a necessary opening of the Church to modernity.

In particular, the Council's Declaration on Religious Freedom, shaped in large part by the American Jesuit theologian John Courtney Murray, seemed to suggest full acceptance by Catholics of the values of religious freedom, toleration, and church-state separation in a pluralistic democracy. No longer, apparently, did non-Catholic Americans have to fear the moral imperialism of Roman churchmen. No longer did they have to fear that bishops would use the civil law to impose sectarian beliefs upon non-Catholic citizens.[3] And no longer did Catholics have to demonstrate the compatibility of their religion with American democratic ideals, laws, and practices. In the aftermath of the 1960 election, it was simply assumed by most Americans that allegiance to Roman Catholicism posed no special obstacle to candidacy for high public office.

These comfortable assumptions were upset by the actions of prominent American bishops during the 1984 presidential election campaign. In an obvious departure from the Catholic hierarchy's established tradition of nonpartisanship in election campaigns, two archbishops and two bishops publicly displayed support for the Republican presidential and vice-presidential candidates.[4] A regional conference of Catholic bishops declared abortion to be the most critical issue of the election while simultaneously denying that the Catholic church was a single-issue church.[5] And in various statements throughout the campaign, the archbishops of Boston, Hartford, and New York insisted that Catholic politicians had a duty to translate religious opposition to abortion into a political position against freedom of choice. In 1984 it seemed that an increasingly assertive American Catholic hierarchy threw caution to the winds and began to tell Catholic candidates how to legislate and Catholic citizens how to vote.

Of course, Catholics were not the only religious leaders to abandon neutrality in the 1984 campaign. They were joined by a variety of mostly conservative evangelical churchmen who invoked God's blessing upon the Republican presidential candidate and urged his reelection because of his position on issues such as school prayer, abortion, and tuition tax credits. Reagan himself provoked an outburst of controversy with his remarks at a prayer breakfast following the Republican convention, when he condemned school prayer opponents as "intolerant of religion." In a major address to a B'nai B'rith Convention, Walter Mondale accused the Republicans of using religion for partisan advantage and of transforming policy debates into theological disputes. Leaders of the National Council of Churches, the American Jewish Committee, and the Synagogue Council of America, disturbed by Reagan's school prayer statements, urged all political candidates to "reject categorically the pernicious notion that only one brand of politics or religion meets with God's approval."[6]

Religion was indeed the surprise issue of the 1984 election campaign; few anticipated that debate about the proper role of religion in public life would rank in importance with discussion of taxes, the government deficit, or nuclear arms and foreign policy issues. Catholics were apparently no different from some other religious constituencies in their aggressive involvement in presidential politics in 1984.

Yet Catholic involvement, centering almost exclusively upon the abortion issue, *was* different, chiefly because it was provoked largely by the nomination of the first female vice presidential candidate ever to run on a major party ticket in American politics. Geraldine Ferraro, a Democrat and a Catholic from New York, had served three terms in the U.S. House of Representatives and had steadily assumed more responsible positions within the Congressional committee structure as well as the Democratic Party.[7] Mondale's selection of Ferraro as his vice presidential candidate electrified a previously unexciting campaign and immediately attracted the interest of voters, especially female voters. Most American men and women celebrated this important "first" in American politics; perhaps few appreciated its enormous significance better than the handful of suffragists, still alive, who had won the right to vote for American women barely sixty years before.

The nomination of a woman for vice president in 1984 was important for some of the same reasons that the election of the first Catholic president was so important in 1960: both events signalled the elimination of unjust barriers to equal opportunity in American politics. Thus many persons sensitive to issues of social justice and sympathetic to the struggle against racial and sexual discrimination rejoiced at the news of Ferraro's nomination. Not so the American Catholic bishops. In contrast to fellow citizens who welcomed this historic advance towards genuine political democracy, prominent Catholic Church leaders reacted to Ferraro's nomination with a concerted effort to undermine her candidacy because of her position on abortion policy. In an unprecedented, partisan attack, then-Archbishop (now Cardinal) John J. O'Connor of New York charged Ferraro with misrepresenting church teaching on abortion. Other prominent bishops questioned whether Ferraro—and other Catholic politicians such as Governor Mario Cuomo of New York—could justify a position of personally opposing abortion on moral grounds while accepting legalized abortion.

In this essay, I shall briefly describe the bishops' efforts to undermine Ferraro's candidacy and then address some of the fundamental questions raised by their political intervention in the 1984 election. I shall first describe Ferraro's position on abortion policy and review the bishops' official statements on political responsibility during 1984, as well as the special comments of individual bishops. Second, I shall raise questions about the appropriateness of the bishops' efforts to undermine Ferraro's candidacy. Third, I shall suggest some reasons for the bishops' attacks on Ferraro. Fourth, I shall argue that the bishops should not have targeted Ferraro for reasons having to do with the defensibility of her position, the historic nature of her candidacy, and some possible long-term effects of their interventions. These include, among other considerations, the risk of making Catholic candidates unelectable and of reviving the anti-Catholic bias which has been present periodically in American politics.

The Bishops' Targeting of Ferraro in the 1984 Campaign

The nomination of Geraldine Ferraro as the first woman to run for vice president on a major party ticket obviously was problematic for the American Catholic bishops. In the decade since the 1973 United States Supreme Court decision legalizing abortion, the American Catholic hierarchy had been engaged in an unprecedented, unparalleled effort to reverse the Court's decision in *Roe v. Wade*. Now suddenly the Democratic vice-presidential candidate was a Catholic woman who, though personally opposed to abortion, supported a woman's legal right to choose (decide) whether to continue a pregnancy.

It was clear that Ferraro thought of abortion as a religious or sectarian issue rather than an ethical issue which transcended denominational belief. In her autobiography, she wrote:

> As a Catholic, I have always accepted the premise that a fertilized ovum is a life, a baby. But others do not always agree. I used to talk about abortion with those of different faiths. Some believed that life began at 'quickening,' the first time the fetus moved *in utero*. Others believed life began at birth. Why should my Catholic beliefs override theirs? I felt very strongly that I had been blessed with the gift of faith, but that as an elected official I had no right to impose it upon others.[8]

While Ferraro accepted her church's teaching that abortion was wrong, she did not believe that she had a moral duty as a lawmaker to translate the church's teaching into civil law. She cited her experience as a prosecutor of rape and child abuse cases in the Queens County District Attorney's office in the mid-1970s, an experience which educated her to an awareness of the complexity of the abortion issue and bred in her a reluctance to use the coercive sanction of the law to exact from non-Catholics adherence to the demands of the church's moral theology.[9] She defended the right and duty of church leaders to address the moral dimensions of public issues such as abortion; at the same time, she insisted:

> I also have my duty as a public official. When I take my oath of office, I accept the charge of serving all the people of every faith, not just some of the people of my own faith. I also swear to uphold the Constitution of the United States, which guarantees freedom of religion. These are my public duties. And in carrying them out, I cannot, and I will not, seek to impose my own religious views on others. If ever my con-

science or my religious views prevented me from carrying out those duties to the best of my ability, then I would resign my office before I'd betray the public trust.[10]

Like many Catholic public officials, Ferraro agonized over the abortion issue and reached her position "as a matter of conscience." She believed her position on abortion policy to be "morally right."[11] She therefore opposed any effort to reverse *Roe v. Wade*, and she supported legislation for federal funding of abortions. Moreover, she was prepared to work for the retention of a woman's legal right to choose.[12] She states in her autobiography that she did not expect her church's blessing for her political position on abortion policy; however, she was not prepared for an attack by church leaders either.

For their part, the Catholic bishops, in several different statements in early 1984, made clear their intention to address a broad spectrum of issues in the election campaign. The official statements of the National Conference of Catholic Bishops (NCCB) and its administrative arm, the United States Catholic Conference (USCC), are noteworthy for their comments on the church's role in the political order.[13] The bishops confidently asserted the importance of the church's participation in public affairs and the right of all, including the church, to be heard in the formulation of public policy. At the same time, they viewed the laity as primarily responsible for activity in political affairs. They restricted the role of the church to analyzing issues for their social and moral dimensions and to measuring public policy against gospel values. Although the bishops maintained that the church had a right and duty to contribute to public debate and help to shape public opinion on important issues of the election, they insisted, "We do not seek the formation of a religious voting bloc; nor do we wish to instruct persons on how they should vote by endorsing candidates."[14] Moreover, they recognized that their political participation could not consist of appeals to the authority of the popes or the Bible but had to be a method of rational persuasion. As Bishop James W. Malone, President of the NCCB, noted after the election:

> In the public arena of a pluralistic democracy, religious leaders face the same tests of rational argument as any other individuals or institutions. Our impact on the public will be directly proportionate to the persuasiveness of our positions. We seek no special status and we should not be accorded one.[15]

With respect to the issues of the 1984 campaign, the bishops repeatedly affirmed a multi-issue moral vision and insisted that "We are not a one-issue Church."[16] Noting that the content of Catholic teaching led them to take positions on many issues, they listed a broad range of topics relevant in an election-year period of national debate: arms control and disarmament, abortion, capital punishment, civil rights, the economy, education, energy, food and agricultural policy, health, housing, and human rights.[17] In their testimony to the platform committees of the two major parties, the bishops suggested that a concern for human dignity and the sanctity of life led them to emphasize two issues in particular: "the prevention of nuclear war and the protection of unborn human life."[18]

Two events led the bishops to retreat from the nonpartisan standard they set for themselves and to become more deeply embroiled in the politics of the 1984 election. The first was a long simmering conflict between Democratic Governor Mario Cuomo of New York and Archbishop John J. O'Connor of New York, which began when O'Connor told reporters on June 24, "I don't understand how a Catholic in good conscience can vote for a candidate who explicitly supports abortion."[19] Cuomo immediately took issue with this statement, construing O'Connor's remark to mean that no Catholic could vote for such New York public officials as Mayor Edward Koch, City Council President Carol Bellamy, U.S. Senator Daniel Patrick Moynihan, and Governor Cuomo himself, all of whom supported legalized abortion. Citing recent lobbying by the Catholic Church which defeated a New York state Equal Rights Amendment, Cuomo complained that "the church has never been this aggressively involved in politics." Concerned that President Reagan had "wrapped himself in religiosity as a self-proclaimed guardian of the nation's morality," Cuomo began a campaign to discuss the proper role of religion in politics.[20]

Cuomo was clearly worried about the Republican Party's open alliance with clergymen of the Religious Right, and the GOP's effort to cultivate Catholic voters with platform positions on abortion and tuition tax credits. But he was also worried about the implications of O'Connor's remark that, as a practical matter, Catholics could vote only for anti-abortion candidates. In self-defense and in defense of Democratic candidates, Cuomo said that "he would make it his goal to shift the public focus from selective moral tests, such as where a candidate stands on school prayer or abortion, to a broader debate over which political party best espoused universal religious values about peace and the poor."[21]

The second event that led the bishops to depart from a policy of nonpartisanship in the 1984 election was, of course, the nomination of Ferraro. Within twenty-four hours of Mondale's choice of Ferraro as his running mate, the National Right to Life Committee, a separate, independent pro-life lobbying group, sent letters to news organizations characterizing the Queens congresswoman as a proponent of "unrestricted legal abortion and Federal funding of abortion."[22] Antiabortion pickets appeared immediately at Ferraro's initial campaign appearances in Minnesota and New York. The Catholic hierarchy, however, was silent on the historic nomination of the first woman ever to have a real chance to serve as vice president. Msgr. Daniel Hoye, general secretary of the USCC, simply said that the bishops' organization would not comment on specific candidates.[23]

Shortly after Ferraro's nomination, however, Bishop Malone, president of the bishops' conference, questioned whether Catholic politicians could separate their personal convictions from their public stance on abortion. In a statement authorized by the Executive Committee of the USCC, Bishop Malone said:

> We reject the idea that candidates satisfy the requirements of rational analysis in saying their personal views should not influence their policy decisions; the implied dichotomy—between personal morality and public policy—is simply not logically tenable in any adequate view of both.[24]

Although Malone disavowed any expression of political partisanship, his comments, taken in context, clearly implied that Governor Cuomo's and Congresswoman Ferraro's views on abortion policy were inadequate from the perspective of the American Catholic hierarchy.

A month later, Archbishop O'Connor broke ranks with the bishops' commitment to nonpartisanship by singling out Ferraro by name and accusing her of misrepresenting church teaching on abortion. Speaking to reporters at an anti-abortion convention in Altoona, Pennsylvania, he accused Ferraro of having "said some things about abortion relative to Catholic teaching which are not true." He made the charge worse by not clarifying it at first. Insisting that he would never tell anyone to vote "for her or against her," O'Connor told reporters:

> The only thing I know about her is that she has given the world to understand that Catholic teaching is divided on the subject of abortion. Geraldine Ferraro doesn't have a problem with me. If she has a problem, it's with the Pope.[25]

Such a direct attack by a Catholic bishop upon a candidate for high public office is exceptional in American politics. It seemed to signal a real effort to discredit Ferraro in the eyes of Catholic voters as a disobedient churchwoman, presuming to defy the patriarchal leadership. When Ferraro asked how she had misstated church teaching, O'Connor pointed to a letter she had sent to Congressional colleagues two years earlier, inviting them to a briefing by Catholic scholars and activists "that will show us that the Catholic position on abortion is not monolithic and that there can be a range of personal and political responses to the issue."[26] Ferraro claimed in response that the disputed sentence was not a reference to church teaching; rather it meant, descriptively, that not all Catholics agreed with or conformed to church teaching on abortion. And she rightly wondered about O'Connor's political motives in raising a firestorm about her alleged misrepresentation at the height of the 1984 election campaign rather than at the time of the letter's publication in 1982.

The American electorate was treated to the spectacle of the Archbishop of New York, in full episcopal regalia, attacking the Democratic vice presidential candidate while neglecting to say anything about the positions of Republican candidates. And O'Connor was not alone in his partisanship. On September 9, 1984, John Cardinal Krol of Philadelphia co-hosted an exuberant reception for Reagan at a Polish-Catholic shrine in Doylestown, Pennsylvania, where he warmly applauded the President for urging aid to religious schools.[27] In a message read at Sunday Masses in all parishes of his archdiocese on October 7, 1984, Krol stated, "Every Catholic is obliged in conscience to oppose abortion both as a personal decision and *as a policy in society.*"[28] Finally, after organizers invited Ferraro to lead Philadelphia's Columbus Day parade, Krol threatened to pull out all the Catholic schools and bands if Ferraro marched. She withdrew, thereby allowing Philadelphia parade organizers to avoid a confrontation with Krol.[29]

On August 10, Archbishop John Whealon of Hartford, Connecticut, stated that it is "irresponsible and even dangerous" for a Catholic politician to express personal opposition to abortion but to refuse to support abortion restrictions. Bishop Edward Head of Buffalo, New York, accompanied Reagan at two public appearances in Buffalo on September 12, and applauded as Reagan criticized the Democrats and urged voters to "put America back into the hands of the people." On September 10, Bishop Roger Mahony of Stockton, California, said Catholic politicians "must attempt to change the law and work to cut off the funds that finance the taking of the life of the unborn" and also must work toward "halting the sinful arms race."[30] Finally, on September 5, eighteen New England bishops, led by then-Archbishop (now Cardinal) Bernard Law of Boston, issued a statement declaring abortion to be the central issue of the election and rejecting "as irresponsible the view that would segregate abortion from the public policy debate on the pretext that this is only a matter of personal opinion and morality."[31] Archbishop Law himself, in an interview with *The New York Times*, described the estimated 1.5 million abortions occurring annually in the United States as a "primordial sin, a primordial darkness" that was corrupting society.[32] He insisted that O'Connor's attacks on Ferraro were not partisan but were prompted by her going farther than other Catholic politicians in saying that the Catholic position on abortion was not monolithic. The hierarchy could not accept division among Catholics in their opinions over the morality and/or the legality of abortion. "That's like saying Catholics for apartheid or Marxists for free enterprise," Archbishop Law said. "A Catholic believes as a Catholic." In other words, Ferraro was not a real Catholic. Abortion had become the litmus test of orthodoxy.

Ferraro's reaction to O'Connor's attack was puzzlement and shock. "His singling me out was highly unusual, a contradiction of the long-standing policy of the NCCB, which strongly opposes the targeting of any political candidate by name."[33] O'Connor persisted in belittling Ferraro—refusing, for example, to invite her to the important Al Smith Dinner—an annual archdiocesan fund-raising event named for the first and, until Ferraro, only New York City Catholic to win national nomination to executive office.[34] Other bishops picked up O'Connor's cue. Throughout a press conference designed to respond to one she had held in central Pennsylvania, Bishop James Timlin of Scranton referred to Ferraro as "Geraldine," a mark of familiarity that under the circumstances sounded patronizing and belittling. Timlin accused Ferraro of being "a secular humanist," and contended that her pro-choice position was less acceptable than the similar stand of Republican vice-presidential candidate George Bush.

> It's a little different, because Geraldine is a Catholic and is making clear she is a Catholic. Mr. Bush is not, and, as I hear it, he's holding out just for rape. Geraldine is saying it's all right for anyone.

Timlin said that to win the church's acceptance, Ferraro must "say that she is personally against abortion and would do all she can within the law to stop the slaughter of innocent human beings."[35]

The exchange between O'Connor and Ferraro provoked an intense debate about the relationship of religion, morality, and politics. Some of Ferraro's fellow Catholic officeholders leaped to her defense. Senator Edward Kennedy and Governor Cuomo recognized that the harassment she encountered might soon be visited upon them, and both spoke in her behalf. Senator Kennedy made an effort to distinguish inherently public from intrinsically private issues. He said that he personally opposed abortion but felt that both procreation and religion were private matters, and he would not presume to impose his belief on someone else. Kennedy argued, further, that it is not inconsistent for Catholic politicians to encourage church political action on the arms race and to discourage it on abortion. "Issues like nuclear arms are inherently public in nature . . . and, here, religion and religious values must appeal to our common conscience—and to the government itself," he explained.

> The church can persuade an individual not to have an abortion, but the church cannot persuade an individual to restrain the nuclear arms race. By its very nature, this is a choice that belongs to the state—and not to the different, independent judgments of each citizen.[36]

In an address at the University of Notre Dame, Governor Cuomo discussed the relation between religious belief and public morality. Cuomo's speech stands out as a landmark of the 1984 campaign, a pioneering discussion of the complexities of church-state relations in the United States and of what it means to be a Catholic in a secular society committed to religious freedom. We shall analyze the address in detail below.

Reviewing the activity of the American Catholic bishops during the 1984 election campaign, I am struck by the frequency and intensity of their pronouncements upon the abortion issue. The sheer volume of comments seems to indicate that, for the bishops, abortion was the paramount issue of the election. Despite public professions of strict nonpartisanship and commitment to a broad respect-for-life ideology, the bishops' single-minded focus on abortion led them to be partisan and to behave in ways disparaging of public officials and of the vocation of politics. I suspect that the main reason for their unusual behavior in 1984 was the challenge they perceived in the candidacy of a Catholic female nominee who was pro-choice.

The Bishops' Critique in Comparative and Historical Perspective

The inappropriateness of the bishops' behavior is best illustrated by a comparison of their treatment of Ferraro in 1984 with their treatment of Catholic candidates for national office in 1928 and 1960. It is now generally conceded, for example, that the presidential campaign of Alfred E. Smith, Democratic Governor of New York and the first American Catholic presidential nominee, went down to defeat largely because of anti-Catholic bigotry.[37] While diocesan newspapers and parish pulpits were used by low-level clergymen to support Smith's candidacy, the Catholic hierarchy made no official statements during the 1928 campaign. Judging from the bishops' statements during the 1920s, they were more concerned with anticlericalism in Mexico than with anti-Catholicism in the United States.[38] Smith was left to defend himself, which he did, insisting upon the validity of the First Amendment and the constitutional declaration that no religious test shall be applied for public office.[39]

Again, when John F. Kennedy was running for President in 1960, the Roman Catholic hierarchy was largely silent on the fact that Kennedy, who was to become the nation's first Catholic President, opposed some church policies, including aid to parochial schools and the appointment of an ambassador to the Vatican.[40] No archbishop so much as uttered a peep when Kennedy said, "I do not speak for my church on public matters—and the church does not speak for me."[41] Kennedy took a more extreme position than did Ferraro on the relation between a lawmaker's religious beliefs and his duties as a public official. Yet in 1960, making allowance for Protestant fears and hostilities, Catholic leaders did not object when Kennedy declared that in public life he would follow his conscience rather than his church. In 1984, Ferraro took a position more conservative than Kennedy's only to become embroiled in a long, lacerating argument with the bishops over abortion policy.[42] Comparisons between the bishops' conduct in 1960 and 1984 were not lost on Ferraro. As she wrote, "The fear in Kennedy's time was that his Catholic beliefs would influence his public policy. . . . In 1984, the fears of a very vocal minority were that my Catholic faith would not play a part in public policy."[43]

Why did the bishops, so quiet in 1928 and 1960, suddenly find their voices in 1984? Why did they treat Ferraro differently from Kennedy?

Not only were the bishops very vocal in 1984; they were openly and inconsistently partisan. Although the NCCB had issued a much publicized pastoral letter on war and peace in 1983, most bishops said precious little about arms control, defense expenditures, and the nuclear freeze in 1984—even though there were clear differences between the major parties on these issues.[44] Moreover, the NCCB deliberately postponed the release of the first draft of their economics pastoral—which was openly critical of Reagan administration policies—to a week after the election so as to appear nonpartisan.[45] No such restraint appears to have characterized the behavior of certain bishops on the abortion issue. Although the NCCB specifically cautioned against a single-issue emphasis in the election, the statements and actions of Cardinal Krol and Archbishops Law and O'Connor suggested that the only issue leading members of the hierarchy really cared about was abortion.[46]

The impropriety of the bishops' attack on Ferraro is illustrated conclusively by its selectivity. It did not escape notice that Ferraro was being criticized for holding the same position on abortion policy that the most prominent male Catholic politicians in America—Senator Edward Kennedy, House Speaker Thomas P. "Tip" O'Neill, Senator Daniel Patrick Moynihan, Congressman Peter Rodino—had held, unchallenged by the hierarchy, for over a decade.[47] Clearly, Ferraro was being singled out by the bishops in ways that were novel in American politics. In 1976, for example, Catholic church leaders met to discuss the abortion issue with the Democratic and Republican presidential candidates. Both Jimmy Carter and Gerald Ford allowed that they were personally opposed to abortion. But they different on abortion policy, Ford supporting the idea of a constitutional amendment that would grant each state the right to set its own standards governing abortion while Carter opposed such a constitutional amendment, but also opposed federal funding of abortions. Following their meetings with the two candidates, the bishops neither endorsed Ford nor attacked Carter. Nor did they circulate pastoral letters to churchgoers criticizing the personally-oppose-but-publicly-support position of these two candidates.[48]

In 1980, when the choice was clearer—the Democrats favoring reproductive freedom while the GOP supported a human life constitutional amendment—the bishops still did not target Jimmy Carter or endorse Ronald Reagan in the way they singled out Ferraro in 1984.[49] Given their balanced, even-handed approach in the previous two presidential election campaigns, the bishops' differential treatment of a female candidate in 1984 seems anomalous and requires an explanation.

Some Explanations of the Bishops' Anomalous Behavior

Why was Ferraro's candidacy so deeply troubling to the hierarchy? Undoubtedly, her support of a pro-choice policy on abortion was galling to the bishops because she took that position seriously and was informally associated with interest groups—Religious Coalition for Abortion Rights and Catholics for a Free Choice—that had lobbied to keep abortion legal.[50] Moreover, in her statements during the campaign, Ferraro did not always give an adequate or full account of her position on the dichotomy between private morality and public policy. As one analyst remarked, "Perhaps if it had arisen in terms of capital punishment, feeding the hungry, and clothing the naked, the links between her private beliefs and public responsibilities would have been clarified."[51] Yet in the heat of the election campaign, Ferraro had neither the time nor the leisure—as did Mario Cuomo—to think through this complex question in a way that would advance the public debate. Also, it seems clear from Ferraro's book that she is more of a practical politician than a scholar of jurisprudence.

However, these explanations only scratch the surface; we are still left with a puzzle. What needs explaining is why Ferraro's candidacy engendered such animus among the bishops, in contrast to the candidacies of other politicians—Protestants as well as Catholics, but all men—who held similar positions on abortion. A clue to the answer may be found in language. Ferraro was the first candidate for national office in American politics to use the first person singular when discussing abortion. Up until 1984, candidates for high public office tended to talk about abortion in the abstract; however, when Ferraro said, "I firmly believe, given my current situation, that I could never have an abortion. I am not so sure, however, if I were the victim of rape and faced with a pregnancy question, whether or not I would be so self-righteous,"[52]—when she spoke in those terms, the concrete dilemma that abortion signifies to women could no longer be dismissed. Ferraro's candidacy personalized the abortion issue. As she remarked in her autobiography:

> I was a dangerous pro-choice spokesperson. I was a Catholic. I was a woman, a mother. It was one thing for Catholic men to speak in the abstract about a woman's right to abortion, as Governor Mario Cuomo would so eloquently in his speech at Notre Dame on September 13th. . . . It was quite another to have a high-profile Catholic woman support the issue, and so personalize it. Mario Cuomo could talk about abortion. I could actually have one.[53]

Ferraro's personalizing the issue may have elicited a stereotypical response from some bishops for whom the most prominent aspect of her candidacy was her gender. (Women in politics typically encounter this kind of stereotyping, often being assigned to legislative committees on education, aging, childcare and other "women's issues" rather than to committees on the military or banking and finance). These bishops tended to identify her with so-called women's issues such as abortion rather than with all the other issues commonly debated in a presidential election campaign. Such sexist stereotyping may account in part for the bishops' differential treatment of her candidacy.

Ferraro's candidacy symbolized more than abortion, however; it signified the changing social roles of women, which church leaders find difficult to accept. Seeking to understand the peculiar anger the bishops displayed toward Ferraro, novelist James Carroll wrote in *Commonweal* that

> Catholic clergy have long accepted the tenuous hold their authority has over men, but what they can't stomach are uppity women. . . . The church is suspicious of the new roles women are claiming for themselves and, in fact, in its alliance with the religious right's campaign for "family values," its tacit opposition to the Equal Rights Amendment, and its rigid adherence to traditional teaching on sexuality, the church upholds an image of womanhood that would make those new roles impossible.[54]

On this reading, it was not only Ferraro's views on abortion policy which were suspect; her entire effort marked a departure from traditional expectations about the proper areas of women's service in society. Ferraro may have been a traditional wife and mother, but she was also something of an insubordinate, a maverick—or a pioneer, depending upon one's perspective—when contrasted with members of the Rosary Society in the typical Catholic parish of the 1950s.

In the end, Ferraro was suspect because she was beyond the control of the bishops. They had no access to her since she was not a clubmember of any association of powerful men in church, politics and business. The career patterns of women in politics are, of course, different from those of men.[55] Although Ferraro was a protégée of House Speaker Tip O'Neill, she was also secretary of the Women's Congressional Caucus, and she had ties with feminist organizations such as the National Organization for Women and the National Women's Political Caucus. It is conceivable that she evoked the bishops' censure because she fit the generalized description of "woman" in Simone de Beauvoir's *The Second Sex*: in contrast to male public leaders, she was strange, alien, and irredeemably OTHER—and therefore inferior (since maleness has been the definition of normalcy).[56] Ferraro could be treated differently by the bishops—in ways that were patronizing, sexist, and openly partisan—because she was a woman.

Evaluation and Implications

The bishops' efforts to undermine Ferraro's candidacy were inappropriate, imprudent, and indicative of underlying attitudes toward women which are plainly, unconscionably sexist. For reasons having to do with the defensibility of her position, the historically progressive nature of her candidacy, and the possible long-term effects of these political interventions, the hierarchy should not have made her the target of their attack.

First, a perfectly good case can be made as to why Catholic lawmakers can and should support a pro-choice position on abortion policy. The case was made rather elegantly by Governor Cuomo in his Notre Dame address. To the bishops' assertion that Catholic lawmakers have a moral obligation to challenge the legal status of abortion, Cuomo responded that there was nothing in church doctrine that required him to accept the political judgment of the bishops that the best way to combat abortion is to seek to outlaw it. Insisting that Catholics are not required to seek to have every church teaching enacted into law, Cuomo outlined a complex argument involving, first, a commitment to religious freedom, tolerance, and civic peace in a pluralist society; second, a recognition that religious belief probably cannot be translated into public policy in the absence of a broad consensus; third, a consequentialist assessment of the probable failure of antiabortion laws in reducing the incidence of abortion (it would be "Prohibition revisited," according to Cuomo); fourth, a suggestion that Catholics, who support the right to abortion in equal proportion to the rest of the population, should not use the law to compel non-Catholics to practice what Catholics themselves do not observe; and, fifth, a recommendation that pro-life and pro-choice forces could unite behind policy measures that would give women greater support and genuine choice in situations of unwanted pregnancy.

In making these arguments, Cuomo appealed to Catholic political thought, which has always acknowledged that the translation of religious values into public policy is a matter not of doctrine but of prudential judgment. The church's traditional thinking about the state, law, and politics recognizes that not every sin need be made a crime, and that prudence and calculation of the consequences of public policies are essential in a well-ordered society, particularly one of divided religious allegiance. Quoting their 1983 pastoral letter, "The Challenge of Peace," Cuomo noted that the bishops themselves recognize

> that the Church's teaching authority does not carry the same force when it deals with technical solutions involving particular means as it does when it speaks of principles or ends. People may agree in abhorring an injustice, for instance, yet sincerely disagree as to what practical approach will achieve justice. Religious groups are entitled as others to their opinion in such cases, but they should not claim that their opinions are the only ones that people of good will may hold.[57]

Secondly, the historic character of Ferraro's candidacy should have served to restrain the bishops' political adventurism. If we situate the Ferraro nomination within the context of women's continued exclusion from American politics, we may appreciate the seriousness of the bishops' errors during the campaign. While women are a majority (approximately 53 percent) of the population, they hold only 14.8 percent of state legislative seats, 6 percent of gubernatorial posts, and only 4.7 percent of congressional seats.[58] By any measure, they are grossly underrepresented in the halls of power in this country. In this context, Ferraro's nomination represented a significant advance in the struggle for political equality. Were the American Catholic hierarchy fully committed to the struggle for equality and equity for women, I suspect they would have refrained from the excesses of a partisan, single-issue attack on Ferraro. Instead, because of the highly visible attacks of several prominent bishops, the Catholic church appeared to be reactionary rather than progressive, and failed to celebrate the history-making candidacy of the first woman ever to be nominated by a major party to high national office.

Finally, one must note some possible long-term implications and consequences of the bishops' political interventions in the campaign. The 1984 election seems to have exposed a troubling rift between church leaders and politicians. As a result of the bishops' narrowly focused attacks on Ferraro, the major political parties may think twice before nominating Catholic candidates to high office in future elections. Moreover, the bishops' behavior led in part to the Committee for Concerned Catholics' advertisement in *The New York Times* on October 7, 1984, stating that there exists a diversity of opinion on abortion within the church and the theological community. The controversy over this ad, and the resulting repressive actions of church-related agencies towards the lay signers, and especially toward twenty-four sisters (religious women) who signed it, have not served the American church well.[59] Non-support of women's rights, the unelectability of Catholic politicians, the chilling of dissent within the church—these are high costs to pay for insisting that Catholic teaching on abortion be translated into civil law (and be made legally binding upon non-Catholics).

Early in this essay I commented that the 1960 election symbolized the end of anti-Catholic bias (bigotry) in American politics. I have come to the conclusion that the bishops' behavior during the 1984 campaign may have reawakened old fears of "Catholic Power" in the United States. *The New York Times* hinted at this in an editorial of September 15, 1984:

> It might as well be said bluntly: . . . the Catholic bishops' effort to impose a religious test on the performance of Catholic politicians threatens the hard-won understanding that finally brought America to elect a Catholic president a generation ago.

Pastor Richard Neuhaus and *Village Voice* columnist Nat Hentoff cried foul, but evidence of the old fears kept cropping up.[60] A broad coalition of Protestant churches, both mainstream and evangelical, filed suit against the Reagan Administration's exchange of diplomats with the Vatican, charging that it violated the First Amendment prohibition against the establishment of religion. This—after the exchange had been approved with little opposition in 1983.[61] Rabbi Arthur Hertzberg, writing in *Commonweal* shortly after the election, raised the specter of Catholics using civil law to "impose" their beliefs upon non-Catholic Americans.[62] Catholics themselves took umbrage at the thought that any bishop could dare tell a citizen how to vote.[63]

We have here the basic anxieties and fears that gave life to anti-Catholicism in American history: fear of foreign control by the papacy in Rome (in this case, a trickle-down papacy which influences American politics indirectly through episcopal appointments and the setting of doctrinal priorities); fear that pastors would tell church members how to vote, thus forming a Catholic voting bloc; fear that a Catholic minority would use civil law to impose its sectarian beliefs upon non-Catholic Americans; fear that bishops would tell Catholic lawmakers how to legislate; fear that an authoritarian, hierarchically structured church would not instill in its members the habits of freedom of thought and civic initiative essential to democracy; fear that, if the bishops did this to Ferraro, who was one of their own, they would do worse to non-Catholics were they ever to gain a majority; fear that, in the end, American Catholics don't take seriously religious freedom, the right to dissent, and the duty to tolerate dissenters because these are not values within the ethos or the structure of Catholicism itself. These are some of the fears aroused by the statements and actions of the American bishops during the 1984 campaign.

These fears are deeply troubling for Catholic as well as non-Catholic citizens. They suggest that perhaps the American church did not change very much between the 1950s and the 1980s. To be sure, there has been a great change in the church's life in the United States: the election of Kennedy signified that American Catholics had come of age politically, socially, and economically. The church weathered the aftershocks of Vatican II and seems now to be trying to strike a balance between the function of legitimator and the role of critic in American culture. Reaction to abortion is part of this struggle; for if the church bowed to the realities of secular society and did not require that public policy reflect its teachings on issues such as contraception, divorce, and remarriage, it drew the line on abortion. Since 1960, the spirit of Vatican II has led to a growing activism on the part of the American bishops as they articulate their concerns about economic justice, war and peace, and human rights. Undoubtedly, they have also observed the increased political activism of the religious right, with its single-issue emphasis and its targeting or "hit list" tactics. The combined effect of these changes may account in part for the difference between the bishops' silence in 1960 and their audibility in 1984; for in this most recent presidential election, a confident, post-Vatican II church hierarchy asserted itself by calling Catholic political leaders to account in a way that was simply unthinkable a generation ago, when Kennedy was elected.

But if there are discontinuities between the elections of 1960 and 1984, there are also continuities. The bishops' behavior in 1984 suggests that clericalism and triumphalism have not disappeared from American Catholic life, and that Catholics and non-Catholics alike must define the proper sphere of their activities in order to resist episcopal encroachment upon the rights, prerogatives and responsibilities (duties) of laypersons. This was the great contribution of Governor Cuomo in 1984: he defended the autonomy of the political sphere, he sought to protect the politician's turf.

The historian David O'Brien has remarked that "religious liberty remains an experiment and church-state separation, far from settling the question, structures a continuing conversation about religion and public life."[64] One may welcome the contributions a newly assertive Catholic church can make to American public life while insisting at the same time that limitations be placed upon its political activities. A chief requirement is non-partisanship: churches in American society are accorded certain privileges and immunities, like immunity from taxation, in return for which it is reasonable to demand that they not engage in partisanship, which involves the allocation of power. Non-partisanship means the church should avoid endorsing candidates and should not draw up voting instructions for Catholic citizens or legislators. Political endorsements by religious leaders are potentially divisive and violate American custom and tradition. As Cuomo stated, "Our innate wisdom and democratic instinct teaches us that these things are dangerous." Above all, church leaders should not invoke different standards for male and female candidates.

The contrast between the bishops' even-handed treatment of male candidates—Catholic and Protestant—in previous elections and their negative reaction to Geraldine Ferraro's candidacy in 1984 illustrates that, despite American women's slow but steady gains in electoral politics, the belief that "politics is a man's world" is still widely shared by powerful elites in American society. It is disturbing to realize that such stereotypical views about "woman's place" are held by leading churchmen of a major religious denomination. It is even more troubling that these partisan attacks on the first woman ever to run on a major party ticket for the vice presidency came from church leaders ostensibly committed to the elimination of sexism in society and the realization of social justice for all, including women. Perhaps it is not surprising that a church which does not accept equality of the sexes within its own organizational structure also does not accept full political equality of women and men in secular society.

Notes

1.   See Susan J. Carroll, *Women as Candidates in American Politics* (Bloomington, Indiana: Indiana University Press, 1985), chapters 5–9. Also Naomi B. Lynn, "Women and Politics: The Real Majority," in Jo Freeman, ed., *Women: A Feminist Perspective* (Palo Alto: Mayfield Publishing Co., 1984), pp. 402–22.

2.   On December 23, 1965, Cardinal Spellman, arriving in South Vietnam for a five-day Christmas visit, was asked by newsmen, "What do you think about what the United States is doing in Vietnam?" He answered, "I fully support everything it does." Then, paraphrasing the words of the nineteenth-century naval hero, Stephen Decatur, the cardinal added, "My country, may it always be right. Right or wrong, my country." As reported in a dispatch from Saigon in *The New York Times*, December 24, 1965, and cited by Dorothy Dohen, *Nationalism and American Catholicism* (New York: Sheed and Ward, 1967), p. 1.

3.   I should explain what I mean by the statement that "the bishops would use the civil law to impose sectarian beliefs upon non-Catholic citizens." I refer here to the bishops' use of the political process to enact laws which reflect Roman Catholic beliefs — sectarian beliefs that are religiously derived and religiously justified but which are not shared by citizens who are non-religious or from a different denomination. In particular, I refer to clerical use of the political process in a partisan fashion to endorse political candidates or to otherwise influence which candidates get into office. As for lobbying in legislatures, the Roman Catholic and other churches do have a right to articulate their views in, for example, testimony before Congressional committees. However, churches, it seems to me, are more than interest groups. They have a special duty to attend to the common good and to universal values of peace and justice.

4.   The *National Catholic Reporter*, September 21, 1984, pp. 21–22. The bishops were: Edward Head, Bishop of Buffalo, New York; James Timlin, Bishop of Scranton, Pennsylvania; John Whealon, Archbishop of Hartford, Connecticut; and John Cardinal Krol, Archbishop of Philadelphia, Pennsylvania.

5.   "The Responsibility of Citizenship," Statement of the Bishops of Massachusetts, New Hampshire, Vermont, and Maine, September 5, 1984, reprinted in Daughters of St. Paul, ed., *Life, A Gift of God: U.S. Catholic Leaders Speak Out on Life Issues* (Boston: Daughters of St. Paul, St. Paul Editions, 1985), pp. 191–95. See also *The New York Times*, September 5, 1984, p. A20.

6.   *National Catholic Reporter* (NCR), September 21, 1984, p. 22.

7.   By 1983, Ferraro had a valued seat on the House Budget Committee and a leadership post within the House Democratic Caucus. The Democratic Party had also selected her as Chair of the Party Platform Committee in 1984.

8.   Geraldine A. Ferraro with Linda Bird Francke, *Ferraro: My Story* (New York: Bantam Books, 1985), p. 215.

9.   Ibid., pp. 215–18.

10. Ibid., p. 227. Also see her statements on abortion in the Vice-Presidential debate with Republican candidate, George Bush, as reported in *The New York Times*, October 12, 1984, pp. B5–B6.

11. Ferraro, *Ferraro: My Story*, p. 218.

12. In remarks on abortion policy made during a speech to the National Women's Political Caucus annual meeting in June, 1985, Ferraro emphasized a woman's right to decide. She did not emphasize this aspect of her views on legalized abortion during the 1984 campaign. See *The New York Times*, June 29, 1985, p. 8. See also *Women's Political Times*, vol. 10, no. 3 (July/August 1985), pp. 3 and 11, speech by Geraldine A. Ferraro to the National Women's Political Caucus convention in Atlanta, Georgia, June 27, 1985. In that speech, Ferraro stated: "Abortion is a personal decision—not a political one. Each woman must choose for herself, based on her values, beliefs and her particular situation. That choice is hers to make, and it does not belong to Jerry Falwell or Ronald Reagan." *Women's Political Times*, p. 11.

13. These statements include: "Political Responsibility: Choices for the 1980s," USCC Administrative Board, *Origins* 13:44 (April 12, 1984), pp. 732-36; Bishop James W. Malone, "USCC Statement on Politics and Religion," *Origins* 14:11 (August 23, 1984), pp. 161-63, reprinted in Daughters of St. Paul, *Life, A Gift of God*, pp. 28-33; and Bishop James W. Malone, "The Bishops and Partisan Politics" (statement of Bishop Malone as President of the USCC and made at the request of the USCC Administrative Board, October 14, 1984) *Origins* 14:19 (October 25, 1984), pp. 289-91; also printed in *The New York Times*, October 14, 1984, p. 26, and in Daughters of St. Paul, *Life, A Gift of God*, pp. 82-87.

14. USCC Administrative Board, "Political Responsibility: Choices for the 1980s," *Origins* 13:44 (April 12, 1984), p. 733. (*Origins* is the National Catholic Documentary Service, a publication of the United States Catholic Conference, Washington, D.C.).

15. Address of Bishop James W. Malone, President, to the general meeting of the National Conference of Catholic Bishops, excerpted in *The New York Times*, November 13, 1984, p. A22. *Origins* 14:24 (November 29, 1984), pp. 384-90.

16. Bishop James W. Malone and USCC Administrative Committee, "The Bishops and Partisan Politics," *Origins* 14:19 (October 25, 1984), pp. 289-91; reprinted in full in *The New York Times*, October 14, 1984, p. 26.

17. USCC Administrative Board, "Political Responsibility: Choices for the 1980s," *Origins* 13:44 (April 12, 1984, pp. 734-35.

18. Bishop J.W. Malone and USCC Administrative Committee, "The Bishops and Partisan Politics," *Origins* 14:19 (October 25, 1984), pp. 289-91; reprinted in *The New York Times*, October 14, 1984, p. 26.

19. Earlier, the bishops of New York State had issued an election-year statement, "Abortion: The Role of Public Officials," on April 6, 1984, in which they described as "radically inconsistent" the position of public officeholders who say they personally oppose abortion but do not wish to impose their views upon others. The bishops called on "all in public office and positions of authority to oppose legalized abortion by support of a constitutional amendment." *Origins*, 13:46 (April 26, 1984), pp. 759-60. Archbishop O'Connor's remark of June 24, 1984 was reported in *The New York Times*, June 25, 1984 and repeatedly thereafter in the controversy with Governor Cuomo.

20. *The New York Times*, August 3, 1984, p. A1.

21. Ibid. The conflict between Archbishop O'Connor and Governor Cuomo was later defused at a ninety-minute meeting between the two men on August 23, 1984. Cuomo said he believed that he and the Archbishop still disagreed over how to

handle the issue of abortion, but that this was a disagreement over political tactics and not church teachings. With respect to public policy, Archbishop O'Connor supported a constitutional amendment banning abortion. Governor Cuomo said he agreed with church teaching that abortion is wrong, but did not agree that outlawing abortion would prevent it. Cuomo also stated his belief that it is discriminatory to permit abortion but then prevent women from obtaining them by denying medicaid funds.

22. *The New York Times*, August 4, 1984, p. 6.

23. Ibid.

24. Bishop James W. Malone, "USCC Statement on Politics and Religion," *Origins* 14:11 (August 23, 1984), p. 163. This statement was released on August 9, 1984. The press release accompanying this statement explained that "Bishop Malone made his comments in a statement authorized by the Executive Committee of the Catholic Conference, the national level action agency of the Catholic Church. Besides Bishop Malone, the members of the Executive Committee are Archbishop John L. May of St. Louis, Vice President of USCC, Archbishop Thomas C. Kelly of Louisville, Archbishop Bernard F. Law of Boston, and Archbishop Edmund C. Szoka of Detroit." Daughters of St. Paul, *Life, A Gift of God*, pp. 28–29, and pp. 32–33.

25. *The New York Times*, September 9, 1984, p. 34.

26. Geraldine A. Ferraro, Introductory Letter, "The Abortion Issue in the Political Process: A Briefing for Catholic Legislators," (Washington, D.C.: Catholics for a Free Choice, 1982), p. 1. This briefing was held on September 30, 1982.

27. *National Catholic Reporter*, September 21, 1984, p. 22.

28. John Cardinal Krol, "Protecting God's Precious Gift," A Message to be Read at All Parishes of the Archdiocese of Philadelphia, on Respect Life Sunday, October 7, 1984; reprinted in Daughters of St. Paul, *Life, A Gift of God*, p. 53.

29. Geraldine A. Ferraro, *Ferraro: My Story*, pp. 231–32.

30. *National Catholic Reporter*, September 21, 1984, p. 22.

31. Daughters of St. Paul, *Life, A Gift of God*, p. 192. The text of this statement was reprinted in *Origins* 14:14 (September 20, 1984), pp. 217–218 and reported in *The New York Times* September 5, 1984, p. A20.

32. *The New York Times*, September 23, 1984, p. E2.

33. Geraldine A. Ferraro, *Ferraro: My Story*, p. 223.

34. Ibid., p. 275. The Al Smith Dinner in New York City is a nonpartisan affair at which the New York Archbishop hosts the presidential and vice-presidential candidates of the two major parties; it is nonpartisan and generally characterized by good humor in the midst of a presidential election campaign. In 1984, Democratic candidate Walter Mondale declined to attend because he had to prepare for the upcoming presidential debate with Ronald Reagan; the expectation was that his vice-presidential running mate, Ferraro, would attend in his stead. There was a precedent for this; in 1972, Richard Nixon declined to attend and his vice-presidential candidate, Spiro Agnew, was present. However, in 1984, an invitation to Geraldine Ferraro was not forthcoming from the New York Archbishop.

35. As reported in *The National Catholic Reporter*, September 21, 1984, p. 22.

36. Senator Edward Kennedy, Address of September 11, 1984, reprinted in *Origins* 14:14 (September 20, 1984), pp. 218–20; also reported in the *National Catholic Reporter*, September 21, 1984, p. 22.

37. See the recent, definitive account of the 1928 election by Allan J. Lichtman, *Prejudice and the Old Politics: The Presidential Election of 1928* (Chapel Hill: University of North Carolina Press, 1979), p. 321, in which he states, "Of all possible explanations for the distinctive political alignment of 1928, religion is the best."

38. See Hugh J. Nolan, ed., *Pastoral Letters of the U.S. Catholic Bishops*, vol. 1 (1792–1940) (USCC: Washington, D.C., 1984), pp. 337–65; also James Hennesey, *American Catholics: A History of the Roman Catholic Community in the United States* (Oxford University Press, 1981), pp. 246–53.

39. See Alfred E. Smith, "Governor Smith's Answer to the Religious Bigotry of the Presidential Campaign, September 20, 1928," in John Tracy Ellis, ed., *Documents of American Catholic History* (Chicago: Henry Regnery Company, 1967), pp. 616–21; also Edmund A. Moore, *A Catholic Runs for President: The Campaign of 1928* (New York, 1956) and James A. Pike, *A Roman Catholic in the White House* (Garden City, N.Y.: Doubleday and Company, 1960), pp. 17–45.

40. It was 166 Catholic laypersons who came to Kennedy's defense on October 5, 1960, issuing an eloquent defense and clarification of the American Catholic citizen's support for religious liberty and church-state separation in the United States. See "The Issue of Religious Freedom in a Presidential Campaign," in John Tracy Ellis, ed., *Documents of American Catholic History*, pp. 652–54. The Catholic bishops issued a brief statement on January 25, 1960, protesting racial and religious bigotry, especially recent anti-Semitic attacks on synagogues and churches. See Hugh J. Nolan, ed., *Pastoral Letters of the U.S. Catholic Bishops*, vol. 2, pp. 232–33.

41. Speech of John F. Kennedy before Greater Ministerial Association of Houston, Texas; reprinted in Theodore H. White, *The Making of the President 1960* (New York: Atheneum, 1967), pp. 391–93.

42. Wilson Carey McWilliams, "The Meaning of the Election," in Gerald Pomper et al, *The Election of 1984* (Chatham, N.J.: Chatham House Publishers, Inc., 1985), p. 171.

43. Geraldine A. Ferraro, *Ferraro: My Story*, pp. 211–12.

44. The *National Catholic Reporter* stated that, at a Catholic social-action directors' gathering in March, 1984, USCC officials said they would not translate the May 1983 nuclear weapons pastoral letter into specific weapons policy proposals. The church was said to make its most important political contribution when it "defines the issues," not when it takes specific legislative stands, explained Father J. Bryan Hehir, the USCC social development and world peace director. *National Catholic Reporter*, September 21, 1984, p. 21.

45. On May 25, 1984, Archbishop Rembert Weakland told the Catholic Press Association that the Catholic bishops did not want their economic pastoral letter "immediately politicized," so its contents would be kept secret until after the November 6 election. To prevent leaks, even the bishops would not be allowed to see the draft until they arrived in Washington for a November 10, 1984 meeting of the NCCB. *National Catholic Reporter*, September 21, 1984, p. 21.

46. It should be noted that other bishops did criticize the single-issue emphasis of these Catholic leaders; in a statement released late in the campaign, twenty-two bishops led

by Bishop Thomas Gumbleton of Detroit and Carroll Dozier of Minnesota took issue with their episcopal colleagues for failing to emphasize the importance of the nuclear arms race. But perhaps this came too late; by October 22, 1984, when it was released, the damage to the Ferraro candidacy had been done. See NC Documentary Service, *Statement by 23 Bishops on Nuclear Arms*, released in Washington, D.C., October 22, 1984.

As indicated by this statement's release, the bishops were apparently internally divided over the conduct of some leading churchmen during the campaign. Some speculated that an intramural struggle was taking place between Cardinal Bernardin, who favored a multi-issue approach, and Archbishop O'Connor, who supported a single-issue emphasis on abortion) for leadership of the American Catholic hierarchy. See Joe Klein, "Abortion and the Archbishop," *New York*, October 1, 1984, p. 39, and *National Catholic Reporter*, September 21, 1984, p. 2.

47. See Mary T. Hanna, *Catholics and American Politics* (Cambridge: Harvard University Press, 1979), chapter 5, pp. 148–99, and *Congressional Quarterly Weekly Report*, February 4, 1978, pp. 258–60, for the voting records of Catholic members of Congress on abortion policy since 1973. It should be noted that, if the bishops were selective about which politicians they attacked, there was also a self-selection process among the bishops concerning who would attack. Ferraro's own bishop, Francis J. Mugavero of Brooklyn, did not publicly criticize Ferraro in 1984 for her position on abortion. But his neighbor, Archbishop O'Connor, did.

48. See the following statements of the bishops in 1976, all collected in Hugh J. Nolan, ed., *Pastoral Letters of the U.S. Catholic Bishops*, vol. 4 (1975–1983): "Political Responsibility: Reflections on an Election Year" (February 12, 1976), pp. 129–37; "Political Responsibility: A Resolution of the Catholic Bishops of the U.S.," (May 6, 1976), pp. 146–47; "Resolution of the Administrative Committee, NCCB," (September 15, 1976), pp. 157–58. Also see "Statement of U.S. Bishops President Archbishop Bernardin" (July 1976) in Daughters of St. Paul, *Yes to Life* (Boston: St. Paul Editions, 1977), pp. 291–92. For an analysis of the bishops' statements during the 1976 campaign, see Maris A. Vinovskis, "Abortion and the Presidential Election of 1976: A Multivariate Analysis of Voting Behavior," in Carl E. Schneider and Maris A. Vinovskis, eds., *The Law and Politics of Abortion* (Lexington, Mass.: Lexington Books, 1980), pp. 184–205; and Gerald Pomper et al, *The Election of 1976: Reports and Interpretations* (New York: David McKay, 1977).

49. Gerald Pomper et al, *The Election of 1980: Reports and Interpretations* (Chatham, N.J.: Chatham House Publishers, 1981).

50. On April 28, 1983, Congresswoman Ferraro gave a speech at a breakfast meeting of the Religious Coalition for Abortion Rights (speech available from RCAR); she also participated (by circulating a letter to Congressional colleagues) in the Briefing for Catholic Legislators prepared by Catholics for a Free Choice, held on September 30, 1982 (see note 26 above).

51. Margaret O'Brien Steinfels, "Personal Perspective," *Christianity and Crisis* 44:19 (November 26, 1984), pp. 436–37.

52. *The New York Times*, September 12, 1984, p. B9. See also Geraldine A. Ferraro, *Ferraro: My Story*, pp. 215–16.

53. *Ferraro: My Story*, p. 222.

54. James Carroll, "On Not Skipping the Sermon," *Commonweal* November 2–16, 1984, pp. 604–5.

55. See Marianne Githens and Jewell Prestage, *A Portrait of Marginality: The Political Behavior of the American Woman* (N.Y.: David McKay Co., 1977).

56. Simone de Beauvoir, *The Second Sex*, trans. H.M. Parshley (New York: Alfred A. Knopf, 1953), pp. xv–xxix.

57. Mario M. Cuomo, "Religious Belief and Public Morality " (lecture to Department of Theology, Notre Dame University, September 13, 1984), *Human Life Review*, vol. 11, nos. 1 and 2 (Winter and Spring 1985), p. 34.

58. These statistics obtained as of December 1986, and are provided by the Center for American Women in Politics, The Eagleton Institute, Rutgers University, New Brunswick, N.J.

59. As reported in *The New York Times*, December 15, 1984, p. 1; *The New York Times*, December 19, 1984, p. A16; *The New York Times*, December 20, 1984, p. A20. See also *Origins* 14:31 (January 17, 1985), entire issue. This controversy has continued for one and one-half years, culminating in a second ad placed by the Committee of Concerned Catholics in *The New York Times*, March 2, 1986. Of the ninety-seven signers of the original ad, twenty-four women religious and four men religious were threatened with expulsion from their communities if they did not publicly retract their views. As of this writing (December 1986), no one has been expelled.

60. Richard J. Neuhaus, "Of Moral Legitimacy and Democratic Governance," letter to the editor, *The New York Times*, September 25, 1984; Nat Hentoff's column in *The Village Voice*, September and October 1984.

61. *The New York Times*, September 23, 1984, p. E2.

62. Arthur Hertzberg, "The Case for Untidiness," *Commonweal*, November 30, 1984, pp. 655–56.

63. James Finn, "What Archbishop O'Connor Didn't Say," letter to the editor, *The New York Times*, September 5, 1984, p. A22.

64. David O'Brien, "American Catholics and American Society," in Philip J. Murnion, ed., *Catholics and Nuclear War* (New York: Crossroads, 1983), p. 16.

8

The Fall of Icarus:
Gender, Religion, and the Aging Society

Constance H. Buchanan

Aging is a problem modern life has thrust with new urgency onto the agenda of American women. No one interested in the welfare of contemporary women and in changing the social patterns that constrain their lives can afford to overlook the questions raised by the aging society. The proportion of elderly people in this country has been rising rapidly in recent decades, and experts predict that by the year 2030 every fifth American will be sixty-five or older. While longevity has been increasing, the population of elderly has itself been growing older. Since women are living approximately seven or eight years longer than men, the majority of these elderly are female. Further, the "old-old," those in the age group seventy-five and over, are predominantly female.[1]

It is not only the fact that women are living longer but also the negative image of aging in American society that underscores the importance of aging as an issue for women. Negative assessments of aging and of elders affect the treatment of older people in this country as individuals and as a social group. More than a decade ago, Robert Butler first referred to such negative assessments as "ageism" and called attention to the need for systematic investigation of its effects on public and private response to aging.[2] Today, whether it is blatant or subtle, negative assessment of aging persists. It is evident in the belief that elders have limited social value and thus may be entitled only to limited rights, and that they no longer contribute significantly to society but instead are a social burden. Fundamental to this belief, despite evidence to the contrary and the fact that only 5 percent of older adults in America are institutionalized at any given time, is the all-too-common exaggeration of intellectual and physical limitations experienced by older people. The negative image of old age in this country rests on the assumption that it is a state of being characterized chiefly by universal and inevitable decline—by dependence.

To shed light both on the image of aging and the situation of women in American culture, this essay will focus on basic social values and attitudes. In particular, it will examine the role of religious thought and practice in shaping these values. Through the ethical norms and meaning they carry, religious symbols, images, and ideas play a powerful role in fashioning and articulating what sociologist Steven Tipton has called the "moral knowledge" of society.[3] The roots of this moral knowledge run deep, as anthropologist Clifford Geertz argued in analyzing the important cultural as well as psychological and social functions of religion. By describing the way things are and the way they ought to be, religion has helped fashion the cultural patterns of meaning that shape personal and collective experience in America. It has been a major force defining basic cultural conceptions embedded in these patterns, including conceptions of human being and the individual.[4]

For these reasons, it is important to explore the influence of religion in America on basic social patterns that determine to a significant degree the ways in which we live and grow old. Analysis of religious ideas, attitudes, and practice has much light to shed on social assumptions about aging and their relationship to other assumptions shaping dominant cultural norms for human being. Such an analysis suggests that conceptions of aging are part of a larger framework of cultural conceptions of human being. These conceptions must be critically assessed: they affect the formulation of public policy—both policy on aging and the larger system of social policies of which aging policy is an integral part. Analysis of religion will also enable us to speculate about the impact of religion on the condition of women in an aging society.

Religion and Aging

Any analysis of American religious attitudes toward aging must focus on Christianity and Judaism. These biblical traditions have provided the primary religious influence in the shaping of American society and culture. Yet few scholars in religion or other disciplines have investigated religion and aging as a personal, social, or cultural issue in American history. The subject of aging and religion has yet to appear in a significant way on the agenda of American intellectual life. Even more striking is the extent to which, historically, aging has been largely unaddressed as a topic within Christianity and Judaism; this remains the case today. Aging appears as a significant issue in these traditions only at the level of national and local institutional policy and practice—not in religious thought. It is, therefore, with these policies and programs that an analysis of religious attitudes toward aging must begin.

Historically in America, Christian and Jewish religious bodies have been pioneers in providing care and shelter to the elderly. In most traditions, this practice evolved into what has become modern religion's central response to older people, the sponsoring and operating of nursing and retirement homes. Yet it was not until the 1970s and the early 1980s that Christian traditions reached the point of incorporating in their national agency structures and policies a mainstream focus on aging. Within Judaism, major emphasis on elders began somewhat earlier.

Today, two developments in particular are making aging an issue within American churches and synagogues. The first is the rapid growth of the aging population within the traditions themselves. In most Christian denominations a large percentage of the membership is age fifty-five or over; in some, such as Methodism—which is now, after the Roman Catholic and the Southern Baptist churches, the third largest church in the United States—fifty-five or over is also the fastest-growing age group.[5] Yet it is interesting to observe that aging is an issue so new to most Protestant denominations that complete and comparable statistics are not always available. Nevertheless, according to denomination reports, 43 percent of the membership of the Methodist Church was fifty-five or over in 1982; 25 percent of the United Church of Christ was over sixty-five in 1982; more than 50 percent of the United Presbyterian Church was over fifty years of age in 1981; 56 percent of the membership of the Episcopal Church was over fifty in 1981; and in 1983 a Unitarian Universalist Association study found that 27 percent of an average size parish or fellowship was over sixty.[6]

A second major stimulus to the recognition of aging as a religious issue is the advocacy of this growing older population within their congregations. In several large Christian denominations—the Methodist, for example—older members are leading the way in formulating policy and structural changes designed to recognize older people as a constituency within the church and to identify aging itself as a religious issue. In the Presbyterian Church, response has been systematic and highly developed. This is due largely to Maggie Kuhn, a church official who provided denominational leadership on aging and also public leadership through founding the Gray Panthers, the highly visible American advocacy group for elders.

Institutional response varies tremendously across the spectrum of Jewish and Christian traditions with regard to funding, program development, and, especially, the extent to which policy and objectives have been articulated.[7] These policy and program statements, issued either by the religious bodies themselves or by the implementing groups established within them to address aging, reveal the image of aging and the status of older people within the traditions. Both emerge not primarily from descriptions of institutional life but rather from the prescriptions for change in communities of faith offered by these statements.

The existence of these institutional efforts to address aging and their nearly uniform orientation toward advocacy point to the central problem revealed by policy and program statements: despite rich religious resources and injunctions for a positive view of aging, both older people and the experience of aging itself have been and still are largely overlooked in religious communities. The primary need that some religious traditions identify is to make elders and aging what they are not now, a central concern of communities of faith. Religious institutions view themselves as especially responsible for promoting justice and compassion in society. And when that society includes a growing population of older people and a prevalence of ageism, elders are increasingly perceived as a social group suffering discrimination and therefore particularly vulnerable. Hence, religious traditions often view themselves as having a special social responsibility for elders. Their institutional literature on aging focuses on the need for religious advocacy for the rights of older people on local and national policy levels on a range of issues that includes housing, income, education, health, nutrition, and protection from crime. Further, religious bodies perceive themselves as responsible for the spiritual well-being of older people, which is understood as an essential part of the quality of extended life that can be nourished by no government agency or other social institution.

Yet it is not simply a sense that ageism and aging are crucial problems in society at large that leads religious bodies to urge that aging be made a central concern of communities of faith. Religious literature on aging also deplores the negative attitudes, stereotypes, and age-discriminatory practices that confront the old *within* religious institutions. The Christian church's slowness to respond to elders is often attributed to ageism. The director of Kansas City's Shepherd's Center, an innovative ecumenical, community-based program that provides older adults with a range of services and an alternative to institutional care, has noted that

> Unfortunately, the church has itself tended to incorporate societal stereotypes of older people. The aging process has been identified with disease, deterioration, and death. Getting old is bad news, even in the community of the "Good News."[8]

The literature on this subject reveals the widespread failure of religious institutions to deliver adequate and effective pastoral care to elders, pointing to a basic lack of knowledge on the part of religious leaders and laity alike about the experience of aging and the distinctive needs and contributions of older adults. It suggests that educational programs on aging be developed and included in the professional and continuing theological education of religious leaders, as well as at the congregational level for the laity, in order to change prevailing negative images of the old. In addition to advocacy and education, most programs on aging mounted by religious traditions emphasize the need for continued delivery of care and services to the aging, including pastoral counseling, friendly visiting, emotional support, food, legal aid, transportation, medical care, housing, and hospice care.

One of the most revealing aspects of these policy and program statements is the attention some draw to the fact that it is the norm in religious traditions for older people to be viewed as passive and dependent recipients of care and services. These statements criticize ministries that provide institutional support in a manner that promotes the image of old people as needy, for such an image helps to create and sustain their dependency. They propose instead a conception of ministry that rejects paternalism.

The literature also points up the failure of organized religion to perceive the elderly as full participants in the spiritual, governing, pastoral, and social dimensions of the lives of communities of faith; or as resources for the tradition's larger mission in society. Elders too frequently are seen as in some sense no longer fully human, contributing members of the tradition; as having lost their capacity for passionate engagement with issues, work, or other people. Their role is perceived to shrink and their status to decline with age. Recognizing this, some of the literature warns of the degree to which the very vitality of a tradition is increasingly dependent on the inclusion and full participation of this growing and too frequently marginal population. Yet vitality is not commonly associated with elders. Another measure of the depth of the ageist assumption in religious institutions is the suggestion in some religious literature that a congregation made up largely of older adults may be viewed as in decline and therefore less likely to attract ministers.[9]

Far less common in the religious literature than this concern for the dignity and self-determination of elders is recognition of the diversity that characterizes the experience of aging. Older adults tend to be viewed as an homogeneous group and aging itself as a uniform experience that is universally shared by all those beyond a certain age. Aging is understood as a predominantly male, white, and Western reality. There is little awareness of the distinctive experience of women and even less of that of racial and ethnic minority groups. This is a point to which we shall return.

While in recent years religious institutions have responded increasingly to ageism and to older people, theological interpretation of aging is still extremely rare. Aging has never been either a significant focus of or source for religious thought in most major Western traditions. What relatively brief contemporary pieces have been written represent initial, small steps toward a theology of aging and often accompany either descriptions of programs on aging sponsored by religious bodies or collections of articles in the field of pastoral care.

Attitudes toward aging in religious thinking tend to mirror existing contradictions in religious institutions and practice. On the one hand, theological reflections on aging underscore the biblical and theological resources in Judaism and Christianity for a positive view of aging and elders, pointing to those positive images of age ("A hoary head is a crown of gold" Prov. 16:31) and injunctions to respect the old ("Honor your father and your mother" Exod. 20:12 and Deut. 5:16) that represent a view in sharp contrast with the ageism of contemporary society. On the other hand, theological treatments tend to mingle advocacy and strong compassion for older adults with negative images of elders and of aging itself. As a result, while many of these treatments are clearly motivated by the desire to promote the loving care and acceptance of elders, their very conceptions of aging and of older adults conflict with and undermine this motive.

Much of the existing theological reflection on aging seeks to address the indignity and dishonor suffered by older persons, but at the same time uncritically sustains a common theological understanding of aging as disease. This common understanding is clearly set forth by Pierre Teilhard de Chardin, a scientist and modern Christian thinker who visualized human life as shaped by forces of growth and diminishment. Teilhard de Chardin viewed aging as the overwhelming of the forces of creative power (activity) by those of disintegration (passivity): "that slow, essential deterioration which we cannot escape: old age little by little robbing us of ourselves and pushing us on towards the end."[10] Here, in this conception of aging as disease and diminishment, as deterioration and decline, lies the root of theological ageism. All too frequently this root goes undetected, with the common result that many theologies of aging begin with the unexamined presupposition that aging is a state of loss and go on to explain, justify, and unwittingly promote this fundamentally negative view.

The religious conception of aging as a state of loss defines that loss as loss not only of the component parts of personhood, but also of personhood itself. Often this is so even for those religious thinkers who want to emphasize the gains of aging, for such gains are defined most frequently precisely in terms of the older person's loss of self. The state of loss brought about by aging is regarded as a state primarily of intellectual, social, professional, physical, and sexual decline. It is a state in which independence becomes dependence, potency becomes weakness, self-sufficiency becomes submission, and competence becomes uselessness.

In short, aging is understood as the loss of active adulthood, a state of being characterized by nothing so much as the loss of intellectual capacity and creativity. In language that also implicitly connects attributes of aging with those of traditional femininity, one writer likens age to a "second childhood," in which

> we move into what some have called a receptive mode of consciousness—as opposed to an action mode—where images and free association within space take precedence over temporal, logical thinking, with its desire for prediction and control.[11]

The belief that aging inevitably involves decay of the mind—loss of reason and of the potential for intellectual achievement—is crucial to a theological understanding of the further major loss represented by aging: loss of social identity and competence. Most theological reflection uncritically accepts the equation of aging with disengagement from work and public life, focusing primarily on loss of meaningful activity, of mastery, and of the social role and status mastery gave.

Some religious interpretations of aging propose benefits derived from this state of loss, benefits that might be seen as mitigating. The tendency here is to interpret the aging state as one in which these benefits are made possible by physical decline and loss of the institutionally credentialed, active, achieving self:

> In the receptive mode of consciousness we can be freed from egocentricity, from always worrying about our public image and the quantifiable success of our efforts . . . To share, to tolerate, to affirm, to be independent of the need to prove oneself— all these are the gifts of age and of the receptive mode of consciousness, as opposed to the action mode of systemic thought and institutional definition of the self.[12]

From this perspective, the individual's retirement from public roles is regarded as making possible acquisition of new values, new ways of being, and even a certain kind of meaning that is assumed not to have been present or possible before the onset of advanced years. Some Christian writers define this meaning as finding the freedom and honesty to address the "real questions" that were avoided previously, those existential questions related to "life as 'being'"[13] One writer sees in aging a new freedom for the individual to express personal values and beliefs that the pressures of professional life had made it necessary to hide.[14] Another writer speaks of retirement as playing a "religious function" in freeing the individual to find new levels of self-worth.[15] And the theology of aging in Judaism provides one of the fullest statements of aging as a time for self-realization, "the highest point of development," with its view of old age as "the Sabbath of the soul."[16]

Nevertheless, most theological reflection on aging attempts to use established theological categories to interpret and often to rationalize the state of loss aging is thought to represent. This is especially evident in the Christian writings. One theologian addresses this method explicitly, arguing that to avoid creating a separate theology of aging, "the basic Christian theological affirmations are to be applied to the specific questions that arise in connection with aging and the aged."[17] The Christian categories of love and justice are those most frequently applied, and this commonly leads the writers to insist in the face of the injustice and loss that elders experience on the need to assert their value and dignity, on God's unconditional love and acceptance of each individual, and on the presence of meaning in every stage of life.

When traditional theological categories are brought to bear, the acceptance of a conception of aging as a state of loss and decline can lead further to a view of aging as human finitude—even as sin. So, for instance, the Protestant emphasis on justification by faith allows the perceived "uselessness" of retired people to be seen as redeemed by God: "the religious community will celebrate the special witness of this stage of life: an emptying out of credentials and a celebration of the grace-filled uselessness of the children of God."[18] When aging is equated with finitude, the role of older persons in religion becomes that of exemplifying human limitation:

> Growing old involves deterioration and loss. The body loses its vitality and becomes prone to disabilities. Personal relations are ended by distance and death. And one's own self-integrity may be diminished by outer events and inner deterioration. The Church needs the continual reminder by the aging of these vicissitudes due to human finitude and sin. The elderly need to be reminded by the Church of the necessity of accepting finitude and forgiveness.[19]

The work of two systematic theologians who have written about aging offers a critical perspective on treatments of aging in pastoral theology. Both theologians reject an approach to aging that views the theological task as delineating a religious response to a social problem. They reject the assumption implicit in this approach that religion is an inert body of beliefs that provides answers to questions arising out of individual and collective social experience. Instead, both view the task of a theology of aging as more appropriately the analysis of the interaction of religion and culture. Specifically, they propose that negative attitudes toward aging and elders are shaped by basic meanings or conceptions in religion and culture that must be critically assessed and transformed.

For David Tracy, the task is one of comparatively analyzing the fundamental meaning of time in both religious symbols and "our common cultural experience" of aging. He assesses the ability of religious symbols to illuminate in new ways important dimensions of the experience of aging, to disclose new understanding.[20] For Tracy, however, it is "general human meaning factors" that constitute the proper focus for theological analysis, not the particular study of age or aging, which he leaves to the life sciences.[21] Tracy argues that the eschatological symbols of Judaism and Christianity reveal that the sources of meaning in human life lie not in any one moment of time but in the diversity and constant mix of moments (past, present and future); so that one moment has no exclusive or greater value compared with others, and time is no longer seen "as a series of atomic moments that tends to co-opt the young, imprison the mature, and forget the old."[22]

For Lucien Richard, however, aging is not a problem of time, but of the meaning of personhood in religion and culture. Richard understands aging primarily as a question of theological anthropology, of basic perceptions of human being. More specifically, Richard sees ageism as a result of the perceived movement of older people from a culturally-valued model of human being to a culturally-devalued model of human being:

> Aging is perceived as the loss of independence, autonomy, power . . . The fear of
> becoming old in a society is determined by the fear of losing those elements which
> constitute one's life's goal, and are perceived as the foundation of self-worth and of
> personhood.[23]

It is this loss that Richard believes a theology of aging must address. He sees the problem underlying ageism in church and society as the human inability to accept loss and negation, or to affirm conditioned autonomy and freedom. And he finds in Christianity the symbolic resources for revaluing the two existing models of personhood so that the ideal model is no longer that of autonomy, self-centeredness, and the will to power, but rather that of dependence, self-emptying, and lack of mastery. In terms of this revaluation, human fulfillment would come to mean, he proposes, not power and being-in-itself, but surrender to limitation and self-giving.

Theological Anthropology and the Aging Society

Analyzing the images of aging and attitudes toward elders that prevail in religious institutions and religious thought uncovers the depth of ageism in religion. It suggests that at the heart of ageism in American religion and culture is the perception that to become old is to lose one's humanity, to become somehow less than fully human. In short, it brings us to the underlying question of human being, suggesting that this question is central to investigations of the aging American society.

Religious treatments of aging reflect and reinforce two cultural conceptions of human being. These two conceptions govern definitions of aging and are asymmetrical, representing differentially valued models of human being. The first of these models is presented as the ideal, the second as deviation from the ideal. The first is assumed to be normative for human life, and the second deficient and undesirable. The ideal model associates normative or "real" human being with the following characteristics: independence, freedom, reason and creativity, action, mastery and achievement, participation in the public world, economic and social power, physical strength, sexual potency, and growth. The secondary model associates deficient or "not really real" human being with the opposite characteristics: dependence, limitation, lack of reason and mental activity, passivity, lack of competence, separation from the public world, economic and social marginality, physical weakness, sexual disinterest, and stagnation.

Aging most often is understood as involving movement from the first, normative form of human being to the second, deficient form. These two conceptions of human life are thus linked in definitions of aging to an implicit and sometimes explicit model of the underlying pattern of human life. They at once presuppose and describe what is all too often in religious thinking, as in psychology, taken to be the normative human life cycle. This life cycle is implicit in such American characterizations of old age as "fading fast," "over the hill," "finished," and "out to pasture."[24] While recognizing its many individual and cultural variations, most scholars nevertheless assume that this life cycle is "general," "human," a "basic sequence," and an "underlying universal pattern" that orders "the seasons of life."[25] Frequently referred to both within and outside of religion as the "peak/slope" model of human life, this life cycle is understood as a pattern of growth and decline, expansion and diminishment, creation and destruction. It is a pattern in which the meaning of human life is located in the possession of vigor, promise, and the time in which to fulfill that promise; in work that is central to existence and has significant consequences for self and others; and in the achievement of recognition, authority, and power. In short, it is a pattern in which life has an heroic quality, or at least the potential for that quality; in which man (*sic*) strives to "occupy the center stage of his world"[26]

The focal point of this standard human life cycle is mid-life, a time when the heroic striving for infinitude begins to be reversed by the reality of human finitude. The path of upward development that leads to independence and power, the goals of maturity, is followed by a downward path of decline toward death. The mid-life crisis in adult development (or the mid-life transition, as Daniel Levinson, perhaps its chief analyst, prefers to call it) is understood to mark the point at which the individual perceives growth to be turning inevitably into decline, at which the illusion of immortality becomes the awareness of mortality. Levinson describes this mid-life point in these terms:

> A man at mid-life is suffering some loss of his youthful virility and, often, some insult to his youthful narcissistic pride. Although he is not literally close to death or undergoing severe bodily decline, he typically experiences these changes as a fundamental threat. It is as though he were on the threshold of senility and even death.[27]

Most theological reflections on aging, even those that attempt to argue for an understanding of the gains aging represents, assume the same peak/slope model. They point to the power of this model to shape human life:

> We are trained to become competent managers of ourselves and our dependents. All these skills are signs of our acquired independence and prove that we have left dependency behind us, that we have "made it". . . . If this is the maturational goal or ideal, how upsetting it is when events in the life cycle force us to surrender it bit by bit.[28]

In this conception of the normative life cycle, aging necessarily becomes, like the plunge of mythic Icarus into the sea, a fall from glory or from the hope of glory. Nor is this model of human life a recent one in American religious thinking. In a "Sermon to Aged People," delivered in 1805, a preacher gave a startlingly similar description of old age:

Once we were men; now we feel ourselves to be but babes. Once we possessed active powers; now we have become impotent. Once we sustained our children and ministered to them with pleasure; now we are sustained by them. . . . Once we were of some importance in society; now we are sunk into insignificance. Once our advice was sought and regarded; now we are passed by with neglect and younger men take our place.[29]

The question of aging, therefore, must be understood as one that itself raises even more fundamental questions about prevailing conceptions in American religion and society of human being and the human life cycle. Aging takes its meaning from this larger conceptual framework and is valued and defined primarily in relation to two norms: the location of fulfillment in the peak of mid-life and of its meaning in independence and power. In this context, religious and nonreligious attempts to reinterpret aging positively are doomed to failure. Defined in terms of the perceived cultural norms for human being and the life cycle, aging must be understood as defeat, surrender, and resignation. It is this negative conception of aging that underlies the hostility and discrimination of ageism in contemporary society.

Theological analyses of aging articulate these dominant cultural norms for human being and the life cycle. By examining the anthropology embedded in these analyses, we can deepen our understanding of these norms. Like Levinson, theologians claim to be objective in their focus on aging as a general, universal human experience. This is true of those who assume an historically constant, widely-shared human experience in their analysis of aging, and especially true of those, like Tracy, who resist exploring even the specific experience of aging—leaving that to the life sciences—in favor of attending to "general human-meaning factors" such as time.

In fact, however, the experience commonly described in these treatments of aging is not universal but particular. While most claim to examine aging as a human problem, they actually examine aging as a male problem in contemporary society. With few exceptions, analyses draw on the experience and perspectives of men as their primary source for definitions and interpretations of aging. In meaning, as in language, the anthropology embedded in prevailing conceptions of aging equates male being with human being and male development with human development. So the developmental experience considered culturally normative for men is universalized and identified as normative for human beings: independence, freedom to pursue individual potential, power—and the loss of all three.

That this experience is *not* the human norm can be illustrated by examining at least one other kind of experience in American society, that of women. The experience and perspectives of women are distinctive. Yet in religion as in almost every field, these have never until recently been a significant focus of scholarly investigation. Nor has the experience of women been a primary source for conceptions of aging, despite the fact that women constitute a majority of the American population and a rapidly increasing majority of older adults. On the basis of several initial studies, however, it is possible to suggest briefly some of the ways in which aging might be understood differently if analyzed as the experience of women rather than of men.

Women's experience of aging, in both its negative and its positive dimensions, is determined in large part by the different cultural norms and social conditions that shape women's development and lives. Foremost among these has been the traditional assumption that for women biology is destiny: the capacity to bear children has been understood as providing the meaning for and determining the pattern of women's lives. Until very recently in American society, this understanding has provided the basis for the perception of childbearing and childrearing as women's natural work, and of the private or domestic sphere as women's proper place. In contrast with men, a woman's usefulness or uselessness has been defined primarily in terms of her sexuality.

Traditionally, neither work, the public world, nor economic and social power has been viewed as central to women's lives. In fact, as psychologist Carol Gilligan has pointed out, not only have women been missing from accounts of human development based on the study of men's lives, but the developmental process of separation, autonomy, and individuation viewed as normative for adults has not been viewed as normative for women.[30] Women's lives have thus been regarded as restricted and static, lacking in fundamental ways the freedom of self-definition and the achievement of adult maturity. Theologian Judith Plaskow has described women's experience as traditionally characterized by the failure to find and take responsibility for a self, by the "narrowness of the not-chosen life."[31] This truncation has defined a norm for women's lives that distinguishes them from men's. In the words of Simone de Beauvoir:

> women, both young and old, may perfectly well lay claim to authority in private, but in public life their status is always the same—that of perpetual minors. The masculine state, on the contrary, changes with the passage of time: the young man becomes an adult, a citizen, and the adult an old man.[32]

In short, because women traditionally have not been perceived in the same way as men to have promise or a future—to possess the potential for assuming public authority, claiming social status and power, and doing work that has important consequences for the self and others—the aging of women cannot be defined as the loss of these things.

Further, initial studies of women's distinctive experience suggest that it is a mistake to assume universal patterns of development, a common human life cycle, or a general human meaning of time. One study suggests that for many contemporary women mid-life is a positive time of self-discovery characterized by looking ahead, not by a sense of imminent mortality:

> the issues and upheavals Levinson describes are, in fact, rare in the lives of the women we studied. We found no evidence that these or the anxiety and depression that define the midlife crisis appear around the ages of forty to fifty. And women rarely spoke of measuring their accomplishments against their expectations, or of concern about "time running out." Of course, many women had no youthful goals to measure their performance against, except to get married and perhaps have children . . . and those who were just beginning to build careers in midlife rarely expressed concern about time running out.[33]

While women's own interpretations of the meaning of their lives and of aging are not yet available to any significant degree, we do have evidence that in fact, for many, aging offers new freedoms from the constraints of childrearing and homemaking, new opportunities, and even some degree of liberation from traditionally defined feminine sex-role behavior.[34] On the other hand, there is some indication that the rapidly lengthening life span of women makes them concerned not about having too little time left, but rather too much.[35]

Further, years lived alone and the prospect of such years is a major factor in women's experience. For many women, the shorter life spans of men mean the loss of a husband and of male companionship in later years. The resulting loneliness may be complicated for many who have lived lives shaped by dependence. The research of sociologist Helena Lopata suggests that traditional gender assumptions and roles in American society, particularly by making women dependent on men, are responsible for the dysfunctional lives of many of the widowed women who constitute the majority of older women. Lopata specifically points to the traditional socialization of women away from independence, from norms of action to build, shape, and maintain their own personal, social, and economic lives. As a result, she argues, social structures that create women's dependence leave many women ill-equipped for old age and even for the use of available services. Lopata describes the experience of large numbers of women over fifty:

They have never been trained to take the initiative in societal engagement, to analyze their needs and the societal resources that may meet them, to plan steps of action necessary for the utilization of such resources, to undertake these steps and to flexibly change definitions and behavior as their life circumstances change. They have relied on automatically engrossing support systems, dependent on the husband as the connecting link between them and the society outside of the narrow circle of relatives and friends involved in these support systems.[36]

At the same time, other studies challenge prevailing images of the lonely, helpless widow, providing new evidence of the capacity of older women for coping with adversity and for living alone.

A further aspect of old age for women is that, whether single or married, they are traditionally viewed as caretakers of the ill and of elderly relatives. As the number of elderly increases in society, especially the "old-old," people aged seventy-five and over, more women aged sixty to sixty-four are likely to become responsible for their care.[37] But perhaps the most salient characteristic of women's distinctive experience of aging is economic. Aging is an important factor in the trend toward the feminization of poverty that has developed in this century and has begun to escalate in recent years. Women are more likely than men to experience poverty in old age; one study shows that in 1984 women accounted for 71 percent of people in poverty aged sixty-five or over. The same study points to the double burden of race and sex in old age, showing that in 1983 41.7 percent of all older black women and 23.7 percent of those of Spanish origin had incomes below the poverty level.[38]

This brief sketch illustrates how aging might be seen differently if gender were employed as a significant category of analysis. Yet attention to gender alone is insufficient. Such further variables as race, ethnicity, and class, and their impact on the developmental and social experience of women and men, are equally important if we are to obtain a more complex and realistic analysis of aging as human experience. The fact that these variables have been for the most part overlooked, is also the result of the anthropology that is embedded in existing treatments of aging, theological and otherwise. The equation of maleness with the human norm in this anthropology has resulted in the exclusion of all who, like women, have not shared that freedom from limitation that is perceived as normative for the lives of men.

When male norms are used as the standard for human life, the experience of others, including unprivileged men who are denied full social access to this normative male experience, is seen as marginal rather than as offering alternative perspectives on aging. The experience of women, blacks, ethnic minorities, the poor, and even of the elderly themselves comes to be defined only by its difference from the established standard. Having no reality or content other than deviance, this great range of experience goes unexplored because it is understood not to exist on its own terms. As psychologist Ellen Langer found in a study of the cognitive dimension of perception of and behavior toward the deviant, "deviance is a category that typically relies for its definition on another category with which it is mutually exclusive."[39] Differences among individuals and groups become secondary. In the words of Clifford Geertz, distinctiveness comes to be seen as "accidental deviation from the only legitimate object of study for the true scientist: the underlying, unchanging, normative type."[40] It is for this reason that both the experience and the voices of those viewed as abnormal, even of the old themselves, are all too often missing from the study of aging.

Anthropologist Jean LaFontaine has demonstrated how differences in physiology become the basis for cultural inequality and exclusion from the exercise of power in society.[41] In short, it is no coincidence that critics of prejudice against the elderly in religion and society see connections between ageism, sexism, and racism:

> Ageism is a form of discrimination that is comparable to racism and to sexism. It involves a process of systematic stereotyping . . . founded on the conviction that personhood must be understood in terms of independence and autonomy and that its developmental trajectory is a process toward a peak with an upward and downward slope on either side.[42]

On the basis of the physical characteristics of age, sex, and race, whole groups are defined as not fully human. In prevailing conceptions of aging, the unexplored experience of these groups comes, therefore, to represent marginal humanity.

Ageism and the Promotion of Normative Human Being

Examining the conceptual framework that shapes prevailing religious attitudes toward aging deepens our understanding both of the meaning and the negative meaning of aging in American society. It reveals that aging is culturally defined from a male perspective and represents on the level of individual existence the inevitable loss of adulthood and manhood, and the movement from privileged status to unprivileged status, from full humanity to marginality. In society at large, this definition is part of a social pattern that locates independence in mature males, especially privileged males, and dependence in older people, as in such other diverse groups as women, racial and ethnic minorities, the poor, and children.

Such examination illuminates a conceptual model in which full humanity is identified in modern America with men at mid-life, who are seen as the major source of vitality and dynamism in society. In terms of aging, this conceptual model has several major consequences. First, it promotes and defends male privilege, and particularly the power of privileged males at mid-life. Second, it provides the basis for social constraints on the behavior of older adults, with age serving as a principle of differentiation that shapes both individual behavior and social relations.[43] This leads to a third major consequence, the creation of an additional dependent group in society—people over sixty-five years of age—and further loss of important human resources.

Scholars and practitioners who wish to address ageism cannot do so effectively as long as they work within the conceptual framework that shapes existing definitions of aging. Until that framework is revised, arguments against the injustices of ageism will be in vain. So too will be attempts to find a remedy for ageism by trying to equalize or reverse the valuation of the normative and marginal models of human being implicit in conceptions of aging, for such attempts necessarily involve affirming or promoting the attributes and experience of marginality. Some scholars in religion may argue that the uselessness of older people is "grace-filled," or that dependence and self-negation represent a model of greater value for human life. Others outside of religion may propose that old age has compensating or even greater meaning than earlier years in the life cycle. But any such attempts to undo ageism cannot be successful because they accept as given a dualistic conception of human being in which the very characteristics of the two models presuppose and reflect an irreversible asymmetry of greater and lesser value.[44]

Ageism and this dualistic conception are products of a larger set of dominant cultural conceptions of the nature of human being, individualism, and fulfillment that support and are in turn supported by social institutions and arrangements. These conceptions are shaped by underlying cultural assumptions and norms. Until these assumptions and norms are recognized and critically evaluated, we cannot effectively address negative assessments of aging and older people; neither can we develop conceptions of aging and policy strategies that are more adequate for an aging society. It is especially important to recognize and critically assess the fundamental assumption shaping all of these cultural conceptions: that male experience of the dominant ethnic group is normative human experience, that white male being is human being.

Recognizing the importance of the normative issues at stake in aging as a social problem brings us back to another of the questions with which we began: the role of religion in an aging society. Religion is of crucial importance to the process of critically evaluating and reconstructing prevailing conceptions of aging and the individual. Analysis of contemporary religious understandings of and attitudes toward aging has shown that these are largely consistent with understandings and attitudes that prevail more broadly in society. Furthermore, negative assessment in religion of old age is not a modern development but can be found in the thought of major figures who shaped the history of Christianity—for example, in *De vera religione* (*Of True Religion*) by St. Augustine:

> After the labours of young manhood, a little peace is given to old age. But it is an inferior age, lacking in lustre, weak and more subject to disease, and it leads to death. This is the life of man so far as he lives in the body. (xxvi. 48)[45]

With regard to aging, the pattern of religious institutions is much like that of other social institutions despite what some see as their unique resources for critically transforming the largely negative social image and experience of aging. To the extent, then, that paternalistic and negative attitudes toward aging persist in religious thought and practice, one possibility is that unconsciously, or in spite of its best conscious efforts, religion may help to reinforce ageism in society in the coming decades.

It may help to do so not only because of the negative image and status of aging itself within religion, but more fundamentally because of traditional religious ideas about human being and the individual. An extensive and growing body of scholarship in religion examines how these religious ideas have been shaped traditionally by the cultural assumption equating male norms with human norms; and how in turn religion has helped to legitimize and reinforce this fundamental assumption in society and culture.

Until the normativity of male experience in the anthropology of Christianity and Judaism is assessed critically, efforts to address ageism in religion will not be successful. Further, religion will continue to reinforce existing social conceptions of human being and individualism which take male experience as the human norm. This will be especially true if the social impact of the religious right with its emphasis on "traditional religious values" continues to grow. Without this critical assessment of religious anthropology, religious efforts to contribute to the creative transformation of aging as a personal, social, and cultural pattern will continue to be seriously undermined.

Conclusion

The aging society, by drawing our attention to the meaning of aging, raises deeper and broader questions about the narrowness, exclusivity, and destructiveness inherent in traditional religious and cultural conceptions of human being. For women in particular, it raises questions about uncritically appropriating conceptions of the self and the life-cycle dominant in American culture.

The diverse experience of those who have been marginalized in American society provides materials for constructing a more adequate and complex conception of aging. It also provides critical perspectives for evaluating existing norms for human being and individualism, and resources for reconstructing these norms. This experience may challenge the view that aging is responsible for the loss of self, suggesting that that loss may be connected instead to equation of the self with power and independence. This equation, considered culturally normative for men, may in fact rob a man to a significant degree of his individuality and over the years impoverish his development of the meaning of his life. It may, while appearing to do otherwise, provide a narrow and paradoxically self-undermining foundation for the self.

The experience of women and others whose lives have been shaped by limitation may help pose such questions as the following: What is the meaning of independence defined as the opportunity to conform to established standards for success? What is the meaning of autonomy that celebrates self-sufficiency and isolation from others? What is the meaning of power that all too often is used in pursuit of self-interest and privilege? What is the meaning of individualism if self-realization and self-expression must wait until old age? And what is the meaning of freedom in a life shaped by and measured against such norms?

In short, the aging society presents a challenge to American religion and American culture. That challenge is the questioning not simply of how women and men grow old, but rather of how individually and collectively they live.

Acknowledgments

This article grows out of my work as a consultant to the Carnegie Corporation's multi-year Project on the Aging Society. I am especially grateful to the Project for stimulating my interest in the social and policy dimensions of aging and for the rich interdisciplinary exchanges it sponsored. I am, of course, also grateful for Carnegie's support of the preparation of this article. Several colleagues took the time to read and make valuable comments on an initial draft. For this and, even more, for always intriguing discussions, I am grateful to Clarissa Atkinson, Gordon Kaufman, Margaret Miles, George Rupp, and Sharon Welch. For her lively interest in the project and help in collecting materials from religious traditions, my thanks also to Irma Gonzalez.

Notes

1. Jacob S. Siegel and Cynthia M. Taeuber, "Demographic Dimensions of an Aging Population," in *Our Aging Society: Paradox and Promise*, ed. Alan Pifer and Lydia Bronte (New York and London: W. W. Norton, 1986), pp. 81 and 86; and in the same volume, Gunhild O. Hagestad, "The Family: Women and Grandparents as Kin-Keepers," p. 147.

2. See especially Robert N. Butler, *Why Survive?: Being Old in America* (New York: Harper & Row, 1975).

3. Steven M. Tipton, "The Moral Logic of Alternative Religions," in *Religion and America: Spirituality In a Secular Age*, ed. Mary Douglas and Steven M. Tipton (Boston: Beacon Press, 1982), p. 103.

4. See Clifford Geertz, *The Interpretation of Cultures* (New York: Basic Books, 1973), pp. 123–24, and for a discussion of the importance of religion as a source of notions of the "really real." See also in this volume chapters on "The Impact of the Concept of Culture on the Concept of Man" and "Ethos, World View, and the Analysis of Sacred Symbols."

5. The size of the Methodist Church is described by Kenneth Briggs in his report on the 1984 Methodist General Conference, "The Methodists Elect 19 to Leadership," in *The New York Times*, July 29, 1984, p. 19; its rapidly aging membership is noted in a petition to the 1984 General Conference of the United Methodist Church calling for creation of a Task Force on Older Adult Ministries (Source: The General Board of Global Ministries.)

6. Figures reported in *Summary of Legislative Actions Taken By 1984 General Conference of the United Methodist Church*; in the *Resource Book on Aging* (New York: The Board for Homeland Ministries of the United Church of Christ); in "Abundant Life for Aging People: Our Vision and Our Calling," in the *Report of the Task Force on Ministries with Aging Persons* (The United Presbyterian Church (U.S.A.), 1981), p. 4; in "Aging and the Church: Promise, Performance Potential," a brochure of the Episcopal Society for Ministry on Aging, Inc.; and in "The Aging UU", *Newsletter of the UUA Committee on Aging*, vol. 2, no. 1.

7. The Task Forces on Aging of the Presbyterian Church (U.S.A.), the United Methodist Church, and the United Church of Christ have produced systematic and highly-developed program statements and resource guides.

8. Elbert C. Cole, "Lay Ministries With Older Adults," in *Ministry With the Aging*, ed. William M. Clements (San Francisco: Harper & Row, 1981), p. 253.

9. Thomas B. Robb, "The Presbyterian Church's Response to Aging" (Presbyterian Office on Aging paper, 1984), p. 2.

10. Pierre Teilhard de Chardin, *Le Milieu Divin: An Essay on the Interior Life* (London: Collins, 1960), p. 60.

11. Urban T. Holmes, "Worship and Aging: Memory and Repentance," in Clements, *Ministry*, p. 96.

12. Ibid., p. 97.

13. Ibid., pp. 104–5.

14. Paul W. Pruyser, "Aging: Downward, Upward or Forward?," *Journal of Pastoral Psychology* (Winter 1975), p. 116.

15. Evelyn E. and James D. Whitehead, "Retirement," in *Ministry*, p. 134.

16. Robert L. Katz, "Jewish Values and Sociopsychological Perspectives on Aging," *Journal of Pastoral Psychology* (Winter 1975), pp. 148–49.

17. Martin J. Heinecken, "Christian Theology and Aging: Basic Affirmations," in *Ministry*, p. 76.

18. "Retirement," in *Ministry*, p. 134.

19. Robert Neale, "Theological Basis for Ministry With the Aging," in *Resource Book on Aging*, published by the United Church Board for Homeland Ministries, Health and Welfare Division.

20. David Tracy, "Eschatological Perspectives on Aging," *Journal of Pastoral Psychology* (Winter 1975), p. 121.

21. Ibid., p. 132.

22. Ibid., p. 132.

23. Lucien Richard, "Toward a Theology of Aging," *Science et Espirit*, vol. 34, no. 3 (1982), p. 274.

24. *Why Survive?*, p. 2.

25. Daniel J. Levinson, *The Seasons of A Man's Life* (New York: Balantine Books, 1978), p. 6.

26. Ibid., p. 35.

27. Ibid., p. 26.

28. Paul Pruyser, p. 109.

29. Quoted in Carole Haber, *Beyond Sixty-Five: The Dilemma of Old Age in America's Past* (Cambridge: Cambridge University Press, 1983), p. 3.

30. For an analysis of the absence of women from psychological theory see Carol Gilligan, *In A Different Voice: Psychological Theory and Women's Development* (Cambridge: Harvard University Press, 1982); also, for the classic research demonstrating the double standard for maturity in traditional sex-role definitions, see Broverman, I., et al., "Sex-role Stereotypes: A Current Appraisal," *Journal of Social Issues* 28 (1972): 59–78.

31. Judith Plaskow, *Sex, Sin, and Grace: Women's Experience and the Theologies of Reinhold Niebuhr and Paul Tillich* (Washington: University Press of America, 1980).

32. Simone de Beauvoir, *The Coming of Age* (New York: Warner Books, 1973), p. 134.

33. Grace Baruch, Rosiland Barnett, and Caryl Rivers, *Life Prints: New Patterns of Love and Work for Today's Women* (New York: New American Library, 1983), p. 239.

34. For a discussion of the phenomenon of sex-role reversal in old age with particular reference to religion see, for instance, Barbara Myerhoff, "Bobbes and Zeydes: Old and New Roles for Elderly Jews," in *Women in Ritual and Symbolic Roles*, ed. Judith Hoch-Smith and Anita Spring (New York and London: Plenum Press, 1978), pp. 207–41.

35. *Life Prints*, p. 240.

36. Helena Z. Lopata, "The Older American: Social-Psychological Needs" in *Ministering to the Elderly: Perspectives and Opportunities* (Wichita: Institute on Ministry and the Elderly, 1977), p. 8.

37. Charlotte Conable, et al., *Older Women: The Economics of Aging* (Washington: WREI, 1980), p. 2.

38. Sara E. Rix, *Older Women: The Economics of Aging* (Washington: WREI, 1984), p. 13.

39. Ellen J. Langer, "A New Perspective for the Study of Deviance," unpublished paper, Harvard University, Department of Psychology and Social Relations, p. 23.

40. *Interpretation*, p. 51.

41. J.S. LaFontaine, ed., *Sex and Age as Principles of Social Differentiation* (London: Academic Press, 1978), p. 1.

42. *Theology of Aging*, p. 274.

43. *Sex and Age*, p. 3.

44. For an analysis of the asymmetry of gender assumptions and its significance for reconstructing the traditional conception of God as Father, see Rosemary Ruether in *God as Father?*, ed. Johannes-Baptist Metz and Edward Schillebeeckx, Concilium Series, no. 143 (New York: Seabury Press, 1981).

45. St. Augustine, *Of True Religion*, trans. J.H.S. Burleigh (Chicago: Henry Regnery Co., 1964), p. 44.

9

Finding a Self:
Buddhist and Feminist Perspectives

Anne Carolyn Klein

Overview of the Issues

To gain a sense of self that is genuinely one's own, and not a projection or product of patriarchy, is an important focus of concern for many women today. The background of this issue is complex and the feasibility of the project linked with our understanding that complexity. Western conceptions of an individual as the creative agent of his world, a construct much embellished in the last five hundred years, is today seriously challenged in the human sciences.[1] The theories of Freud, Marx, Foucault, or Kohut, for example, suggest that as individuals our responses and actions are largely, if not exclusively, shaped by external circumstances such as class, up-bringing, and social structure. Indeed,

> much of the intellectual history of the present century can be read in terms of a fundamental tension in the representation of an individual, a dismantling of the classical figure, and a simultaneous effort to reconceive it.[2]

That classical figure is of course male, and the privileged intellectual history also predominantly male. I note this familiar fact by way of introducing the complexities and possibilities that ensue in developing a feminist theory of selfhood and identity using categories and paradigms from a traditional, embedded Buddhist culture that in many respects mirrors the one vanished from the West since medieval times.

Yet it is partly the traditional cultural context in which Buddhist theory raises questions about the nature of self that makes these theories relevant to women today. Women still must contend with the expectation that they will focus on or at least fulfill traditional roles as wives and mothers, and that they will function in society through the reflected identity gained from husbands and children. Although parallel expectations were once also incumbent on men, this has long since been questioned and repudiated by them; men are able to "reconceive" their status as individuals. "Individuation" has meant, by and large, the emergence of consciously chosen work and attitudes from the grey background of homogeneous roles and expectations. Men as a group have proceeded further in this direction than women, although their apparent freedom has brought its own limitations regarding what is acceptable for a man to be or do.[3] Feminists do not necessarily wish to follow the direction of male individuation, despite an insistence on freedom from women's roles as men have constructed them. Thus, when it comes to questions of how and what kinds of identity or selfhood are achieved and bestowed in our culture; the current unraveling of assumptions surrounding male individualism can open much fruitful discourse, but it should not lull us into thinking that men and women necessarily are struggling with the same issues, or that they share personal and social histories.

Among contemporary North American women, search for a strong and fresh identity is often motivated by the urgent need to avoid a patriarchal style of identity. This latter involves, by definition, a sense of self which is neither chosen by women nor in their best interest. From a feminist perspective, the oppositionality that characterizes patriarchal styles of selfhood is pernicious. An identity crucially maintained through opposition, whether this manifests itself as actual exclusion of others or as the projecting onto others of unwanted elements of oneself, is to be avoided.[4] Class, racial, national, and sexual chauvinism all rest on a style of identity which, regardless of content, is characterized fundamentally by its need to express unassailable differences between oneself and others. Indeed, to maintain such an identity *requires* an ideology that entails, in the words of Susan Griffin, "the creation of another, a not-I, an enemy."[5] Some other paradigm of selfhood is needed. But what? Is it possible or even desirable to avoid all oppositionality? Can we distinguish differences without setting in motion the dance of dualism and conflict? Is it possible, in short, to find or imagine a functioning and powerful selfhood that is not so predicted on an exclusionist ontology of identity that in creating strength it also creates a basis for rejecting those who do not share this "identity?" What is the significance of one's relationships to individuals, groups, or cultures in forming such a non-exclusive identity?[6] In exploring these issues we will have to contend with a possible tension between (1) the importance of relationships to a healthy sense of self, and (2) the crucial need to have an identity that is experienced as genuinely one's own and not the making of another. To put this another way, many women seek a style of identity that is powerful, yet favors the relational over the individual.

Indeed, feminist endeavor has a vision of empowered persons who, in the words of the French feminist Hélène Cixous, have "no commerce with a love that stultifies the strange."[7] Strength without stridency, an identity of embrace rather than distance, is a more subtle achievement than the physical or psychosocial brute force with which societies and individuals are accustomed to create themselves. The difficulty here is partly that both language and the reflective process operate by way of exclusion—that is, dualistically. Thus, modern French feminists approach the dilemmas of identity by creating new ways of thinking and, especially, writing.[8]

Buddhist philosophy, with its radical questioning of common assumptions regarding identity, seems particularly relevant to the developing feminist agenda. Buddhism offers a critique of hyperindividualism as well as a positive view of an interdependently understood identity. Furthermore, Buddhism is important because it is not organized around one of the principal disjunctures in Western thought, the bifurcation of epistemology and ontology,[9] and the sub-split within epistemology between experience and knowing. Feminists in this country are just beginning to understand that these fissures in the intellectual landscape are inhospitable to women. At the very least, the separation of these areas contributes to the abstractness of modern philosophy, against which feminism seeks to develop theory anchored in and relevant to experience.

To this end, Buddhist literature offers much to explore in an attempt to further understand and change Western conceptual schemes that women find problematic. Buddhist writings are particularly valuable in opening two issues crucial to our discussion: categories of subjectivity and ontological questioning. For reasons I will suggest below, an expanded vocabulary of subjective states may be an important step in bridging epistemological and ontological areas of inquiry. In most Buddhist traditions, ontological and epistemological considerations are intimately and explicitly entwined. The attention given to ontological descriptions of persons or things is matched by detailed epistemological explanation[10] of what takes place in the mind or subject who knows this. Certainly, theories of what mind is and how it works are foundational to assumptions and questions regarding the nature of selfhood. Such theories of mind also figure strongly in current North American feminist exhortations to groundedness, clarity, and recognition of be-ing.

In developing the relevance of specific Buddhist material to feminist questions and criteria regarding selfhood, I will focus mainly on theories and practices in Indo-Tibetan Buddhism, especially the Gelukba order's discussion of the Middle-Way Consequentialist (Prasangika–Madhyamika) school of Mahayana thought. I will suggest that the way in which this material frames what it understands to be a profound search for identity uncovers a dynamic congruent with the one being developed by feminists.

Psychology and Ontology

The purpose of Buddhist theory and meditative technique in general is to develop particular subjective states, many of which belong to categories of personal growth and styles of identity that, as we will elaborate below, do not at present figure significantly in Western developmental models. Western psychology emphasizes the "vital importance of developing a sense of continuity, identity, and ongoingness in existence."[11] From the Buddhist perspective, this type of secure identity, though foundational to development, is intrinsically problematic, a source of chronic dissatisfaction. Western philosophy, in raising crucial questions about the ontology of identity, does not clearly elaborate how the philosophical insights it offers affect the epistemological state of the subject. Western psychology, in focusing on the subject, tends not to examine the assumed ontology of the self whose development it charts, and therefore does not envision a stage of development that depends on questioning this. Feminist critique in this country seems to imply a place for such development when it notes on the one hand the necessity for a strong sense of consciously chosen selfhood, and recognizes on the other the deeply relational nature of identity. Their critique turns on two central axes, questions regarding the content of women's identity as women would create it, and questions regarding the ontology that undergirds both particular content and the overarching experience of self. What I call "content" has to do with the emotional or psychological character of self, and "ontology" with the existential structure of that self.

Buddhist observations on the stages of personal development presuppose the presence of an appropriately functioning psychological self and address themselves primarily to an ontological critique of the self. Unlike the developmental levels of Western psychology, Buddhist theories seem to begin with an adult rather than a child. Their further premise is that erroneous ontological assumptions about both self and other govern virtually all other experiences of self. Spiritual growth— development beyond the state of merely viable identity—is charted in terms of the relinquishment of increasingly subtle errors regarding the ontology of self.[12] Similarly, the female quest for selfhood highlighted here involves ontological as well as psychological issues. In furthering discussion of the latter through Buddhist material, we will have to contend with the Buddhist claim that certain ontological truths are available only to particular subjective states. For example, direct insight of what Buddhism calls the empty nature of the self—a special quality of oneself—is only experienced by a mind conjoined with specifically defined styles of stability, clarity, intensity, and, ultimately, insight.[13] Such factors, largely outside the vocabulary of current psychological language, nonetheless presume much of what the West regards as psychological well-being. I emphasize this because it seems clear to me that the modern feminist engagement, like the Buddhist one, is with styles of personal development that expand the classical dimensions of psychological health. It is easy to see that the same psychological health associated with assured self-constancy can accommodate unfortunate and ultimately unhealthy tendencies such as self-inflation, denigration of others, or narrowness of vision.

The assumption that ultimate ontological truths are available to human subjectivity—to perception—has much to do with the unified unfolding of ontology and epistemology in Buddhist and other traditions that uphold the possibility of "sacred knowledge." Despite problems inherent in this claim, feminists also seek an understanding pertinent to both being and knowing.

Concern for the experiential content of this self, for such basic requisites of psychological health as self-esteem and internal cohesiveness, is therefore to be joined with an examination of the experienced ontological structure of that self. Buddhist analyses of these matters are in my opinion significantly consonant with important elements of feminist reflection. However, the relevant Buddhist discussions of self and selflessness—persons and the emptiness of persons—have never taken account of gender as a category governing analysis. Even though the wisdom of selflessness is frequently characterized as female,[14] to my knowledge no one within the 2,500-year-old tradition has analyzed Indo-Tibetan theories and practices connected with emptiness in the context of how they do or do not speak to women. I am not yet prepared to suggest how such an inquiry might proceed in Asian countries where Buddhism is practiced; I do think it possible to find relevance to questions significant for women in North America.

A small but influential group of modern feminist writers describes selfhood primarily in ontological terms. Mary Daly, though more than willing to encourage an identity antagonistic to males, characterizes woman ontologically as "rooted in the intuition that Powers are constantly unfolding and creating, communicating, Be-ing more."[15] Further, as Marilyn Massey points out, French feminists like Cixous and Irigaray, taking as their starting point woman's experience of her own unfettered body, also focus on the almost-paradoxical vision of an identity that is both self-contained and non-exclusive.[16] For Cixous, woman is to know herself as "a moving, limitlessly changing ensemble . . . an immense astral space not organized around any one sun that's any more of a star than the others."[17]

Emphasis on knowledge through the body is also important in the work of contemporary North American writers such as Carol Christ and Adrienne Rich. My purpose here is to suggest another way of thinking of a strong self whose power does not depend on its ability to oppose, project, or conceive itself as radically separate. The process entails both epistemological and ontological considerations.

In order to explore a subjective style relevant to feminist interest in a non-oppositional *modus operandi*, I will turn first to a Buddhist discussion of the mental state of awareness. Buddhists in general consider awareness salutary in its own right as well as an essential subjective component in accomplishing further growth, particularly insight into the actual ontological status of the self. The topic of awareness therefore leads to analysis of ontological principles pertinent to an identity that incorporates but moves beyond the "healthy ego" that Western patriarchal culture deems optimal. In this context we will also be able to contrast Buddhist discussions of emptiness with a form of nihilism that has been appropriated by recent feminist thought.

Accessing Experience

As a style or category of subjectivity, awareness is in several ways significant in enabling a non-oppositional or non-ideological sense of self. From a feminist perspective, awareness is a non-oppositional mental posture that is at the same time self-empowering. Let us try to analyze why.

First, simple awareness can watch internal processes without interfering with them.[18] It entails no oppression of oneself by an ideal — patriarchal or otherwise — against which one is measured. A number of Western feminists have written about the importance of such self-awareness. The "wandering" chronicled by Mary Daly, wherein a new naming presages an "entrance to the Arch Image,"[19] requires awareness and self-knowledge. Doris Lessing, herself much influenced by another tradition of sacred knowledge, Sufism, makes awareness the starting point of Martha Quest's spiritual odyssey in *The Four Gated City.* Quest learns how to render herself "alive and light and aware";[20] she knows the advantages, walking in the London rain, of having "her head cool, watchful, alert."[21] She knows too the sense of "a quiet, empty space, behind which stood an observing presence."[22]

The "observing presence" is an important dimension of experience. It permits self-knowledge without the crippling weight of an ideal against which one inevitably falls short.[23] Engagement with ideals can become potentially debilitating self-negation which also distracts from self-understanding. Contrasting oneself to an ideal is debilitating if, despite an explicit message of striving and optimism, there is stronger implicit emphasis on one's present unsatisfactoriness. The daily bombardment of *Cosmo*-style advice for make-overs, and media injunctions to deodorize, paint, and polish, operate on the same principle. Fear of falling short of ideals is, especially for "religiously" oriented persons, a great obstacle to self-knowledge, particularly when, under the guise of offering hope for improvement, the present state is demeaned.

The paradigm of struggle against self is well known in religious and secular practice. Mary Daly, in *Pure Lust*, scathingly satirizes Christian ascetics, seen as emblematic of patriarchal religiosity, for glorying in denying who they were in order to be something else. She calls such self-denial "sado-ritual." Such oppositional striving against self may or may not be peculiar to patriarchy. Whatever its efficacy in some situations, it has built-in dangers for women. It makes self-knowledge difficult, especially for a woman in a patriarchal culture that is eager to tell her exactly who she is or should be (preferring, actually, to gloss over any possible difference between these). The less sense she has of her own integrity, the easier it is to drive the message home. This is one reason why the struggle toward ideals is, as Judith Plaskow says, a practice for those who already possess a certain kind of strength.[24] Socially constructed ideals are an excellent way of controlling those who can be persuaded they should live up to them. They require maintenance of an oppositional identity if one is to maintain self-integrity in the face of them. Buddhist literature makes the point that manipulation, like all oppression, depends on unconscious ontological assumptions regarding the self that oppresses and is oppressed.

Thus seen, the potential disadvantages of a quest for self, or any religious quest, that is dominated by ideals are fourfold: (1) hindering self-knowledge, (2) demeaning the self, (3) providing a means by which one may be manipulated and (4) continuing the oppositional style that many feminists explicitly seek to overcome.

In short, self-knowledge can be much hampered by the presence of demanding ideals. It can be stymied further by excessive admiration of the ideal in question. Yet, ideals are often intrinsically appealing, beckoning one to merge with them, so that a person without a strong sense of self is likely to be engulfed by them. The patriarchal solution seems to be to match the strength of an ideal with the strength of one's own individuality. In addition to the difficulty, in some contexts, of distinguishing these, this is unacceptable to most feminists. It simply perpetuates oppositionality. Admiration for an ideal needs to be balanced by an equal degree of self-knowledge. Otherwise, in addition to the perils just noted, one becomes impatient for personal change while at the same time remaining in a kind of personal vacuum, a vacuum thinly veiled off from awareness by unrealistic expectations. Self-abandonment, which must be distinguished from the Buddhist understanding of selflessness or emptiness,[25] is the result of allegiance to an idea. It is easy to acquire. A few years ago I overheard a conversation between two American practitioners of Buddhist meditation. One, speaking with a kind of rosy excitement, turned to another and asked, "How has meditation changed you?" She appeared to expect some kind of success story of triumph over unwanted personality traits. The object of this inquiry, not responding to her eager anticipation, said, "Change? I don't want to change. I just want to *be* there."

It is often hard to "be there." However, an observing awareness offers a religious endeavor or self-cultivation that does not operate via oppressive ideals. Awareness as a means for getting in touch with one's own experience is crucial here. It is uncritical, it simply sees and accepts. This non-judgmental awareness constitutes groundedness; it is the beginning of constructive personal power. Awareness can facilitate access to one's experience, but it will not resolve all the issues. It will not illuminate, for example, the extent to which experience is culturally conditioned; nor will it determine new directions of endeavor. It will not necessarily vitalize activity.[26] Yet, Buddhist traditions maintain that simply by its presence, uncritical awareness is salutary. Being aware of an experienced weakness, defect, or confusion relieves the drain caused by trying to pretend that it does not exist. Psychologists might call it "owning one's feelings." Acknowledging feelings takes power from them and gives it to the conscious self. Mistaken ontological assumptions about that self are not altered, but the conditions for growth are provided. Growth can then take place, not without effort, but without the kind of fight that can divide the self from the source of its strength. Such awareness is not simply a self-consciousness in which one experiences oneself as an object, but, as we have seen, has specific subjective qualities of its own—among them clarity, energy, buoyancy.[27] Further qualities develop as simple awareness becomes associated with greater degrees of stability. In addition to accessing experience and offering a method of empowerment that is not demeaning, awareness is important to women because it is, in and of itself, grounding.

Valerie Saiving, the first feminist theologian to express how the failings of women *as women* are different from those of men, suggests that distractibility and diffuseness, the lack of an organizing center or focus, are among the chief female "sins."[28] Sustained awareness speaks directly to this need for focus. Again, it facilitates focus without depending on an external goal or threat to galvanize it. In this sense also it is non-oppositional. Moreover, the capacity for careful observation is often strong in women. Doris Lessing writes:

> Old people, servants, children, slaves, all of those who aren't in control of their own lives, watch faces for minutes signs in eyes, gestures, lips, as weather-watchers examine the skies.[29]

To watch others in this manner, however necessary, is a defensive maneuver, not an empowering one. To draw on this same skill in observing oneself so that one can then observe others in the context of knowing the observer, is finally to become a true participant, capable of purposeful, aware engagement with others.

Thus, awareness may have specific significance for women. It enhances understanding of one's own experience, reduces distractedness, and grounds activity. It also presents a potential hazard: too much fascination with awareness can drain energies from other important areas of endeavor.[30] As with most things, balance is required.

Let us consider the value of non-oppositional awareness in a particular Buddhist understanding of selflessness or emptiness. On the basis of awareness, and in the context of having a healthy degree of self-constancy, one becomes familiar with one's own assumptions regarding not only the healthfully constant self, but the reified status of that self. Subsequent analysis will challenge the latter but not the former. One thereby opens the possibility of experientially separating the continuity essential to psychological health from mistaken reification of the self. Only when one can identify reification of the self in terms of one's own experience is one ready to reflect on whether or not such a self is a delusion. We will consider the Buddhist observation of and reflections about the reified self, and then consider the relevance of these to the feminist agenda of a non-oppositional, grounded self.

A Question of Self

Before meditation on emptiness or selflessness commences, one needs to become thoroughly familiar with the ordinary experience of self. One observes, uncritically and without correction, the existential status naturally attributed to it. For example, one might observe that when the strong sense of "I" is discerned, no matter what its psychological content, it seems to have a certain locus and a certain style or ontological ambience that appears to combine elements of mind and body but at the same time seems different from them. It is important to note that there is no one way the ontologically misconstrued self "should" appear, and there is no immediate critique of its contents. The point is to allow one's natural way of perceiving the self to unfold. Later it will be subjected to analysis, but only after the initial phase of identifying the ordinary sense of self has been navigated. Because this sense of self may initially be unclear, the classic Buddhist advice is to observe closely at times of strong emotion such as happiness, indignation, greed or sorrow.[31] It is precisely when strong feelings arise – for example, when one is defending against an unjust accusation, in a state of fright or exultation – that one can detect the self that one will defend, rescue, or to which one will give pleasure. These feelings do not define self, but they do enable one to identify the self that has these experiences. Weeks or months of observation are recommended to gain familiarity with one's own way of conceiving self. This is considered the most difficult phase of the process of coming to understand what Buddhists mean by selflessness. Indeed, Tsong-ka-pa, a fourteenth-century Tibetan yogi and scholar, devotes to this topic nearly half of his discussion of the special insight (*lhag mthong*) into emptiness.[32]

Tsong-ka-pa begins his discussion of special insight with emphasis on awareness of one's present state. He describes the ordinary experience of selfhood in ontological terms:

> Just as, for example, in order to ascertain that a certain person is not here, you must know the person who is not here [375a] so in order to ascertain the meaning of "selflessness" or "non-inherent existence," you must identify well that self, or inherent existence, which does not exist. [Otherwise] . . . you will not unerringly ascertain the negative of it.[33]

The self observed by ordinary awareness and then denied in theories of selflessness is not a psychological self characterized by certain personality traits, dominant emotions and so forth. It refers rather to a *style* of selfhood, to the ontological or existential status of such a self. Specifically, it refers to the assumption of a greatly exaggerated existential status. In the language of Buddhist philosophy, this reified sense of self is known as true or inherent existence. This term signifies, in part, the sense of something as massively existent, unambiguously findable or concretely identifiable, as one can point to a rock and then pick it up. It is this self, but not self in general, that is to be negated. In the Buddhist perspective this concept of "true existence" easily becomes the basis for an overbearing sense of hierarchy and thus provides fuel for oppression. According to the Prasangika-Madhyamika system, the most subtle forms of a misapprehension are innately present, not learned or socially constructed.

The word "self" in the Buddhist term "selflessness," although a literal translation, can be quite misleading. The "self" negated in the theory of selflessness is synonymous, not with person, but with inherent existence; in this sense one can speak of the selflessness of stones, trees, and so forth. The unthinking attribution of status to others, and the appropriation of it for oneself, is considered by Buddhists to be the lived ontology that underpins all oppression. Or, to use Foucault's term, this misconception provides in Buddhist theory the "surface of inscription for power"; in the Buddhist context this signifies one's susceptibility to being overpowered by perceptions and feelings founded on that basic error.[34] Identifying one's experience of self is considered essential because it gives access to this error. Analyzing or denying such a self will have no significance unless one first identifies implicit conviction in it.

Many feminists, aware of how extensively men have controlled women's minds and bodies—the very constituents of self—distrust the idea of "finding" a true or natural female self.[35] They emphasize the need to recognize the patriarchally sustained one and then, implicitly at least, to move to a different, more genuinely rooted, experience of self. The dynamic of discovering the apparent, manipulated sense of self with the expectation of redefining self parallels the Buddhist use of awareness to identify, and subsequently correct, the ontologically mistaken sense of self.

But how can a different sense of self occur? There is tension between the feminist perception of a need to re-create self and the assumption that there is an as yet undiscovered presence of a true female way of being.[36] The Buddhist perspective emphasizes an inquiry that proceeds from awareness of experience, regardless of how culturally conditioned this may be, and leads to ontological insight. The self of untutored experience is, from different perspectives and at different points in the exploration, both undermined and valorized. However, not even the qualified valorization of the presently experienced self suggests that one will find one's deepest identity through awareness of it. Further, because contemporary understandings of "identity" pertain to matters of character and feeling rather than to ontology, there is no Western parallel to the contemporary concept of a "search for identity" in Buddhist terms. Rather, in the Gelukba approach, one comes to grips with a self or identity that is the basis on which one receives and is overpowered by the projection of others. In the long run, one can identify a viable self of a wholly different ontological order, and this identification will ultimately be accompanied by profound changes in one's character and relationship with others. Unlike many feminists, however, Buddhism does not concern itself with complex psychological analysis of the self. The focus remains ontological because the addiction to inherent existence is the basic characteristic of mind that predisposes one to oppressing and being oppressed, or to any other form of suffering. It is the assumed existential status of the oppressed and confused self as well as of the empowered and prideful self that is at issue. This status is not problematic for spiritual reasons—as with Christian pride, for example—but because it provides a basis for unethical behavior and experience.

The method for bringing to light this ordinarily unnoticed sense of inherent existence is itself non-oppositional. It consists of a simple, uncritical awareness of one's own view of inherent existence—that is, of one's own sense of "I." Moreover, unless this term "inherently existent 'I'" is seen as descriptive of some aspect of experience, however subtle, it will be irrelevant for both Buddhists and feminists. This reified ontology can be experienced even when one's identity is unclear in terms of social role or psychological content. That is, one can feel "I don't know who I am" and still have a mistakenly reified sense of the "I" who does not know.

Thus one begins with awareness of one's own experience. This is not, as we have seen, because such perception is entirely correct, though such awareness may be more correct than other kinds of subjectivity—but because awareness, rather than any grand ideal, is regarded as the starting point of religious life and philosophical discourse. Moreover, as already indicated, all afflictions come about through dependence on an innate error, a particular reified self. Since this self is an important support of oppression, Buddhist emphasis on undermining this sense of self is of interest to persons who seek a nonoppositional, non-idealizing approach to issues of identity.

To this point we have discussed one style of subjectivity that Buddhists consider useful in accessing one's present experience of self. I will now turn to a description of the ontological qualities of the self that is denied in Indo-Tibetan Buddhism, and of the self that is affirmed; then I will distinguish both selflessness and the mind that understands selflessness from certain forms of Western nihilism.

The Ontological Self

The self of ordinary experience is described with varying degrees of subtlety in Gelukba texts. These descriptions pertain mainly to the ontology of the experienced self, rather than its content. Except in its discussion of compassion, seen as central to the project of Mahayana Buddhism, specific feelings or personal qualities are not emphasized. Attention centers on more widely applicable ontological patterns of the experienced self. Typical of the Gelukba position is this statement by one of the foremost contemporary scholars from that tradition, the present Dalai Lama:

> There are many different ways in which the person or I appears to our minds. In one way, the I appears to be permanent, unitary, and under its own power; in this mode of appearance the I seems to be a separate entity from mind and body with the person as the user or enjoyer and mind and body as what is used or enjoyed.[37]

Feminists have also expressed concern about such a depiction of self and have envisioned a different way of being. This would not mean that a woman is, in the words of Hélène Cixous "an undifferentiated magma but that she doesn't lord it over her body or her desire."[38] "Lording it over" requires precisely the reified self, a self which is a fundamental component of the patriarchal self. Seeing self as distinct from a mind and a body in this manner opens the way to an oppositionality between self and mind or body, as well as between mind and body. For Tsong-ka-pa and the philosophical system of Prasangika in general, however, this exemplifies a relatively superficial mistaken sense of self. It is not the most deeply ingrained sense of self. Belief in it is easily dispelled by the reasoned reflection that will occupy the next phases of analysis. After all, it is argued, if the self were as independent of mind and body as it sometimes seems, it should be possible to experience this self, one's own or others', without any reference to mind or body. And this is patently not the case.[39] Yet, one could overcome oppositionality and still be mistaken regarding the nature of the self. The Dalai Lama, again referring to well known Gelukba categories, describes a more subtle, but still ontologically overbearing, sense of self:

> In another mode of appearance the I seems to have its own substantially existent or self–sufficient entity but to be of the same character as mind and body. There are both innate and artificial [or learned] forms of consciousness that conceive the I to exist in accordance with this appearance. . . . Another is the appearance of the I as if it exists inherently; our innate misconception of I is a consciousness which views the I in this last way as concretely existent in accordance with this appearance. This form of misconception exists in all beings, whether they have studied and been affected by a [religious or philosophical] system or not.[40]

The point is not that one *consciously* mistakes the self's ontology in this way, but that we all operate under the assumption that this is the case. It is this unintended assumption that must first be identified by non-oppositional awareness.

Subsequently, one subjects this sense of self to analysis. Without specifying how the analysis works,[41] I will describe its method. The mode of understanding is not textual but experiential. That is, having observed how the existential or ontological status of the self is ordinarily experienced, analysis is used to test whether a self like this could actually exist or not. Such reflection progresses in stages from the merely intellectual to an experiential integration of emptiness, the absence of reified selfhood. In early and middle stages of analysis, the intellect itself proceeds dialectically—that is, oppositionally. Because it is directed at undermining the ontological basis of its own oppositionality—the conception of inherent existence—it is able finally to undercut all inherently existent oppositionality, but not oppositionality in general. The possibility of hierarchical and other differences still exists, but not the ontological support that is the chief factor making differences problematic. For example, high and low are strictly relative designations, one cannot exist except in relation to the other; within nominally established differences, high and low have the common quality of being empty of reified or inherent status as high or low.

The conclusion that the self does not exist at all is not drawn, but rather that the self is utterly unreifiable, non-inherently existent. Understanding this emphasizes the contingent, dependent, interconnected, and non-autonomous nature of the self's existence. An active, effective self exists, but not in any sense independently. Again, the fact that persons do not exist in this way is, according to Prasangika, the most subtle emptiness qualifying the self. Only when this emptiness or selflessness is fully known can one discover the self affirmed in this Buddhist system, a fully functioning self which certainly exists, but its existence has no ontological fixedness. Although viable as an agent and object, the self affirmed in Buddhism is dependently constituted.

It is created through association, rather than separation, and in relation, rather than from nothing.

Theories of emptiness and interdependence frame ontological dynamics crucial to current North American feminist reassessments of the inclusive and relational context of identity formation. In this view, other persons are not merely mirrors facilitating self-knowledge, but "the self is known in the experience of connection, defined not by reflection but by interaction, the responsiveness of human engagement."[42] The experience of emptiness discussed above is associated with the development of a compassionate sense of relatedness in which self and other are seen not as oppositional but as relative designations, like the far and near banks of a river.[43] The identity of each is utterly contingent on the other. This much is easy to understand. Mahayana texts suggest however that the real import of this perspective cannot be perceived so long as one maintains a reified sense of self or other. Emptiness theory is therefore crucial to the full development of relational understanding and compassionate involvement.

Broadly speaking, emptiness theory runs parallel to current feminist observations of the mutuality of self and other as constitutive of personal identity. For both Buddhists and feminists, however, the question remains: how does one live within this recognition, even if one takes it to be true? Is it something to be brought to consciousness at will? Is it only descriptive or is it also prescriptive? If the latter, what, precisely, does it prescribe? How might it influence individual behavior or social praxis? At the very least it calls attention to the foolishness of paying excessive homage to human autonomy. A case in point is our own culture's loyalty to an illusory independence. This glorification of independence may partially explain the low esteem in which the difficult and vital tasks of childbearing, child rearing, and primary education are held. Social, economic, and institutional failure to support parenting may stem in good measure from a deeply-rooted unwillingness to value the utter dependence all adults have had as children on the work of parents, and primary or secondary school teachers—most of whom are women. Moreover, in many colleges and universities, teaching, at its best a powerful expression of relationship, is not valued as much as "Lone Ranger" scholarship. There is an irrational but powerful clinging to the idea of "self-made" autonomous men.

According to psychologists such as Carol Gilligan and Nancy Chodorow, many women in our culture find it more accurate to think of themselves in terms of connectedness than separation. Because most models of powerful selfhood available to us in modern life feature autonomy and separateness, women who do not wish to claim power in this way often decline to claim it at all, partly because more appealing styles of power do not readily present themselves. A woman may react to the available model of power by behaving meekly, or she may experience herself only as helpmate to others, as incapable of further aspirations. The personal cost of such a stance is discussed widely. Scholars have emphasized the psychological and social context of this posture, but there is another sphere of influence operative regarding woman's sense of self, the ontological sphere.

Self-abandoning behavior is not merely a drain; it also fails to get at the ontological root of the issue. In the Buddhist view, it is not only the powerful, confident person who has an ontologically overwrought sense of self. A person with a fragile psychological self or low self-esteem is just as likely to have this, although the ontology of that self may be less accessible to awareness. To realize that one need not be attached either to a highly *or* lowly esteemed self is to open a fresh possibility of self-identity. This does not mean that ontological concerns necessarily take precedence over psychological ones. It would be foolhardy for anyone with an overly fragile sense of self to engage in a process which undermines her identity when what is needed on the psychological level is a stable, organized self.[44] Ontological inquiry may however strengthen the sense of self in a different way. To express this possibility in Western terms: the Buddhist analysis of self might help alleviate a person's tendency to become a reflecting pool for projections. Why? Because in the Buddhist view the ontologically inflated self is the fabric of the sail—the confidence or lack of it, for example—that catches the wind of such projections. Such a sail blows an erratic course. An ontologically false sense of self is distracting, leaving one at sea, ungrounded.

What potential do the principles associated with the Buddhist discussion of selflessness have to open non-oppositional reconstructions of individual identity? We can only evaluate this by considering once again, and from a different perspective, some subjective styles associated with this endeavor.

Mahayana Buddhist texts emphasize that the process of coming to understand non-inherent existence, or emptiness, involves a radical reorientation of the subject. Many subjective experiences are cultivated, such as simple awareness, an unshakable concentration known as calm abiding which is accompanied by physical and mental joy and agility, an increased benevolent concern for others, and a sense of no longer being entirely cut off from sense objects or from other persons. Awareness participates in a larger process of growth, not by moving toward ideals but by making possible insights that alter the state and—

thereby the content—of one's interiority. The insight into emptiness, facilitated by awareness, leads to an empowered compassion.[45] The relationship between such insight and concern for others is an important principle in Mahayana Buddhism. Insight, and its affective counterpart, compassion, are crucial for the Buddhist enterprise of ultimate liberation. To quote from Saraha, one of India's great Buddhist yogis:

> One who enters into emptiness without compassion
> Will not find the most excellent path.
> Yet, should one cultivate only compassion
> One will not attain liberation, but remain in cyclic existence.[46]

In Indo-Tibetan Mahayana Buddhism, neither compassion nor an understanding of selflessness comes to full flower without the other. Moreover, insight into the ontological principle of interrelatedness engenders understanding of interpersonal connectedness and hence in Mahayana is fundamentally conjoined with compassionate concern for persons who are no longer seen as other.[47] In other words, the subjectivity involved in experiencing emptiness is characterized by emotional richness. This is important to notice, because Buddhist emptiness has often mistakenly been associated with inner deadness and with certain forms of nihilism.

How then is emptiness distinguished from nihilism? What might distinguish it from, for example, Novak's "experience of nothingness," of which North American feminist theory has made considerable use? These terms must not be confused because of their semantic similarity. To do so would be to obscure the respective relevance for feminist issues of identity. In describing the distinction between Western "experience of nothingness" and "emptiness," I will refer to emptiness in two different ways: as a theoretical perspective and as a focus of experience. It is important to contrast descriptions of the experience of emptiness with descriptions of the experience of nothingness in order to take account of the ontological implications of each.

Emptiness and Feeling Negative

In *The Experience of Nothingness* Novak writes that "To choose against culture is not merely to disobey, it is to die."[48] For Novak, "the source of the experience of nothingness lies in the deepest recesses of human consciousness, in its irrepressible tendency to ask questions."[49] Here nothingness signifies, in part the bleakness and alienation that results from not seeing one's own reality mirrored in the larger one and the way this experience motivates many, many questions. Women have often described their own situation in these terms. Moreover, incessant questioning can be exhausting. Mary Daly, paraphrasing Simone de Beauvoir, observes that "women who have perceived the reality of sexual oppression usually have exhausted themselves in breaking through to discovery of their own humanity with little energy left for constructing their own interpretation of the universe."[50]

The angst associated with Novak's nothingness is something that "may lead either to madness or to wisdom."[51] In either case angst is a passageway, not an end point. Thus, as a focus of experience, its place in the developmental spectrum in which it is embedded is different from that of the realization of emptiness. Emptiness is not an experience that one passes through to something better, as in the mythic paradigm of a descent into hell. Rather emptiness is an awareness one continually cultivates so as to integrate it into more and more aspects of one's life, including one's relationship to others. Moreover, as understood in Buddhist Middle-Way (Madhyamika) systems, emptiness is not the void that Novak describes as "full of danger, insanity, destructiveness, rage."[52] Realization of emptiness is not a recognition, despairing or otherwise, of a lack of *telos* in life's trials, even though it undermines the ontological status of *telos*, as well as of the self that seems to require it. Nevertheless, both *telos*, construed in Buddhist terms, and self are valid constructs.

Whereas Novak's nihilism involves recognition of a lack of meaning, emptiness theory questions the ontological status of agents while preserving the meaning of their actions as valid.[53] Nihilism in general denies a posited totality of a whole—whether God or something else—on which one can depend and through which one incurs value. Madhyamika, agreeing that such a conception limits human possibilities, takes the discussion of emptiness and associated topics in epistemology to include a vast range of possibilities. Compassion, mental clarity, and energy are positive concomitants of understanding emptiness. These results do not depend on dismissing the world as illusion and offering a more stable realm; the world is said to be illusion-like, not "mere" illusion, and neither more nor less, ontologically, than emptiness itself. Insight into emptiness does not result from pushing aside one's experience of the world, but by observing it more closely. Unlike the experience of nothingness that Novak discusses, the emptiness discussed in Indo-Tibetan Madhyamika does not signify a state of alienation.

The new possibilities connected with realizing emptiness in this tradition are primarily developments in the person, not escape to another realm. In Buddhism the discussion of emptiness or selflessness aims at developing specific subjective insights and experiences. Emptiness does not become a focus for Buddhists simply because it is considered true. Emptiness is central to Buddhist theory and practice because realization of this is salutary in the short term and transformative in the long one. In order to have a direct experience of emptiness, as opposed to mediated, conceptual understanding, however vivid and psychologically affective, certain qualities of mind must be present. The factor of mindfulness discussed above must be developed and combined with other factors so that one achieves the pacification of mind known as calm abiding. This is the lowest form of concentration with which it is possible to cognize emptiness directly. Calm abiding is always associated with mental and physical joy. Meditators from many traditions, Buddhist and non-Buddhist, attest to the connection between mental concentration and pleasurable physical feelings. Therefore, in terms of its psychological aspect, the experience of emptiness is not one of emotional nothingness. Although some form of joyful release may follow Novak's "experience of nothingness," joy is not an integral part of the nihilistic perspective itself.

Emptiness as Inalienable

Having discussed the subjective features associated with emptiness, we can turn to ontological considerations. In addition to being the focus for specific experience, emptiness is an ontologically descriptive term. As such it is an ingredient in the dynamic agents as well as the inanimate objects of the world. It is, in short, an immanent quality of existing things, having no existence apart from them. This is another factor distinguishing Madhyamika emptiness from Novak's nothingness. The latter is part of alienation, the former of integration. For Buddhists, both the theory and experience of "emptiness" undermine psychological or ontological self-sufficiency and confirm the existence of a self that is ontologically relational and whose primary emotional characteristic is compassion for others. Indeed, in Prasangika-Madhyamika interdependent existence is the necessary reciprocal meaning of emptiness; it is as all-encompassing a rubric as emptiness itself. Emptiness or selflessness is described as altogether compatible with functionality and existence. Both its religious significance and its potential import for feminist experientially-based theories of selfhood lie in this functionality.

Moreover, as an ontological theory, emptiness is descriptive of self as well as other, and contradicts the ontological oppositionality that feminists see as characterizing the patriarchal self, and which Buddhists see as characterizing an ontologically overwrought sense of self.

Emptiness is often credited with a generative quality that nothingness, used in the ontological sense of *ex nihilo* does not possess. Unlike the nothingness or nihility which in Nishitani's pithy phrase "lies on the far side of phenomena,"[54] emptiness is part and parcel of all that it qualifies, and has no existence except as a quality of these things. Thus it is compatible with activity in ways that nihility is not. For all these reasons, emptiness "lies on the near side" of being, it is not "some point recessed behind the things that we see with our eyes and think of with our minds."[55] Rather, these are suffused with the quality of emptiness. Neither emptiness nor the sense-objects it qualifies can exist without the other. The *Twenty-Five Thousand Stanza Perfection of Wisdom Sutra* states:

> It is like this: a Bodhisattva [an altruistically motivated seeker of highest enlightenment] is empty of being an inherently existent Bodhisattva. A Bodhisattva's name is also empty of being a Bodhisattva's name. Why? It is their nature. It is like this: it is not that form is empty on account of emptiness; emptiness is not separate from a form. A form itself is [that which is] empty; just [that which is] empty is also the form.[56]

Emptiness is co-extensive and integrated with people and things, not set apart from them. To know emptiness therefore is not to be preoccupied with "the negation of everything that is."[57] Emptiness is not seen as opposed to being, but as an inseparable quality of all that exists. Thus, emptiness itself is empty—not a paradox, but a logical unfolding of the principle that nothing inherently exists. The theory of emptiness can help articulate the possibility of a strong identity not predicated on exclusion of unlike members. This is largely because the meaning of emptiness, which negates much of what is ordinarily conceived about the ontological nature of self, other, and the world, *simultaneously* underscores the interdependent, relational co-existence of self, other, and the world.

In these ways, the Prasangika-Madhyamika theory of emptiness parallels feminist critiques of patriarchy by questioning the ontological assumptions on which patriarchal power is premised. Moreover, and especially important for feminist thought, emptiness theory offers an option for a transformative perspective that need not, though it sometimes does, gain its leverage from a point outside the sphere of love, work, and relationship that is the domain of feminist endeavor.

Self-Concepts and Societies

In what ways, if any, might insights gleaned from Buddhist materials support, enrich, or shed light on the social issues women face today? On what basis do we even begin to assess this? Cultural disparities make it difficult to base judgment solely or even primarily on how women fared in traditional Buddhist societies. That they tended to have somewhat more respect and independence than their non-Buddhist Indian or Chinese counterparts does not clearly indicate how Buddhist theory might pertain to today's feminist concerns. In addition to the difficulty of taking the situation of pre-modern Asian women as a primary indicator here, there are other complexities.

Emptiness, understood as a quality of things and people, is equally compatible with terrorists, pacifists, misogynists, and feminists. As a quality of things therefore, emptiness is not a governing principle; it does not favor ontologically one type of quest over another. As a quality to be acknowledged or experienced however, emptiness does favor certain types of attitudes. We have also noted that the mind which understands or experiences emptiness is of necessity focused, clear, and inclined to be ethical, active, and compassionate. Any ethical or social implications of emptiness theory must derive primarily from the features and empathies of the mind engaged with it, and from the kind of society seen to foster the ontological and epistemological implications of this theory.

The further import of emptiness theory has to do with perceived integration of emptiness with, rather than its alienated distinctness from, those things and beings which are empty—that is to say, everything and everyone. This integration purveys an ontological model whose implications are at odds with much that is fundamental to patriarchy. The error of inherent existence that emptiness theory counters is a form of projection. According to the most prevalent system of Madhyamika such "projection" is automatic: it results from the erroneous way in which we make assumptions about what seems to inherently exist, and thus about the way things are by their very nature. By extension then, emptiness theory disputes the presumption that others, and in particular women, are by their nature persons to be molded by patriarchal projections in the name of family, culture, and tradition.

Emptiness theory undercuts patriarchal hierarchy in another way as well. It proposes the equal ontological *value* of all things and people, even though their functions may be assessed hierarchically. For example, in the "Advice to Singala Discourse,"[58] Buddha indicates the reciprocal, if not altogether equal, responsibilities between child and parents, student and teacher, master and servant and so forth. Although hierarchy is not questioned, each group is due specific forms of consideration and recognition from the other. This is similar to accepting equality before the law without at the same time asserting the equal talents of each individual. By contrast, patriarchy has often equated functional status with value. This results in the view that power inheres in the individuals and is not interdependently constituted. Emptiness theory can recognize existent hierarchies while maintaining the equal ontic value of each constituent.[59] Emptiness theory may not favor a particular social structure; yet, those who develop an understanding of emptiness presumably will also understand the interdependent nature of any social structure, and perhaps therefore may be freer from the constraints or rigidity of the patriarchal subject-object dyad. Whether this might bring about social change in North American culture as it has not in Buddhist cultures, and what sort of change that might be, cannot be predicted.[60]

Historically, emptiness theory has co-existed with intricately hierarchical societies in India, Tibet, China, and Japan. The Buddhist *sangha* or spiritual community itself, however, has not always reflected the hierarchical arrangement of the larger society. Indeed, since the inception of Buddhism, a distinction has been made between how the Buddhist spiritual community should operate and the politics of society at large. When the Buddhist community was initially formed in India during the fifth century B.C., economic welfare and social stability were primary concerns. These were judged to be best maintained by supporting the monarchical institutions of the time.[61] Considerable emphasis was placed on the benevolent concern rulers should evince toward their subjects but the then-current tendency toward monarchy went unquestioned. The principle of benevolence was considered more important than egalitarianism. In other words, as is also true in Buddhist doctrines of karma and ethics, a king's or government's motivation and actual effect on persons was considered more crucial than social structure as such. Hierarchy itself was not repudiated. At the same time, the relational status of all constituents in the social hierarchy was emphasized.

In contrast to the larger social order, the Buddhist *sangha* operated by consensus.[62] "Every member of the *sangha* was regarded as having equality of rights in any deliberation concerning the life of the community."[63] This egalitarian trend deserves notice. Nevertheless, for a variety of reasons, the community of nuns was structurally subordinate to the community of monks, and younger monks subordinate to their elders. I. B. Horner has suggested that the former aspect of this structure was primarily a concession to Indian society. When Buddhism arose in the fifth century B.C., the sanction of female clergy was itself a radical departure from centuries of tradition. At that period in Asia only the Jains had begun to offer similar opportunities to women. In any case, the legislated subordination of the community of nuns to that of monks does not seem to have been questioned. At the same time, there was open recognition of the equal spiritual possibilities for men and women, and in this important though not conclusive sense women and men—two groups in an institutionalized hierarchical relationship—were equal.[64]

Conclusion

Despite all the difficulties we face, many women have found and are finding ways to claim powerful identities that are not extensions of patriarchal value systems. Nevertheless, there are few theoretical models with which we can articulate and broaden such development. The Buddhist literature examined here offers an ontological model of selfhood that is non-oppositional and thus consonant with a feminist tendency to value connectedness over separation as a viable model for establishing identity.

An essential issue to date has been women's efforts to build a psychology of connectedness without addressing directly the assumed ontological status of the self that is so connected. The discrepancy between a psychology emphasizing connectedness and an ontology emphasizing reified isolation is counterproductive. Buddhist analyses of self as active and empty offers one approach to an articulation of selfhood that addresses the tension between social interrelatedness and psychological individuality.

Much of our discussion has focused on emptiness as an ontological theory. We have also considered the experiential dimension of emptiness, in particular the styles of subjectivity that occur in approaching and understanding it. Buddhist analysis here, uniting epistemological and ontological concerns, instances a closing of a major rift in Western thought, a rift currently critiqued by feminists. What we need is precisely to understand the subject—ourselves—*in relation to* the structures by which we organize meaning.

Having discussed the relevance of emptiness theory and the experience of emptiness for feminist questions regarding women's identity, and having distinguished briefly the import of emptiness and nihilism for feminist theory, we moved to its possible social import. This is ambiguous: on the one hand Buddhist traditions state that the effects of understanding emptiness are palpable. On the other hand, even in societies where significant portions of the population were either roughly familiar with or actively cultivating realization of emptiness, no one has yet claimed to discern a clear causal connection between that fact and specific social developments that affected women or men. Perhaps such effects will be hypothesized as our understanding of Buddhist cultures is refined. Still, it will be impossible to verify precisely how a particular given society has been tempered by its doctrines and practitioners of selflessness. Would any given culture have been more or less patriarchal, matriarchal, or hierarchical without exposure to these ideas? Nevertheless theoretical discussions of emptiness in Buddhist literature, including detailed descriptions of subjective styles associated with it, can help refine the categories of ontology and subjectivity on which feminist theory continues to build.[65]

Notes

1. Heller, Sosna, Wellberry, eds., *Reconstructing Individualism*, (Stanford: Stanford University Press, 1986), p. 7.

2. Ibid., p. 10.

3. Ironically, although the main privilege patriarchy claims for its supposed beneficiaries is powerful autonomy, it sets in motion permutations of privilege that are in important ways confining. In commenting on an earlier version of this paper, Richard Niebuhr astutely observed that "one failure of patriarchy as it is commonly understood is that it does not take autonomy seriously enough; it substitutes a private or limited maxim for a true *nomos* or law."

4. See for example Massey's discussion of Rich, Kristeva and Irigaray, *Feminine Soul* (Boston: Beacon Press), pp. 184–88.

5. "The Way of All Ideology" *Signs* (Spring 1982), p. 643.

6. See Carol Gilligan, "Remapping the Moral Domain: New Images of Self in Relationship," in *Reconstructing Individualism*, pp. 237–52.

7. Hélène Cixous, "The Laugh of the Medusa" in *New French Feminisms*, ed. Elaine Marks and Isabelle de Courtivron (New York: Schocken Books, 1981), p. 264.

8. See Donna C. Stanton, "Language and Revolution: The Franco-American Disconnection" in *The Future of Difference*, ed. Hester Eisenstein and Alice Jardine, Barnard College Women's Center (Boston: G.K. Hall & Co., 1980), especially p. 76 ff.

9. For excellent discussion of this see Jane Flax, "Mother-Daughter Relationships: Psychodynamics" in *The Future of Difference*, p. 21ff.

10. Lee Yearley noted these categories to me in a different context, Stanford, January 9, 1987.

11. Jack Engler, "Therapeutic Aims in Psychotherapy and Meditation: Developmental Stages in the Representation of Self" in *Journal of Transpersonal Psychology* 16, no. 1 (1984), p. 25; this is a reworking of Engler's "Vicissitudes of the Self According to Psychoanalysis and Buddhism: A Spectrum Model of Object Relations Development" in *Psychoanalysis and Contemporary Thought* (1983a), 6.1, 29–72.

12. For brief descriptions of these errors, see Jeffrey Hopkins, *Meditation on Emptiness* (London: Wisdom Publications, 1983), pp. 296–304.

13. Geshe Gedun Lodrö, "Calm abiding and Special Insight," unpublished MS, 1979, in discussion of Asanga's Levels of Hearers (*Śrāvakabhumi, Nyan sa*). There are four factors developed in the process of gaining calm abiding (*śamatha, gzhi gnas*). The factor of stability (*gnas cha*) signifies the ability to remain constantly with a chosen object; the factors of clarity refer to subjective clarity (*trang cha*), the clarity of both subject and object (*gsal cha*) and intensity (*ngar*).

14. For discussion of female symbolism associated with Buddhist wisdom see A. Klein, "Non-Dualism and the Great Bliss Queen" in *Journal of Feminist Studies in Religion* (1985), vol. 1. Regarding the relationship between such female symbolism and the lives of actual women in Tibet, see "Primordial Purity and Everyday Life" in *Immaculate and Powerful: The Female in Sacred Image and Social Reality*, ed. Clarissa Atkinson, Constance Buchanan, and Margaret Miles, Harvard Women's Studies in Religion Series (Boston: Beacon Press, 1985), pp. 111–38.

15. *Pure Lust* (Boston: Beacon Press, 1984), p. 30.

16. *Feminine Soul* (Boston: Beacon Press), p. 184.

17. "The Laugh of the Medusa," in *New French Feminisms*, p. 259.

18. For a classic discussion of simple awareness, see the discourse on the "Foundations of Mindfulness" (*Mahà-satipatthāna sutta*), Trans. in *Heart of Buddhist Meditation*, (London: Rider and Co., 1969). For a concise discussion of the development of calm abiding see Hopkins, *Meditation on Emptiness*, 80–90. We can compare this developed awareness, for example, with Hegel's self-consciousness which, in revealed religion is "aware of itself in pictorial objectification, not as yet *as* self-consciousness" *Hegel's Phenomenology of Spirit* VIII.788, trans. by Miller and Findlay (Oxford: Clarendon Press, 1977), p. 589. "Self-consciousness . . . necessarily involves consciousness of self as object . . . [it] is impossible apart from self-objectification" (Mark Taylor, *Journeys to Selfhood: Hegel and Kierkegaard* (Berkeley: University of California Press, 1980), p. 186.) The object but not the *style* of such awareness is focal here. Further, if we accept Donna Stanton's statement that for Hegel "the knowing subject called 'consciousness of self' . . . emerges as a unity and passes through one transcendent act of cognition after another" (in *Future of Difference*, p. 74), this is patently not the case in Buddhism where awareness itself reveals the arising and ceasing of one moment of consciousness followed by another. See also Charles Taylor, *Human Agency and Language*, pp. 80–88.

19. *Pure Lust*, pp. xii and 89.

20. *Four Gated City*, p. 36.

21. Ibid., p. 37.

22. Ibid., p. 38.

23. In the literature on calm abiding, "simple awareness" is distinguished from the function of introspection (*samprajanya, shes bzhin*); this latter is the factor of mind that notices whether faults such as laxity or excitement are present. See Hopkins, *Meditation on Emptiness*, pp. 74–76. A classic distinction between mindfulness and introspection is made in the Shantideva's *Engaging in the Bodhisattva Deeds* (*Bodhisattvacāryavatāra, spyod 'jug*), 1979.

24. *Sex Sin and Grace: Women's Experience and the Theologies of Reinhold Niebuhr and Paul Tillich* (Washington D.C.: University Press of America), 1980.

25. Conversation with Constance Buchanan, Cambridge, Mass., July, 1985.

26. Conversation with Hester Gelber and Rose Anne Christian, at Stanford University, April, 1986 helped clarify this last point. The relationship between vitality or energy and clarity or awareness is an interesting one, especially if one takes account of tantric perspectives. I hope to do so elsewhere; space does not permit it here.

27. For a discussion of the characteristics of mind associated with *any* wholesome consciousness, including simple mindfulness, see Angarika Govinda, *The Psychological Attitude of Early Buddhist Philosophy* (London: Rider, 1969), pp. 120–21. The classic Theravada source for this is Buddhaghosa's *Visuddhimagga* (*Path of Purification*), Shambala, 1976 reprint.

28. Christ and Plaskow, eds., *Womenspirit Rising* (New York: Harper & Row, 1979), p. 37.

29. *The Four Gated City*, p. 247.

30. Conversation with Courtney Thompson, Stanford University, November 1985.

31. Discussed in the chapter "Perfection of Wisdom" of the fifth Dalai Lama's "Sacred Word of Manjushri" translated by Jeffrey Hopkins as "Practice of Emptiness" (Dharamsala: Library of Tibetan Works and Archives, 1974), pp. 11–12).

32. Elizabeth Napper, "Dependent-Arising and Emptiness" unpublished Ph.D. dissertation, University of Virginia, 1985 [forthcoming from Wisdom Publications, London, 1987], p. 106. The text under discussion is "Great Exposition of Special Insight" from his *Great Exposition of the Stages of the Path* (*Lam rim chen mo*). Peking Tibetan Tripitaka, p. 6001, vol. 152.

33. Ibid., p. 269.

34. Michel Foucault, *Discipline and Punish: The Birth of the Prison*, trans. Alan Sheridan (New York: Vintage Books, 1979), p. 50; discussed in Marilyn Massey, *Feminine Soul: The Fate of an Ideal*, p. 40.

35. Conversation with Marilyn Massey, November 7, 1985, Stanford, Calif. For an exemplary discussion of the perils of such an idea, see Marilyn Massey, *Feminine Soul: The Fate of an Ideal*, passim, but especially pp. 26–29.

36. Buddhism also has both these models of discovery and development. As I hope to show elsewhere, this has been a major area of debate among numerous groups of Buddhist exponents.

37. Tenzin Gyatso, the Fourteenth Dalai Lama, *Kindness, Clarity, and Insight* (Ithaca: Snow Lion Publications, 1984), p. 162.

38. *New French Feminisms*, p. 259.

39. For further discussion of this analysis, see Hopkins, *Meditation on Emptiness*, pp. 43–51, 677–97.

40. *Kindness, Clarity and Insight*, p. 262.

41. For discussion of this see Jeffrey Hopkins, *Meditation on Emptiness*, especially Part I, chapters 1–4 and Part II.

42. Carol Gilligan, "Remapping the Moral Domain" in *Reconstructing Individualism*, pp. 240–41.

43. Kelsang Gyatso, *Meaningful to Behold* (London: Wisdom Publications, 1980), p. 236.

44. Harvey Aronson, "Altruism and Adversity: Perspectives from Psychoanalytic Object Relations Theory," unpublished paper delivered at the Tibetan Buddhist Learning Center, July, 1985, pp. 12–16, and Aronson, "Guru Yoga—A Buddhist Meditative Visualization: Observations Based Upon Psychoanalytic Object Relations Theory and Self-Psychology" unpublished paper delivered at American Academy of Religion Meeting at Anaheim, Calif., November 1985, pp. 43–48.

45. For an exploration of how this is empowering and why all forms of compassion are not, see A. Klein "Gain or Drain: Buddhist and Feminist Views on Compassion" *Spring Wind*, Ann Arbor, Mich., vol. 6, nos. 1, 2, and 3, 1986. For a discussion of early Buddhist views on the relationship between insight and compassion see Harvey Aronson, *Love and Sympathy in Theravada Buddhism* (New Delhi: Motilal Banarsidas, 1980), pp. 93–94.

46. Quoted by Nga-wang-den-dzin-dorje in *Ra Dik*, 37.5; trans. Klein unpublished ms. p. 14. Selections from this text will appear in *Tibet Journal*, Spring/Summer 1987. Further reflections on the nature of the subjectivity involved in cognizing emptiness, as I hope to elaborate elsewhere, pertain to classic discussions of the "womb of the Buddha" (Tathāgathagarbha).

47. See chapter 13 of Shantideva's *Engaging in the Bodhisattva Deeds (Bodhisattvacāryāvatāra)* translated and commented upon by Kelsang Gyatso in *Meaningful to Behold* (London: Wisdom Publications, 1980), p. 237.

48. Michael Novak, *The Experience of Nothingness* (New York: Harper Torchbooks, 1978), p. 13.

49. Ibid., p. 14. See also Christ, *Diving Deep and Surfacing*, pp. 14–15. She points out that Mary Daly was the first to notice the significance of Novak's categories for women, first in her review of Novak's book ("Critics' choices," *Commonweal*, vol. 93, no. 21 (February 26, 1971), p. 526, and later in *Beyond God the Father.*

50. *Beyond God the Father* (Boston: Beacon Press, 1973), p. 7.

51. *Experience of Nothingness*, p. 15.

52. Ibid., p. 65. The illuminating despair of which Novak speaks may roughly parallel how some in the Buddhist tradition initially relate to expositions of emptiness. This occurs because of misinterpreting their import nihilistically. Such misinterpretation is taken as a sign that instruction on emptiness is inappropriate for that person at that time. Tsong-ka-pa in the *Perfection of Wisdom* section of his *Clarification of the Thought (dbU ma dgong ba rab gsal)* states that those who will construe the discussion of emptiness to mean that cause and effect are not operative, or that nothing really exists at all—are not suitable even to begin study of the topic of emptiness. (Sarnath, 1983, 119.12.9ff.). Their error results from overextending the significance of emptiness and therefore negating more than is intended. Tsong-ka-pa labels such an error an abandoning of emptiness. Because it denies the interdependent existence of agents, activities, and other phenomena, this view represents a failure of understanding, an abandonment of emptiness.

53. This emphasis is especially strong in Gelukba discussions of emptiness.

54. Keiji Nishitani, *Religion and Nothingness* trans. by Jan Van Bragt (Berkeley: University of California Press, 1982), p. 85 and p. 123 ff.

55. Ibid., p. 123.

56. Quoted in *The Buddhism of Tibet* by H. H. Tenzin Gyatso, trans. Jeffrey Hopkins (London: Allen & Unwin, 1975), p. 73.

57. See Daly's critique of Tillich as unduly fascinated by non-being in *Pure Lust*, 29–30.

58. From the *Dīghanikāya*, iii.180ff.; trans. in de Bary, ed. *The Buddhist Tradition* (New York: The Modern Library), 1969, pp. 39–44.

59. This theoretical framework developed in conversation with Harvey Aronson, October, 1986.

60. There is also the matter of what an individual's involvement with religious practices associated with emptiness might imply for the larger society. That such involvement, even in Buddhist countries, is not likely to be the province of large groups of a portion of the population, does not foreclose the possibility of their having some effect on society. Durkheim, focusing on how ascetics affect the social order, writes:

    > It is necessary that an elite put the end too high if the crowd is not to put it too low. It is necessary that some exaggerate, if the average is to remain at a fitting level. [quoted by Trevor Ling p. 170 from *Elementary Forms of the Religious Life* (New York: Collier Books, 1961) p.3ff].

    This assumes however that those who "exaggerate"—that is, who devote their lives to cultivating and living in accordance with the subjective styles associated with emptiness theory, are somehow significant cultural figures. Generations of women, for example, have lived their lives in ways antithetical to patriarchal perspectives ("unconcerned" with the hierarchies that obtain there) without this factor even being noticed, let alone seen as an example for the rest of society.

61. Quoted by Trevor Ling, *The Buddha* (New York: Collier Books, 1961), p. 3ff.

62. Ling, *The Buddha*, p. 172–74.

63. Ibid., p. 159.

64. See Nancy Falk, "The Case of the Vanishing Nuns," in *Unspoken Worlds: Women's Religious Lives in Non-Western Cultures*, ed. Nancy Falk and Rita Gross (San Francisco: Harper & Row, 1982); see also I. B. Horner, *Women Under Primitive Buddhism* (London: Routledge and Kegan Paul, 1930, reprinted in Delhi: Motilal Banarsidas, 1975).

65. Thanks to P.J. Ivanhoe, of Stanford University, for a careful reading and good discussion of this article.

Contributors

Clarissa W. Atkinson is Associate Professor of the History of Christianity and Associate Dean for Academic Affairs at the Harvard Divinity School. She was a visiting scholar in the Women's Studies in Religion program in 1974–75 and 1975–76.

Karen McCarthy Brown is Associate Professor of the Sociology of Religion at the Graduate and Theological Schools of Drew University. She was a visiting scholar in 1983–84 and a Phillips Scholar in 1986 in the Women's Studies in Religion program.

Constance H. Buchanan is Associate Dean for Program Development at the Harvard Divinity School and has been the Director of the Women's Studies in Religion program since 1977.

Emily Erwin Culpepper received her Th.D. in theology from the Harvard Divinity School. She was a visiting scholar in the Women's Studies in Religion program in 1984–85.

Sheila Greeve Davaney is Professor of Theology at the Iliff School of Theology. She was a visiting scholar in the Women's Studies in Religion program in 1979–80.

Cheryl Townsend Gilkes is Assistant Professor of Sociology at Boston University. She was a visiting scholar in the Women's Studies in Religion program in 1981–82.

Anne C. Klein is Acting Assistant Professor of Religious Studies at Stanford University. She was a visiting scholar in the Women's Studies in Religion program in 1982–83.

Amy Schrager Lang is Associate Professor of Literature at Massachusetts Institute of Technology. She was a visiting scholar in the Women's Studies in Religion program in 1985–86.

Margaret R. Miles is Professor of Historical Theology at the Harvard Divinity School.

Mary C. Segers is Associate Professor of Political Science and Director of Women's Studies at Rutgers University. She was a visiting scholar in the Women's Studies in Religion program in 1985–86.

Index